THE CHILD IN OUR TIMES

Studies in the Development of Resiliency

Edited by

Timothy F. Dugan, M.D.

and

Robert Coles, M.D.

BRUNNER/MAZEL, *Publishers* • New York

With gratitude and love
We each dedicate this book
to our parents

Library of Congress Cataloging-in-Publication Data

The Child in our times : studies in the development of resiliency /
   edited by Timothy F. Dugan and Robert Coles.
      p.   cm.
   Bibliography: p.
   Includes index.
   ISBN 0-87630-528-1
   1. Resilience (Personality trait) in children.   2. Resilience
(Personality trait) in adolescence.   I. Dugan, Timothy F.
II. Coles, Robert.
BF723.R46C48   1989
155.4'182—dc19
                                                                89-515
                                                                CIP

Published by
BRUNNER/MAZEL, INC.
19 Union Square
New York, New York 10003

Foreword

This is a timely, much-needed book, one that reads well and is more than the sum of its parts. As well as a good clinical read, this volume will be a valuable reference to maintain the vital balance necessary as our biological knowledge advances, challenging and enhancing the psychodynamic foundation of our knowledge of human development and psychological therapy.

In the spirit of Sigmund and Anna Freud's creativity and in keeping with the seminal contributions of August Aichorn, Donald Winnicott, Erik Erikson, Peter Blos, and many others, the editors have assembled a stimulating, inspiring, scholarly volume of research reports that document:

- the vital balance of body and mind;
- the extraordinary uniqueness of each individual in the context of epidemiological realities;
- the necessity of maintaining a full awareness of the inventory of each individual's strengths and vulnerabilities;
- the opportunities and burdens presented by the social environment;
- and the aim to achieve consonance and to minimize dissonance when trying to fit the needs of each individual and population group with therapeutic assistance and a facilitating environment that will promote healthy development, and that will mitigate those blemishes, imperfections, and disadvantages that also characterize the human condition.

At last we have a volume in which there is a lucid orchestration of the best knowledge about biopsychological endowment and environmental opportunities and burdens, viewed in a developmental, psychodynamic context, with a frame of reference that presents the individual as a unique moral person who is an authentic representative of his or her society and particular culture. In this volume, health balances illness, biology and psychology belong together, and the individual is not lost in the changing epidemiological patterns of mental health and mental illness that we must take into account regularly and systematically in order to maintain our concern for the individual and in order to enlarge our capacities for planning and prevention.

Albert J. Solnit, M.D.
Sterling Professor of Pediatrics
and Psychiatry, Yale University
Child Study Center and
School of Medicine

Contents

III. ADOLESCENCE: DEVELOPMENTAL STRESS AND ADAPTATION

IV. DEFYING THE VOICE OF DOOM: FROM ADOLESCENCE TO ADULTHOOD

Contributors

RICHARD BERLIN, M.D.
Medical Director, Child and Adolescent Services, Somerville Mental Health Clinic, Somerville, MA; Instructor in Psychiatry, Harvard Medical School at the Cambridge Hospital, Cambridge, MA

STELLA CHESS, M.D.
Professor of Child Psychiatry, Department of Psychiatry, New York University Medical Center, New York City, NY

ROBERT COLES, M.D.
Professor of Psychiatry and Medical Humanities, Harvard University; Faculty, Cambridge Hospital, Department of Psychiatry, Cambridge, MA

RUTH B. DAVIS, PH.D.
Director, CASPAR (Cambridge and Somerville Program for Alcoholism Rehabilitation) Alcohol Education Program, Somerville, MA; Clinical Instructor in Psychology, Harvard Medical School at the Cambridge Hospital, Cambridge, MA

E. VIRGINIA DEMOS, ED.D.
Director, Program in Counseling and Consulting Psychology, Harvard Graduate School of Education, Cambridge, MA

BARBARA BOOK DORNBUSH, B.A.
Former Research Coordinator, Adolescent and Family Project, Boston, MA

TIMOTHY F. DUGAN, M.D.
Instructor in Psychiatry, Department of Psychiatry, Harvard Medical School at the Cambridge Hospital, Cambridge, MA

J. KIRK FELSMAN, ED.D.
Assistant Professor of Psychiatry (Psychology), Dartmouth Medical School, Department of Psychiatry, Hanover, NH

NORMA HAAN, PH.D.
Formerly, Psychologist and Research Scientist, Institute of Human Development, University of California, Berkeley, CA

STUART T. HAUSER, M.D., PH.D.
Associate Professor of Psychiatry, Harvard Medical School; Director, Adolescent and Family Development Project, Massachusetts Mental Health Center, Boston, MA

ALAN M. JACOBSON, M.D.
Associate Professor of Psychiatry, Harvard Medical School; Chief, Mental Health Unit, Joslin Diabetes Center; Associate Director, Adolescent and Family Development Project, Boston, MA

JANCIS V.F. LONG, PH.D.
Clinical Psychologist, The Washington School of Psychiatry, Washington, DC

JOSEPH M. SCHWARTZ, PH.D.
Assistant Psychologist, McLean Hospital; Instructor, Harvard Medical School, Boston, MA

GEORGE E. VAILLANT, M.D.
Raymond Sobel Professor of Psychiatry, Dartmouth Medical School, Department of Psychiatry, Hanover, NH

MARIE ANNE B. VIEYRA, M.A.
Psychology Department, University of Connecticut, Storrs, CT

DONALD WERTLIEB, PH.D.
Associate Professor of Child Study, Tufts University, Medford, MA

Preface

Several years ago I found myself evaluating a suicidal 14-year-old girl in the Cambridge Hospital Psychiatry Emergency Room. She had taken her mother's antidepressant medication following an angry encounter with her mother. The child was born in the United States of Portuguese immigrants. The child was wearing designer jeans and a boldly colored shirt, emblazoned with the name of a well-known rock group. She was sedated at the time of the interview, denied any anger toward the family or her mother, and was apologetic for her behavior. The child was accompanied by her mother, who spoke only a few words of English and who was dressed in the traditional black dress and black head scarf I had come to associate with mothers in Portuguese immigrant families.

We spoke of the possible precipitants of the impulsive suicide attempt. The child had begun receiving phone calls from a neighborhood boy about three months prior to the suicide attempt and this had precipitated considerable conflict in the family. The mother, through a translator, told of her worries about her daughter, her own sense of isolation in general, the moral conflicts presented by her daughter's interest in boys; she also alluded to a sense of abandonment by her husband who worked two jobs and drank too much. The mother oscillated between moments of deep sobbing, seemingly for herself and her thwarted desires, and outbursts of bitter criticism directed at her daughter.

Over the years, this had become a familiar story to me—of well-wishing, God-fearing parents who had left Portugal with the dream of economic success and social freedom, and of immigrant children who struggled between the "old world" values of the parents and "new world" values as visible on the streets of Cambridge and in their local schools.

This 14-year-old wasn't the first child we had seen in this dilemma, nor would she be the last. I felt comfortable in my clinical impressions, buoyed by much experience and well versed in explanatory formulations such as "anger turned inward and directed at the self" or "failed separation." I was comfortable, that is, until this child's older sister arrived in the emergency room.

The older sister was 18 and likewise dressed in designer jeans, but wore an attractive blouse and sweater. She had left her afterschool job in Harvard Square as soon as she heard of her sister's suicide attempt. She confirmed that her younger sister and mother had been fighting about the phone calls from the boy. She also told me of her concerns about her mother's sadness and her father's persistent tiredness. She confided in me that she contributed $30.00 per week to the family's food budget. She then astounded me by telling me, in a very embarrassed fashion, looking away from me and keeping her eyes downcast, that she had been accepted by a local, private college three months ago, including a full scholarship. Although she could commute from home, she planned to go to that college and stay in the dorm. She denied any psychiatric symptoms, said she had a 3.6 average in high school, and told me of her interest in studying computers in college, although she could not tell me how she would then like to apply such knowledge in a career. She had a boyfriend and avoided the encounters with her mother by lying. She had worked an afterschool job for three years and assumed she would in college. She was very worried about her sister, though her mood was bright and she felt hopeful about the future.

How do we formulate the dynamics of the older sister? While psychoanalysis aids us in the characterization of pathology and is generally an excellent beacon light in the journey to address the issues of the 14-year-old girl, what science and guideposts do we have to draw upon in understanding the 18-year-old sister who had likewise been born in the United States and raised by the same family? Some may argue that these questions need not be matters of clinical concern, and they may be correct; but it seems to me that if we are interested in elucidating a truly general developmental psychology, then we must complement our highly evolved thinking about pathology-producing variables with a like measure of thinking about development-sustaining variables. Only in a synthesis of the two forces can we then feel assured that we are indeed understanding development.

For this volume we drew together a group of outstanding clinicians and researchers who were invited to apply their experience, research and ideas to the issues of resiliency. Impetus for this work came from a conference on *The Child in Our Times: Resiliency and Vulnerability—Application to Clinical Practice,* which was sponsored by the Cambridge Hospital, Division of Child and Adolescent Psychiatry, and the Harvard Medical School, Department of Continuing Education. I hope readers find themselves challenged by the breadth of these chapters and stimulated by the variety of topics and case applications.

Timothy F. Dugan, M.D.

Acknowledgments

We would first like to acknowledge the thoughtfulness and dedication of our contributors. They bravely accepted our invitation to attempt a clinical application of the concepts of resiliency. To move from the academic realm of large cohorts and risk approaching the consulting room is indeed a challenging task, and we appreciate their efforts to do so.

We would also like to thank members of the Cambridge Hospital, Department of Psychiatry. The Department, while being a major teaching division of the Harvard Medical School, Department of Psychiatry, is also a program within the Cambridge-Somerville Mental Health Center, a division of the Commonwealth of Massachusetts Department of Mental Health. The Department exists both as a clinical facility providing care to chronically ill patients and their families in the public sector and as an academic center. Over the years, we have been impressed that our faculty have been able to see strengths amidst calamity and have, following Erik Erikson's lead, been able to formulate the adaptive purposes hiding behind even the most destructive behaviors.

In particular, we would like to thank Myron Belfer, M.D., Chairman, for his support in offering the conference and in his encouragement of this publication. Nancy Cotton, Ph.D., John Mack, M.D., and Douglas Jacobs, M.D., were influential in planning the original conference and encouraging an interest in the topic.

And lastly, we thank our patients, who continue to challenge us. That so many of them have maintained hope in the midst of such deprivation and disenfranchisement is a model to us all and a major motivation behind our interest in the topic of resiliency and the publication of this volume.

Timothy F. Dugan, M.D.
Robert Coles, M.D.

Introduction

Throughout her life Anna Freud insisted that children be her teachers—that their astonishing capacities, their vulnerabilities, their moments and longer of knowing adaptiveness, all be acknowledged as important givens, rather than banished with a flurry of portentous or dismissive formulations. In Yale she once said this to an American doctor: "It is a rare day that at least one child doesn't give me pause—make me wonder *what* to think! I suspect that if the time comes that I'm no longer surprised or made to have second thoughts—oh, I'd be ready then to try another occupation!"

I thought of her—the lifelong modesty and tactfulness and open mindedness that characterized her work as a child psychoanalyst—as I read the essays that make up this book. I do not think it presumptuous to believe that she might have taken an interest in what these psychoanalysts and psychiatrists and psychologists have to say—she who learned in the Second World War what boys and girls could manage to sustain emotionally during England's trial under the relentless Nazi "blitz" of 1942 and 1943. On another occasion at Yale she observed that "we have yet to discover what it is that makes for real endurance in children, however difficult their lives." Perhaps we move just a bit closer to such knowledge with the help of these clinical and research papers.

All too often many of us want to nudge even the apparently "normal" child toward the doctor's office or, at the very least, into the arms of some psychodiagnostician, whose theoretical statements claim to account for anything and everything. Even the resourceful and willful child, a smile on his or her face, can be taken care of, so to speak, under such circumstances: what *seems* all right is "really" a sign of looming or eventual trouble. Still, children are able so very often to manage their lives rather well—and if we who own the high theory don't credit them much, or issue among ourselves our grave warnings, then so much the sadder for us, I suspect Miss Freud felt (and with her Erik H. Erikson and August Aichorn). What the chapters in this volume tell, actually, is how persistently various children have pushed us in the direction of curiosity and inquiry, rather than an all-too-assured satisfaction with this or that paradigm of what is, or ought be, in the mental life of our young patients, not to mention the mental life or ordinary boys and girls, by the millions, who sustain various vicissitudes and manage, still, to "keep trucking," as the phrase goes—no matter what some of us may think of their psychological prospects.

The point, of course, is not sentimentality, nor a romanticized portrait of childhood. This book is the result of long and patient work with children on the part of physicians or social scientists who have, no doubt, had their own skepticism as watchdogs of sorts, a reminder that if there is, indeed, "resiliency" to be documented, then the observations ought to be sustained, vigorous, and clearheaded. Nor do any of these authors make extravagant claims on behalf of the children they have come to know. In each case the researcher is trying to understand how it is that particular boys and girls manage, against one or another kind of obstacle, to keep their wits about them, to get on with a reasonably satisfactory or intact life.

Such an understanding is important not only for the sake of psychological justice (that various young individuals be given their due) but also in the interests of a more subtle and knowing child psychology and child psychiatry. Freud knew, all along, that psychoanalysis had to comprehend not only psychopathology, but also the ordinary responses of people to life's everyday challenges. Anna Freud echoed such a dual interest with the title to an important book, *Normality and Pathology in Childhood*. The essays in this current volume are contributions to such a line of inquiry—a series of probes into the various aspects of "normality" by men and women who have put in a long time with children and who realize, as Miss Freud did, that it is hazardous, for sure, to underestimate the possibilities for growth and successful endurance in children, and as well, risky to categorize a child's developmental progress without proper cautionary regard. What seems unpromising may well turn out to be a rather hopeful series of events, even as, of course, a seemingly "well adjusted" child can harbor all sorts of potentially hurtful inclinations—which, all of a sudden, can prompt a decided unraveling of a given personality.

Years ago a girl of six whom I knew—a black child initiating school desegregation in New Orleans, against great odds: mobs, violence, daily threats to her life, ostracism—told my wife and me one day that she hoped she would "get through one day, and then another"; but she also told us that if she did manage to do so, and do so with success, she would have an explanation: "It will be because there is more to me than I ever realized." I thought of that remark as I read these most interesting and suggestive essays—reminders to us who work with children in various ways that we have yet to fully comprehend that "more," although we are most certainly and evidently trying to do so, as this book surely indicates.

Robert Coles, M.D.

Part I

PRECURSORS OF RESILIENCY

1
Resiliency in Infancy

E. Virginia Demos

The goal of this chapter is to explore in detail the variety of factors that may contribute to establishing and maintaining a pattern of resiliency in a young child. The chapter will draw on illustrative data from a longitudinal study begun nearly 30 years ago in Boston, and currently revived under the direction of Dr. Louis W. Sander. I and several colleagues have reanalyzed the data from the first two years of life and produced a psychological profile of each infant in order to do a blind match with the profiles of these same people as young adults. The adult data have been collected and analyzed by a separate team of investigators, also under the direction of Dr. Sander. Our task required us to define meaningful variables of psychic organization that are most likely to show some continuity over the 25–30-year span of this study, and we have been looking specifically at resiliency as such a variable.

In general, resiliency is defined as the capacity to bounce back or recover from a disappointment, obstacle, or setback, but clearly this is

This research was supported by grants from the Spencer Foundation, and from the MacArthur Foundation.

I wish to acknowledge my debt to the other members of the research team who helped analyze these data: Drs. A. Halton, S. Kaplan, and G. Stechler.

not a simple, unidimensional capacity. I used the phrase "pattern of resiliency" above to convey the sense of a plurality of abilities or capacities, and also to suggest the contextual parameters involved. Resiliency, like other comple, psychic organizations, does not function uniformly and automatically, but waxes and wanes in response to contextual variables. Thus, given the demands of this longitudinal study for future recognition, it has been important to identify both the unique pattern of abilities and the range of situations most likely to evoke them for each child.

CHILD ABILITIES

It has been helpful to see resiliency as comprised of an assembly or combination of closely related abilities that seem to work together to produce resiliency, but that can also each occur separately and independently of each other. What abilities are involved? At the very least, resiliency requires that the child take an active stance toward an obstacle or difficulty. If the child simply gives up, then by definition, this is not a resilient response. The capacity to bounce back requires the ability to see the difficulty as a problem that can be worked on, overcome, changed, endured, or resolved in some way. Indeed, most infants seem to be born with this potential and begin life as active problem-solvers, but they can learn to become passive in the face of difficulty, thereby compromising their resiliency.

Another ability, closely related to the first, is the ability to persist and to continue trying to find a way to improve things, or to return to a positive state. Here we are dealing with an optimal range of effort that is difficult to specify. Nevertheless, one or two tries would probably not qualify as sufficient, and 50 tries would look more like perseveration than resilience. Resiliency, then, seems to involve a "reasonable" persistence that avoids getting stuck or bogged down and that seems to know when enough is enough, when to give up on a task, and when to temporarily redirect one's efforts.

But taking an active stance and persisting are still not sufficient to add up to resiliency. Perhaps an example would be helpful here to illustrate the limits of active persistence. One of the infants in the study was developmentally delayed. This child would approach each new task with an active, problem-solving stance and with great persistence, but possessed such a limited repertoire of skills and such limited cognitive capacities that the result was a repetition of the same inadequate response, over and over again: for example, 59 attempts to climb a set of stairs. This child seemed unable to learn from mistakes, that is, was unable to modify future responses on the basis of information obtained from the consequences of prior responses. Thus, resiliency also requires that the child have the capacity to develop a range of strategies and skills to bring to bear on a problem. Clearly, there are large individual differences in terms of levels and varieties of skills and complexity of strategies. And these differences will either enhance or curtail a child's capacity to respond in a resilient manner.

Another closely related factor that affects the degree of resiliency is the scope or range of a child's interests and goals. Theoretically, a variety of skills and strategies can be focused narrowly or broadly. However, in the infants we have been studying, a constriction of interests tended to correlate with a smaller repertoire of skills and strategies, and vice versa—the broader the interests, the more varied and complex were the skills and strategies. Thus, there tended to be a compounding of these two factors, producing a mutually reinforcing process of narrowing or a mutually reinforcing process of expanding. There were some exceptions to this pattern, which will be discussed later.

Resiliency in its most developed manifestation, which would include an active stance, persistence, and the application of a variety of skills and strategies over a wide range of situations and problems, also seems to involve a flexibility, by which I mean, knowing when to use what. Thus, merely applying one's skills and strategies in an automatic way (e.g., in a fixed sequence) to every situation would not qualify as a resilient response. Resiliency requires the ability to discriminate between situations and people and to select only the most appropriate responses from among one's repertoire for each occasion.

And finally, there is a motivational assumption embedded in this combination of abilities which states that one's efforts must be successful and/or gratifying in some way, at least some of the time, in order for resiliency to flourish. The frequency, degree, and kind of success are all important parameters here, and vary from child to child. I will return to this issue later when discussing affective sequences.

Table 1 presents a summary of the data on each of the subjects in the longitudinal study, with reference to the combination of abilities that seem to be related to resiliency. The subjects are indicated by number.* Pluses and minuses have been used to indicate the presence or absence

---

*The sex of the subjects has also been deleted. All reference to the subjects will be in neuter terms until the recognition task by the adult team has been completed.

TABLE 1
Child Variables

	Range						
	Active	Persistence	Social	Objects	Flexibility	Success	Resiliency
1	+	+	+	+	+	+	High
2	+−	+−	−	−	−	−	Low
3	+	+	+	−	+	−	Low−Med
4	+−	+−	+−	+−	+−	+−	Low
5	±	±	+	−	±	±	Low−Med
6	+	+	+	−	+−	+−	Med−Low
7	+	+	+	−	+	+	Med−Hi
8	+	+	−	−	−	+−	Low
9	+	+	+	+−	±	±	Med
10	+	+	+	+	+	+	High
11	−+	−+	−+	−+	−+	−+	Med
12	+−	+	+−	+−	+−	−	Low
13	−+	−+	−	−	−	−	Low
14	+	+	+−	+−	+−	+−	Med−Low
15	+	+	+	+	+−	±	Med
16	+	+	+	+	+	+	High
17	+	+	+−	+−	+−	+−	Med
18	+	+	±	±	±	±	Med
19	+	+−	+−	+−	+−	∓	Med−Low
20	+	+	+−	±	+−	±	Low−Med
21	+	+	±	±	+−	±	Low−Med

of an ability. A sequence of a +− or a −+ indicates a change over time in that particular ability (e.g., it started well, but declined over time; or was not present in the beginning, but developed over time). A stacking of pluses and minuses, one on top of the other, ±, indicates that the ability is present or absent depending on the situation, with the top symbol representing the more dominant mode. As one can see from Table 1, there are a variety of patterns of abilities manifested by even this small number of cases, resulting in varying degrees of resiliency from high, medium–high, medium, low–medium, medium–low, to low. I will refer back to Table 1 and the individual patterns in subsequent discussions.

How do these abilities develop and become sustained within the individual so as to create a reliable, recognizable characteristic that we would call resiliency? It has become increasingly clear during our study of these children that there is no simple answer to this question, that there are inputs from many sources, and that, indeed, the answer may be different for different children. Factors that are present and seem determining in one case may not be present or have the same determining effect in another case. At the same time, however, there do seem to be some general dynamics that apply across cases. Therefore, in describing the kinds and degrees of resiliency these children were able to develop in their first two years of life, and the various factors involved in this development, I will try to preserve the unique patterns of specific cases, while at the same time utilizing them as examples of general principles of organization that seem to be operating across cases. Thus, for example, I have already argued that there is a finite set of abilities which combine to produce resiliency, and that they all have to be present to some degree for the phenomenon to occur. But as Table 1 indicates, there are great individual differences in the time course of these abilities and the degree to which each ability is manifested, whereby unique patterns are generated. By combining the idiographic and nomothetic perspectives and utilizing the creative tension that occurs between them, one can more readily discern the contributions of both.

One of the many factors influencing the infant's capacity for resiliency is temperament or innate endowments. Clearly, not all babies start out with the same characteristics. According to Thomas and Chess (1977), most babies fall into the "easy baby" category, which means that they are innately adaptable and moderately active. This gives them a head start on resiliency. A quick glance at Table 1 indicates that most of the babies in our sample fell into this category. A smaller number of babies will start out life with less adaptability, or with a more passive stance toward the world, or with some sort of developmental or physical deficiency, and thus will require more input from a caregiver to develop resilience. Two babies in our sample, 11 and 13, fell into this category. Child 11 received the extra input necessary for adequate functioning, and child 13 did not.

FAMILY CHARACTERISTICS

This last statement introduces the equally important factor of the caregiver's response to the infant's unique characteristics. Currently, there is much discussion in the literature about the importance of the goodness of fit or match between the infant's characteristics and changing developmental capacities over time, and the caregiver's characteristics, expectations, and ability to provide optimal challenges or "phase-specific experiential nutrients" (Erikson, 1950; Greenspan & Porges, 1984; Sander, 1962; Stechler & Kaplan, 1980; Thomas, 1981). We have found this notion of a fit or a match to involve more than one dynamic. When the match is based on a perception and a valuing of the baby as an autonomous, unique being—in other words, when it is based on an empathic understanding and support of the infant as a separate person (see Demos, 1984, for a detailed discussion of empathy)—then the possibilities for developing resiliency in the child are greatly enhanced.

Table 2 presents characteristics of the families. The first two columns refer to the parents' understanding and support of the child's goals and capacities. Families 1, 11, and 16 were clear cases of these parental capacities, whereas families 2, 3, 5, 12 (and to a lesser extent 8, 13, 19, 20, and 21) show a striking lack of these capacities. A match or fit based on empathy does not require that the child possess characteristics similar to those of the parents. Whatever the degree of similarity or difference, the parents are able to bridge the gap and to make the necessary adjustments in order to appreciate and foster the unique potentialities of their child. In family 11, for example, the baby was born with cerebral palsy, but the mother was able to see the baby's potential, to adapt her caregiving to the baby's capacities, and to work tirelessly to improve the baby's physical capacities. By the end of the two-year period, this child functioned adequately and had achieved a moderate degree of resiliency (see Table 1).

A good fit or match, however, can also occur when the child possesses some important characteristics that are similar to those of the parent. In these cases, the dynamic underlying the parental stance toward the child may be one of identification, rather than true empathy. In such cases, the parent values and supports the child because the child is just like the parent, but tends not to value or support those aspects of the child that are different from parental qualities. Family 10 is a good example of this kind of dynamic. The mother was very vigorous, active, and exuberant, and would characteristically engage in sudden, highly stimulating interactions with her baby—interactions so intense and intrusive that they often horrified the observers. But the infant matched the mother in vigor, activity, and exuberance and would characteristically respond with chortling and laughter. However, the infant was also capable of quieter, more dreamy states that the mother found difficult to accept, and at such times, the mother would try to provoke her child into activity. The mother was also quite intolerant of certain kinds of behaviors at certain times, and would set quick and harsh limits. Thus, as long as the child stayed within the mother's personal realm of recognizable and acceptable behaviors, the mother was a vigorous supporter of her child, but outside of this realm the mother moved swiftly and vigorously to prohibit or change her child's behavior, and required her child to make the necessary adjustments.

In this particular case, however, there were two mitigating factors that helped the child to adapt. First of all, the mother's idiosyncratic bound-

TABLE 2
Family Variables

	Empathy				Affect Sequences	
	Understand	Support	Flexibility	Contain	Pos-Neg-Pos	Pos-Neg-Neg
1	+	+	+	+	+	−
2	−	−	−	−	−	+
3	−	−	−	−	+	+
4	+	−	−	−	+−	+
5	−	−	−	±	+	+
6	±	±	−	−	−	+
7	±	±	+	+	+	−
8	+	−	−	−	−	+
9	+−	±	+	±	+	+
10	±	±	+	+	+	−
11	+	+	+	+	+	−
12	−	−	−	−	−	+
13	∓	−	−	+	−	+
14	∓	∓	∓	−	−	+
15	+	+−	+−	+−	+−	+
16	+	+	±	±	+	−+
17	+	+−	+−	+	+	−+
18	±	±	±	±	+	+
19	∓	−	−	−	−	+
20	∓	−	∓	+	∓	±
21	∓	∓	∓	∓	∓	±

aries encompassed a wide range of behaviors and thus afforded the child many degrees of freedom. Second, the mother was capable of what we have come to call "selective empathy,"* namely, empathy under specific circumstances. For although this mother's stance toward her child was based primarily on identification, there were occasional moments when all of her usual tactics failed to produce the desired result. At such times, this mother could stop trying to force a solution, could step back and empathetically understand her child's situation, and could then alter her behavior accordingly. Later in this chapter I will discuss the importance of this kind of flexibility, as well as other factors involved in this case that produced such a highly resilient child (see Table 1).

This particular combination of a high degree of similarity between child and parent and a parent's identification worked so successfully in family 10 in part because of the specific characteristics they shared,

*I am indebted to Paul Ornstein for this term.

namely, vigor, exuberance, and a high activity level. But the same combination proved disastrous for family 13, whose shared characteristics included slowness and cognitive limitations. Baby 13 manifested an unusual degree of inactivity in the early months and later showed marked developmental delays, but the parents were very pleased and comfortable with these characteristics, saw no reason to actively intervene, and thus left the baby alone for long periods of time. The baby's initial deficits were greatly compounded by this lack of attention; left alone, the baby was unable to develop a repertoire of adaptive strategies and skills, and fell farther and farther behind. By the time this baby could crawl and walk (in the middle of the second year), there was such a paucity of cognitive and manipulative skills that most initiatives and efforts resulted in perseveration, stereotypy, or frustration. This child was one of the least resilient children in the sample.

When there is not a good match or fit between child and parent characteristics, *and* when the parent is unable to bridge the gap through an empathic understanding of the child and to make the necessary adjustments, then the results can vary; however, the possibilities for enhancing the development of resiliency in the child are greatly reduced. Family 8 is a good example of this kind of situation. The baby was vigorous, active, and persistent, and although the mother could at times admire these qualities in her child, she was herself cautious and fearful, and spent much of her time trying to inhibit her child's activities. This child could outlast the mother and withstand her prohibitions, but winning these battles rarely led to the gratification of shared play and an elaboration of strategies and skills, for the mother would withdraw. Thus, without facilitation and support, the child's vigor and persistence gradually took on a driven, scattered quality, seeking novelty by changing objects often rather than through elaboration, resulting in a repetitive sameness with little flexibility and resiliency.

The importance of temperament and infant characteristics as a factor influencing resiliency, then, is a function of parental abilities to adapt to the child. When parents can use their empathic understanding of the child to foster the child's unique potentialities, then the child's characteristics, as determining factors, diminish in importance, except in extreme cases of deficit or temperament, which may set limits on the compensatory possibilities of even the best caregiving efforts. We saw this in family 11, where with extraordinary efforts by the mother, the child was able to achieve a medium level of resiliency, but no higher, at least by the end of two years. When these parental empathic abilities are not present, and the parent relies primarily on identification, then the specifics of the match between the child's characteristics and the parent's characteristics becomes of central importance in determining the outcome.

Another important factor influencing the infant's capacity for resiliency is the degree of resiliency in the family system. This can be manifested in several ways. First of all, families differ in the degree and kinds of flexibility they have in dealing with problems. By problems I mean the myriad ways, both large and small, in which a parent's agenda can differ from a child's agenda. The manner in which these situations are handled provides an important source of learning for the young child, for in such moments the child is emotionally invested in his or her own plan and initiative, and cares a great deal about what happens. Thus, the parent's response conveys information about whether or not that initiative and the emotional investment is valued and respected, about whether or not such disagreements or differences can be resolved and negotiated, and about the style of negotiation and the range of possible solutions or compromises. And because these moments of clashing agendas occur so frequently in the daily lives of families with small children, the power of the learning that occurs is increased by the redundancy inherent in the process of generalizing from one situation to another by means of perceiving variance, namely, repetitions with a difference.

A flexible parent, who does not get stuck in battles with the child, but who can usually manage to find alternative solutions that allow for some gratification of the original plan as well as some compromise, can convey the message that the child's initiative and affective investment are valued and respected, that problems can be solved, and that there are a variety of means of achieving one's goals. Family 1 was a good example of this kind of flexibility and the child quickly began to imitate the mother and display the same capacity for compromise, negotiation, and creative solutions. Family 16 articulated early their commitment to fostering their child's initiatives, and the mother, in particular, devoted much time and energy to facilitating her child's plans. This child was capable of compromise, although the mother rarely insisted on it, and developed a strong expectation that its plans were important and would succeed and a good capacity to carry them out. Family 10 was also flexible much of the time, but, as described earlier, this mother could also be quite inflexible and impose her will on the child, completely overriding the child's plan. Thus, this child had to learn when to give in to mother and when to persist and engage in negotiation.

By contrast to these three relatively flexible families, family 4 represented the opposite extreme. As soon as the child began to display initiative in a persistent manner, (somewhere in the middle of the first year), the parents perceived life as a battle and stated unequivocally, "Baby will fight, but we will win!" They presented this child with a trio of insurmountable forces: a united front, hypervigilance, which included a relentless interference with the child's plans, and the use of shaming and humiliation to obtain compliance. Following an illness at around 15 months, the child finally gave up an active struggle and became listless, wan, and an irregular sleeper and eater. Family 19 was also relatively inflexible and adopted negative techniques to obtain compliance (namely, spankings, angry commands, isolation, and threats of abandonment and banishment), allowing the child only two choices—surrender or defiance. But unlike child 4, whose initiatives were relentlessly interfered with by hypervigilent parents, child 19 was left alone for long periods of time and was able, when alone, to carry out its own plans and to act out defiant fantasies and conflicts around obedience.

There are a number of family patterns that fall in between these two extremes. In two cases, for example, the parents actively provoked and encouraged behaviors in their child that gratified the parent, and actively discouraged or ignored all other behaviors. Thus, in family 3, the mother could not tolerate any dependency on the child's part and punished or ignored demands made on her by the child, or would discontinue a behavior once she realized the child liked it and therefore might start demanding it. At the same time, the mother seemed to enjoy angry, destructive behaviors. The father was more responsive to the child's initiatives and demands, but was not as available as the mother. Gradually, this child became focused on trying to please the mother, rather than on trying to pursue its own initiatives, and increasingly engaged in destructive acts and acts that involved self-inflicted pain (e.g., slamming its body into a cabinet in order to evoke a laugh or a smile from mother). In family 5, the mother ignored the child for long periods of time, but responded when the child was "cute" or "entertaining." This child gradually developed skills as a clown, a mimic, and a flirt, all of which clearly pleased the mother, but gave up trying to develop a whole range of other skills that were not responded to in the family.

Both of these children retained some flexibility, persistence, and creativity (see Table 1) in the prescribed areas of expression allowed to them, but they also both gave up a much wider range of interests and skills and gave up trying to pursue their own initiatives in exchange for winning their mother's approval. Winnicott (1971) has argued that when behavior becomes guided by external stimuli rather than by internal motivations and cues, it is the beginning of the "false self." These two children had begun that process; it was manifested early in the second year of life and was the result of learning to devalue and to *not* attend to internal motivations and cues, and to focus instead on external stimuli, principally those coming from the mother.

Family 7 also selectively responded to their child's behaviors and therefore steered the child in some directions rather than in others; however, the scope of the steering was far less extensive than in the two previous cases, and it occurred in a generally supportive context. Thus, while this mother allowed and helped to make possible the child's play with inanimate objects, she herself did not participate in these activities. But when the child engaged in verbal, social, or fantasy play, the mother was actively involved. This mother also actively trained the child to persist by teasing the child and encouraging the child to fight back. Another characteristic of this mother were her periodic depressions. During such periods she was unable to be her usual responsive self, but she did manage to stay in contact with the child. The child, in turn, learned to adapt to these states by going into a more passive, wait-and-see, observing mode. Thus, the child's resiliency was only moderately compromised and only in specific areas; for example, there was a diminution of joy and excitement and a lack of creative elaboration of plans in relation to play with inanimate objects. There was one other problem area for this child which will be discussed in the next section.

Another facet of family resiliency, closely related to flexibility and perhaps representing another kind of flexibility, involves the family's capacity to contain problems within their original context and set of issues, and to keep them from spreading into other areas and interfering with the child's functioning at other times. In family 7, just discussed above, the mother elicited fear in the child during toilet training. This fear was still in evidence by the end of two years and had not been mastered or resolved, but neither had it spread to other areas. The child was not generally fearful or inhibited, nor did the mother remind the child at other times of this fear, or tease or reject the child because of it. Thus, it remained an encapsulated problem.

Family 10 was also a good example of this capacity. In the last several months of the first year, there was an intense and prolonged struggle between mother and child about going to sleep in the crib at night. The mother would put the child in the crib and walk out of the room, and the child would scream and become frantic with anger and terror and cry intensely for long periods of time. This decisive mother uncharacteristically vacillated, sometimes leaving the child to cry, sometimes picking the child up, and sometimes allowing the child to fall asleep in her arms. The problem persisted at this intense level for several months, but during this difficult period the child did not become more fearful, clingy, or demanding of the mother's presence during the day. Nor did the mother become impatient or angry at the child during the day for not complying with the mother's wishes at night. The problem stayed focused on the child's being left alone in the crib. It was finally resolved when the mother, in one of her rare moments of selective empathy, was able to adapt to the child's needs (instead of insisting on the reverse) and discovered that if she remained in the room for a few minutes after placing the baby in the crib, the baby would calm down and fall asleep.

In these two families, then, whatever difficulties the parents experienced (e.g., feelings of anger, disappointment, guilt, confusion) when dealing with the problem area, they did not allow them to intrude into other interactions with their child at other times of day, in other contexts. These parents seemed to have a strong investment in preserving a positive stance toward their child. I will return to the importance of positive affect in the final section of this chapter.

Other families who did not succeed in containing problems manifested a more inconsistent or mixed stance toward the child, or a less intense involvement in the child's life. Three families in the sample—families 6, 14, and 15—showed a marked ambivalence toward the child, which in each case involved a major interactional issue and thus cut across a wide range of situations and activities. In family 6, the issue involved an ambivalence about closeness. The mother could allow closeness for only so long and then would withdraw, but would become angry if the child turned to another adult for comfort or interaction. In family 14 the ambivalent issue involved enjoyment of life. The mother would encourage or permit the child's participation in an activity, but in the middle of the child's excitement and enjoyment, she would suddenly interfere and prohibit the activity—a veritable killjoy. In family 15, the mother's ambivalence centered around how much support and help to give her child, and yet still make the child tough and strong. Thus, she would usually begin by providing help, but would then begin to tease and frustrate the child. When the child dissolved in tears, the mother would once again become comforting and supportive.

Each of the parents seemed stuck and could only act repeatedly on both sides of their ambivalence at every opportunity. Having failed to resolve these major issues themselves, they were in no position to help their children resolve them. Thus, each of these children was faced with an uncontainable and insoluable problem, and each gradually imposed idiosyncratic constrictions and solutions. Child 6, confronted by the mother with the message, "Don't be dependent, but don't be too independent or attach to another," and with a mostly absent and unsupportive father, gradually became defiant, turned away from help offered by others, and preferred and insisted on doing things alone—clearly a compromise in resiliency. Child 14—faced with a frustrating, interfering, and sometimes hostile mother, who could also be positive and comforting, and with a more positive and responsive, but frequently absent father—gradually became oversensitive to intrusions, narrowed its interests, and defended them with stubborn persistence, resulting in a decrease in resiliency over time. And child 15 had to deal with a mother who offered just enough support to keep the child active, but would also tease, criticize, and withdraw support, and with a more benign, but uninvolved father. This child took on the mother's teasing, aggressive style. Gradually, the early signs of resiliency evolved into an insistent need to be in active control of interactions and into a grim tenseness in pursuing plans.

Family 2 and, to a lesser extent, family 20, represent a different kind of uncontainable problem, namely, a minimal investment in the child. In family 2, although the mother hovered anxiously over the child's physical functions (e.g., eating, sleeping, and bowel movements), her more characteristic stance was to feel overwhelmed and to experience her child's active initiatives as exasperating or bad. Thus, she offered no support, protection, or facilitation, and often tried, unsuccessfully, to curtail the child's activities by yelling at or hitting the child. The father could, at times, facilitate the child's efforts (e.g., he built a little stand so the child could look out the window), but was also harsh and impatient with the child's expressions of distress or fear. The child learned to fear and comply with father, and to successfully defy and oppose mother, thereby existing always in a win or lose situation and never experiencing the middle ground of negotiation, compromise, cooperation, and so forth. Without support for a wide range of initiatives or protection from danger, the child also began to constrict activities and skills. All these factors contributed to a steady decline in resiliency. In family 20, the parents were very young and the mother felt trapped and depressed by parental responsibilities. She developed a breezy, permissive, inattentive, almost negligent style of parenting. The father was somewhat more attentive, but both expected the child to be independent and to work things out on its own. The child became important to the parents as a source of entertainment and pride regarding certain capabilities. But as the child struggled to master a variety of situations without parental help, manifesting a defensive or precocious independence, its plans became more limited, less ambitious, and focused on learning new skills and turning away from people and relationships.

In all of these cases involving an uncontainable problem, the child was faced with a pervasive, insoluable difficulty. Thus, each family had failed to keep the level of challenges within the child's capacities to resolve, and in each case the child responded by constricting its scope in some way. It looked as if each child did so in order to maximize the possibilities for mastery and success or, in other words, to cut the challenge down to a more manageable size. Thus, these children preferred to do the doable, and to avoid or escape from the undoable, even though that choice compromised their resiliency by reducing their focus and repertoire of strategies and skills. The preservation of an area of positive, successful functioning therefore seemed to be paramount.

<h2 style="text-align:center">THE MOTIVATIONAL ROLE OF AFFECT</h2>

This brings us to the final factor influencing a child's capacity for resiliency and one that perhaps provides the motivational basis for many of the dynamics that have already been discussed, namely the importance of positive affect and of affective sequences. According to Tomkins (1962), the positive affects of interest-excitement and enjoyment-joy are experienced as inherently rewarding states and, as such, they can become goals in and of themselves.

> In the case of the human being, the fact that he is innately endowed with positive and negative affects which are inherently rewarding or punishing, and the fact that he is innately endowed with a mechanism which automatically registers all his conscious experience in memory, and the fact that he is innately endowed with receptor, motor, and analyzer mechanisms organized as a feedback circuit, together make it all but inevitable that he will develop the following General Images: (1) Positive affect should be maximized; (2) Negative affect should be minimized; (3) Affect inhibition should be minimized; (4) Power to maximize positive affect, to minimize negative affect, to minimize affect inhibition should be maximized. (1962, p. 328)

In applying Tomkins' formulation to infancy, Sander's work has been particularly useful. He has recently argued (1985) that the capacity for inner experience exists at the outset of postnatal life. Thus, the ego (or self) begins as a state ego rather than a body ego, and the infant's own states, where coherent, recurrent, and desired, become the primary target or goals for behavior. I have argued elsewhere (Demos, 1988) that these early waking states are in fact affect states. Thus, the goal to re-experience positive affect or to recreate the situations associated with the experience of positive affect, while minimizing or avoiding negative affect, can motivate and shape the young child's behavior from birth onwards. The Papouseks come to a similar conclusion based on their experimental work with young infants:

> Infants appear to be just as attracted to the expectation of a pleasurable outcome that accompanies success as they are motivated to avoid the negative affect experienced with too much incongruency, dissonance, or the inability to discover the contingencies and adjust their own behavior accordingly. (Papousek, Papousek, & Koester, 1986, p 99.)

The examples described above, of the children compromising their resiliency in order to avoid failure and to preserve an area of successful functioning, is a good demonstration of the power of positive affect to motivate and shape behavior.

When positive affect is frequently embedded in a sequence of positive affect, followed by negative affect, followed by positive affect, its motivational force is augmented because the child learns that positive affect can be reliably reestablished, that negative affect can be reliably endured or managed or gotten over, and that the child itself can be an active agent in causing these things to happen. Such a sequence can be experienced at the micro level, which would involve momentary shifts in affect. For example, a child experiences interest and enjoyment as it plays, then encounters an obstacle and expresses distress and anger. This expression brings the mother, who helps resolve the difficulty and so the child reexperiences interest and enjoyment. This kind of sequence can also be experienced at the macro level, which might involve a more prolonged struggle that ends in mastery (e.g., family 10's prolonged struggle over the crib which was finally resolved). And it can involve any combination of positive and negative affects. When it becomes a characteristic family sequence, and therefore occurs in many settings and across many issues, it gradually creates in the child a strong expectation that things will work out and that difficulties can be mastered. Translated into motivational terms, the young child experiences one or more of the following: I can do things; I can solve problems; I can endure frustration and discouragement because I know things will get better; bad things don't last long; and so forth. When such a motivational stance is firmly established, the child approaches each new situation with confidence and optimism.

The four families in this sample that produced children with high or medium-high resiliency all shared two characteristics that were either not present or were present to a more limited degree in the other families.* They maximized opportunities for the shared experience of positive affects, and they were quick to reestablish shared positive affect whenever there was a break (e.g., an angry scolding, or an experience of negative affect by the child). Thus, they were frequently engaged in creating positive-negative-positive affective sequences. Mothers 7 and 10, for example, were both capable of sudden, harsh prohibitions, but they would both quickly make up afterwards by hugging and kissing their child. Thus, however intense or distressing and frightening these moments may have been for each child, they were characteristically brief and were reliably followed by an affectionate coming back together. Neither child showed evidence of a generalized fearfulness as a result of these sudden, intense barrages, although child 7 did show persistent fear about toilet training, which seemed to remain an unresolved issue for this pair. Mothers 1 and 16 were not harsh disciplinarians, and therefore did not create such dramatic extremes for their children, but consistently fostered positive exchanges with their children. All four mothers also found ways to help their respective children whenever they experienced distress, anger, fear, or shame in the ordinary course of events. For example, mother 10 would jolly up or distract her child following a frustration or disappointment, whereas mother 1 was more likely to come up with a creative compromise and thereby reestablish a positive, cooperative experience. And mother 16 bent over backwards to try to accommodate her child's wishes, thereby avoiding or quickly remedying negative experiences for her child.

There are many subtle differences in the way these sequences occurred, and these details are important in shaping the child's unique psychic organization and the specific strategies the child is able to use to cope with negative affect or to reestablish positive affect. Ideally, in order for the positive-negative-positive affective sequence to be most effective, the parent has to acknowledge or respond directly to the negative affect as well as help the child reestablish a positive state (e.g., "Oh, those blocks just won't do what you want them to," verbalizing the child's frustration). Then the parent has to offer either instrumental help with

*Family 11 is an exception. It also shared these two characteristics, but because of the child's physical limitations, only a medium level of resiliency was achieved.

the blocks or emotional support (e.g., "Try again, maybe it will work this time"). By contrast, mother 10, for example, reestablished positive affect by distracting or jollying up her child after a frustration or a scolding. At such times, she seems to be teaching the child to forget about what just happened and to move on to something else. This capacity can be very useful in certain situations, but it does not help the child cope directly with the negative affect, nor does it help the child to endure such states when they cannot be quickly forgotten or escaped from.

The other families in the sample represented a variety of affective possibilities. Several families manifested a mixed pattern containing both positive-negative-positive and positive-negative-negative sequences. In family 9 the father was committed to maximizing positive affect and to quickly reestablishing positive affect, but the mother was more focused on the child's behavior than on the vicissitudes of the child's emotional experiences. As the child became more active and assertive (e.g., at around 16 months), the mother became increasingly punitive and harsh. After a scolding, this mother would demand that the child face the wall until it could stop crying, and then that the child apologize and promise to be good before she would forgive the child. Thus, this child was required to master or suppress its negative affect alone, while being rejected and shamed. This child developed an intense fear of hats and reenacted, over and over again in play, a crime-punishment-forgiveness sequence. And although the child continued to be active and persistent, spontaneity was gradually lost as more caution was exercised to avoid doing the wrong thing and being rejected. In family 18, the mother was initially committed to maximizing positive affect, but over the last eight months she became focused on molding the child into an obedient, docile conformist. Throughout, the father manifested a sadistic, teasing style and could suddenly become quite negative and rejecting. The mother did not protect the child from these frightening encounters with the father. In this shifting family system the child developed a number of adaptive strategies—compromise, persistence, defiance, defeat, cautiousness, imitating father, producing ingratiating grins, or backing away from him. But as the pressures for conformity increased, the child became more compliant and inhibited.

Two other families manifesting a mixed pattern of affective sequences (families 3 and 5) were disccused earlier under family flexibility. In these families the parents only encouraged behaviors that gratified them and actively discouraged or ignored all other behaviors, and the children gradually gave up attending to and pursuing their own initiatives and focused on their parents as the sources of important cues. In the earlier discussion I invoked Winnicott's term "the false self" to describe this process. Here I would like to emphasize the affective dynamics involved. I have suggested elsewhere (Demos, 1983) that every affective moment involves three components occurring simultaneously: a trigger or stimulus; the affect *per se,* which involves facial, vocal, and autonomic patterns of expression and experience; and the response, which includes plans, behaviors, and fantasies, as well as memories of similar events in the past. A parental response, therefore, affects all three components of an experience, regardless of the parent's intent. When parents focus on their child's behavior, as did these parents and the mother in family 9 just described, the affective component of the child's experience is not acknowledged, validated, or shared. Thus, opportunities for maximizing the child's interests and enjoyments, invested in many plans and behaviors, or for minimizing and mastering the child's distresses, angers, shames, or fears evoked by ordinary events, are lost.

When these children engaged in behaviors that interested or pleased their parents, positive-negative-positive affective sequences could occur, but the positive affective components of the experience would not be acknowledged and therefore not maximized. And at all other times, when these children engaged in behaviors that displeased or did not interest their parents, there was no effort or commitment by their parents to help the children overcome difficulties or to reestablish positive communications after a scolding. Thus, there were many occasions when positive-negative-negative affective sequences were experienced by these children; for example, the child manifested interest in an activity, encountered a frustrating or distressing difficulty, tried to engage the parent, the parent ignored, scolded, or discouraged the child, thereby compounding the child's original distress and/or anger). In these sequences, the child's positive affects were minimized, the negative affects were compounded and intensified, and the child was then left alone to cope with the consequences. In motivational terms, these children were learning that their affective states and the plans, ideas, and fantasies related to them did not seem to be very important or valuable. They were also learning that by themselves they were unable to develop skills and solve problems, unable to endure or master negative affects, and unable to reestablish positive affects. At such times, they experienced themselves as devalued, ineffective, and helpless. In such a state the need for parents is heightened, and all the children's efforts became focused on obtaining and sustaining their parents' involvement. They began then to shift away from using an awareness of inner states as a useful frame of reference for guiding behavior, and began to develop skills as readers of parental states and availability. Thus, the range and depth of their developmental possibilities, including their resiliency, were narrowed.

In families 20 and 21 the parents were not consistent in their affective sequences. Family 20 has already been described as relatively permissive and inattentive. Thus, although they were often benignly positive, they were not very involved with the child. They also could become punitive when irritable. In family 21, the father was more committed to maximizing positive exchanges with the child and to reestablishing positive affect, but the mother was often unable to separate the child's needs from her own needs; thus, she would fail to comfort the child in situations that she did not perceive as distressing, or she would provoke anger and protest in the child by misreading the child's cues or by persisting in an activity beyond the child's wishes or needs (e.g., overfeeding the child). In these two families no consistent affective sequences were established.

The other nine families in the sample manifested predominantly positive-negative-negative affective sequences, although there were subtle differences between them. Families 6, 14, and 15 were caught in ambivalent stances toward their children and, as described earlier, they constantly created and then spoiled positive experiences for their children. By contrast, families 2, 4, 8, 12, 13, and 19 consistently interfered with or failed to support their children's interests and enjoyments, and compounded and intensified their children's negative states with shaming, punishment, abandonment, or lack of support. Thus, for all of these children, positive affects in interaction with parents almost always led to negative consequences; all of these children, in their own way, gradually constricted and inhibited their interests and enjoyments in an attempt to control, prevent, or minimize the possibilities for experiencing distress, anger, shame, or fear. As a result, their resiliency was severely compromised.

SUMMARY

I have tried to illustrate the plurality of individual capacities and family variables that are involved in developing and sustaining resiliency in a young child. The data were drawn from a longitudinal study and were presented in a transactional context that stressed the active contributions of both parent and infant, the extent of early learning that occurs for the infant in such exchanges, and the central motivational role of affect. The patterns of resiliency for these 21 children were fairly clear by the end of their first two years of life. They represent the best solutions these infants could generate, given the state of their resources at the time and the degree and kind of facilitation and flexibility provided by their caregivers. When this longitudinal study is completed, we will discover whether or not, or to what extent, these patterns remained constant over a 25-year span. Do the highly resilient children remain so? Do those in the middle range gain or lose resiliency? Do the children whose resiliency has already been compromised ever regain some adaptability? What are the determining factors? Are these affective sequences recognizable in their adult lives? Perhaps in a year or two we will be in a position to answer these questions.

References

Demos, E.V. (1983). A perspective from infant research on affect and self-esteem. In J.E. Mack & S.L. Albon (Eds.), *The Development and Sustaining of Self-Esteem,* pp. 45–78. New York: International Universities Press.

Demos, E.V. (1984). Empathy and affect: Reflections on infant experience. In J. Lichtenberg, M. Bornstein, & D. Silver (Eds.), *Empathy II* (pp. 9–34). Hillsdale, NJ: The Analytic Press.

Demos, E.V. (1988). Affect and the development of the self: A new frontier. In A. Goldberg (Ed.), *Frontiers in Self Psychology, Progress in Self Psychology, Vol. 3* (pp. 27–53). Hillsdale, NJ: The Analytic Press.

Erikson, E. (1950). *Childhood and Society.* New York: W. W. Norton.

Greenspan, S., & Porges, S. (1984). Psychopathology in infancy and early childhood: Clinical perspectives on the organization of sensory and affective-thematic experience. *Child Development, 55,* 49–70.

Papousek, H., Papousek, M., & Koester, L.S. (1986). Sharing emotionality and sharing knowledge: A microanalytic approach to parent-infant communication. In C. Izard & P. Read (Eds.), *Measuring Emotions in Infants and Children, Vol. II* (pp. 93–123). Cambridge, England: Cambridge University Press.

Sander, L. (1962). Issues in early mother-child interaction. *Journal of the American Academy of Child Psychiatry, 1,* 141–166.

Sander, L. (1985). Toward a logic of organization in psychobiological development. In H. Clar & L.J. Siever (Eds.), *Biologic Response Styles: Clinical Implications* (pp. 19–37). Washington, DC: American Psychiatric Press.

Stechler, G., & Kaplan, S. (1980). The development of the self: A psychoanalytic perspective. *Psychoanalytic Study of the Child, 35,* 85–105.

Thomas A. (1981). Current trends in developmental theory. *American Journal of Orthopsychiatry, 51,* 580–609.

Thomas, A., & Chess, S. (1977). *Temperament and Development.* New York: Brunner/ Mazel.

Tomkins, S. (1962). *Affect, Imagery, Consciousness, Vol. I: The Positive Affects.* New York: Springer.

Tomkins, S. (1983). The quest for primary motives: Biography and autobiography of an idea. *Journal of Personality and Social Psychology, 41,* 306–329.

Winnicott, D.W., (1971). *Playing and Reality.* London: Tavistock Publications.

2

Coping with Moral Conflict as Resiliency

NORMA HAAN

To state that morality is central in human existence is a truism, but to suggest that certain forms of moral interchange build children's resiliency, while other equally respected forms may leave children vulnerable to life stress, requires more explanation. The intent of this chapter is to support this view with an action-based view of morality that is quite different from formulations of morality that are commonly held by child specialists.

USUAL VIEWS OF YOUNG CHILDREN'S MORALITY

An explicit or sometimes implied conceptualization of the very young's moral capacity is the starting point of all moral theories since it is here

Work on this essay was supported by a Research Scientist Award (K05 MH00258-06) and a research grant (R01 MH37290) to Norma Haan, both from the National Institute of Mental Health. Gary Yabrove's and Paola Theodorou's assistance in preparing this essay was invaluable.

The editors regret to mention that, since writing this chapter, Dr. Haan suddenly died. Her death is a real loss for those studying children's psychological development.

that assumptions are introduced about the basic nature of humans. This first premise is critical since it sets the stage for all subsequent stipulations. Most moral philosophers, as well as Freud, Piaget, and Kohlberg— each with somewhat different reasons—have thought that the young child is basically self-serving. Freud's view of the superego was required by his suppositions concerning the nature of the young child's uncivilized id; Piaget and Kohlberg based their views on the presumption that young children are cognitively unable to recognize another person's position and therefore are also unable to coordinate their own position with another's. Given these suppositions about young children, society's and adult caretakers' responsibility is clear: Children's natural selfishness or self-containment must be replaced by concern for others.

In recent years, however, several bodies of research and observations of young children's morality suggest that Freud's, Kohlberg's, and Piaget's views may not be correct. For instance, the investigators of prosocial behavior offer a different view. In a recent extensive review of some 400 studies, Radke-Yarrow, Zahn-Waxler, and Chapman (1983) conclude that preschool children "are not only egocentric, selfish, and aggressive; they are also exquisitely perceptive, have attachments to a wide range of others, and respond prosocially across a broad spectrum of interpersonal events in a wide variety of ways and with various natures" (p. 484).

Still other researchers, identified as cognitive scientists (for instance, Anderson, 1980), have taken special care to design laboratory experiments of morality that were in small children's cognitive grasp, an obstacle not overcome in many studies of children's morality. They report that preschoolers are able to integrate moral information and make comparatively complex judgments about moral equity.

Then there are Robert Coles' (1980) observations of morality in those very special young children whose life is caught up in the moral-political protests of their embattled parents—black children integrating schools in the South, Protestant and Catholic children in Ulster, Northern Ireland, and others. He states, for instance, about the Irish children:

> These can be pensive lads and lasses, even the wee ones of five and six. They ask me tough questions for which I'm not sure Socrates would have easy replies. . . . (p. 38)

> And what strikes me is not only their seriousness (I suppose you psychiatrist chaps may find that worrisome!) but their consideration for others. These are thoughtful children: they have seen

people struggling and dying for something they very much believe in. . . . (p. 38)

Finally, Zahn-Waxler and Radke-Yarrow have also studied children of parents suffering from bipolar affective difficulties (in Bales, 1984). They affirm a moral phenomenon that is observed in clinical settings. In role reversal, very young children of troubled, especially depressed parents sometimes become profoundly sensitive, concerned, and helpful to their parents. Although clinicians properly worry about such role reversals, we need to notice that young children *could not* take on this kind of responsibility if they were morally incapable.

AN INTERACTIONAL VIEW OF MORALITY

Several Key Ideas

In the past 20 years, psychologists have undertaken the empirical investigation of morality, but they are locked in controversy. All their arguments come down to one basic uncertainty: What is the nature of *the* morality that people use and cherish in their everyday life? (It is not permissible for scientists *as scientists* to propose any other kind of morality.) Despite the present confusion, I have the impression and hope that direct empirical study of practical morality will eventually produce fresh insights about the moral basis of life. The definition of morality that I propose (Haan, 1982, 1985, 1986; Haan, Aerts, & Cooper, 1985) is shaped and influenced by my earlier experience as a clinician, so it is interactional between at least two people; it centers on the ideas that morality is almost always conflictual—since self versus others' interests are involved—and that moral action is motivated by three common human desires: first, the need to feel that one is moral; second, the need to feel that others think one is moral; third, the need to feel that one's world is just. That people desperately need to feel they are moral is no news to clinicians informed as they are by their clients who, even when they voice their guilt and shame, backhandedly proclaim their knowledge of morality. Indeed, Freud's theory of ego defenses entirely depends on the observation that people will go to great lengths to justify their morality. Very small children do the same. Furthermore, Lerner (1980) demonstrated in a series of studies that people also prefer to believe the world is just, another phenomenon often observed by clinicians who attempt to help clients out in their own behalf.

I do not present or defend this interactional formulation here in much detail, since my thesis concerning children's resiliency and vulnerability primarily depends on a different view of very young children's morality as it is now increasingly being seen by various researchers and as it seemed in my recent study of four-year-olds.

This presentation is framed by several points:

1. There is a basic, centuries-old misconstruction of the nature of young children's morality. Although they are generally assumed to lack moral cognizance, I will argue and give evidence to suggest that young children have the *same* basic moral understandings and concerns as adolescents and young adults.
2. However, the quality of moral action taken by any age group fluctuates. This inconsistency varies with the different meanings they draw in interaction with immediate situations. In stressful situations grownups, but especially children, often act badly. Of course, most morally problematic situations are stressful and stress destroys clarity. In other words, the concept of durable and consistent moral character does not seem accurate. Instead, what is taken to be moral character may be consistency in the strategies people use to solve problems of any kind.
3. Frequently observed deficiencies in young children's moral behavior may not be due to incapacity but rather to their greater vulnerability to stress, their objective powerlessness, and frequently to their parents' ascribing to the culturally conventional theory that young children are selfish, an attitude that fixes parent–child interaction and operates educationally like a self-fulfilling prophecy. People who are well-situated—economically, socially, educationally, and emotionally—have more options, so they tend to solve problems better and more consistently. Obviously, young children are not well-situated.
4. If young children do not lack moral understanding and concern but vary more radically in the quality of their moral performance, then other factors—I specifically suggest the quality of their ego functioning in supportive and nonsupportive situations—may explain their moral inconsistencies. In fact, I suggest observed deficiencies in all people's moral functioning can be understood as failures to cope with conflict and the stressful processes of its resolution. Therefore, I suggest that moral understanding is not what develops in moral devel-

opment. Instead, moral performance improves with age because ego skills and capabilities for resolving conflict improve with age.

5. Because moral problems are bidirectional and conflictual, they are best solved when all participants are able to identify the elements of their disagreement accurately and go on to create solutions that respond to their shared identifications. Commonsense evaluation expects this accuracy—people should be accountable and honest during moral conflict. Parenthetically, therapists work with their clients to achieve this kind of accuracy within the transference and in their outside lives. Moral action is likely to be higher quality, too, when protagonists cope since the latter involves negation and distortions, while the former involves accuracy.

If this general argument has worth, it has definite consequences for clinical practice, especially with children and parents. At this point I mention three:

a) If children do have moral understanding, they are sentient human beings who must then be involved in moral negotiations even when they are in error—as children frequently are. It becomes prudent then to preserve their moral honor and participation during the negotiation rather than maneuver them into compliance. If they *do* understand what is going on, at least on an intuitive, emotional level, then discipline becomes a more complex, subtle exchange, and it cannot simply be consistent, firm, gentle correction of children's wrongdoing.

b) If children have moral understanding, then their attempts to protect their own self-interests must be taken seriously rather than cast off as further evidence of their selfishness, as often occurs. In fact, a mark of vulnerable children is that they are often unable to protect their legitimate self-interests.

c) Experiences of helplessness—a main component of human stress—may prefigure childhood vulnerability, while a sense of agency must prefigure childhood resiliency. Probably no human experience produces a greater sense of helplessness than to be a moral victim, that is, to be used or ignored and not recognized as a moral being. Yet if young children do have moral understanding, helplessness may be exactly what they experience when adults assume that they are without moral awareness. The widely held view that children are moral illiterates gives credence to a second

idea that they do not know the experiences of being morally
ignored or used.

A STUDY OF FOUR-YEAR-OLDS' MORAL ACTIONS

To counter these usual views, I describe my study of four-year-olds.
My question is how do pairs of four-year-olds act morally when they are
in moral conflict but the context supports their coping? As in my previous studies of adolescents and young adults, we used a simple situation
which we called NeoPd, meaning New Prisoner's Dilemma. This situation is a slice of life since participants' fates—successes, failures, and
stalemates—depend on their coordinating their actions with one another. The situation evokes two clear moral issues. First, a person cannot
"win" without hurting his or her partner, and if he or she tries to turn
NeoPd into a conventionally competitive game, the other person can
easily stalemate this attempt so neither participant gets any reward. "Success" depends on tacit or explicit agreements to share, demonstrating in
a very practical sense that no person is an island. Second, when participants make agreements—promises if you like—they often and unthinkingly break them. These moral issues are upsetting, emotional experiences for all age groups.

The moral demands of this task were the same as for the older age
groups but various cognitive simplifications of the situation were made
for the four-year-olds so outcomes would depend on moral understanding and not on cognitive competence. Thus, outcomes were concretely
depicted as shown in Figure 1; payoffs in pennies were immediate; only
two children played at a time; and a staff leader supported the children's
coping efforts to prevent overwhelming stress that would have led to
capitulation and tears.

The 40 four-year-olds who participated in this study were from two
adjacent nursery schools; their families were primarily middle class and
75% were White, while Blacks and Asians made up the other 25%. All
pairs who played together were of the same sex except two. The pairs
were considered friends, or even best friends, by the teachers. The staff
leaders took neutral roles but they continuously turned the problem
back to the children. The leaders also tried to help the children *cope with*
the problems. In other words, we aimed to establish *optimal conditions* that
would allow these children to cope and thereby give their best performance, not the defensive performance that they might have given if they
became stressed or adult-compliant. No special instructions were given

Solutions :

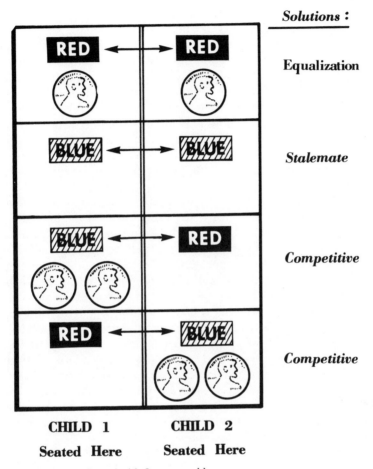

Equalization

Stalemate

Competitive

Competitive

CHILD 1   CHILD 2

Seated Here   Seated Here

FIGURE 1. NeoPd Board used with four-year-olds.

except for the invitation to play a game; in the activity room they were told they would receive pennies that they could take home. They were uniformly eager to get pennies.

In the activity room, the children were seated side by side, and the board, shown in Figure 1, was placed in front of the them. They each had a bowl to contain their pennies. The play required both children simultaneously to place a red or blue card on the table as the staff leader said, "One, two, three, choose." As can be seen in Figure 1, the structure of this task allows three main solutions. First, *equalization,* which occurred when both children played red cards; both would receive one penny. Second, *stalemate,* which occurred when both children played blue cards; neither received pennies. Third, *default* occurred when one child played blue and received two pennies and the other played red and received no pennies. The adolescents and young adults that I had studied earlier produced two additional, more complex solutions and the four-year-olds did also. *Reparation* occurred when the two children agreed that the child who was behind in points would play blue to catch up in pennies, while the child who was ahead would play red and therefore receive no pennies. *Betrayal,* a form of default, occurred when one child deliberately broke an explicit agreement to equalize that he or she had made with the other child.

Equalizing and reparative acts can surely be regarded as evidence of children's general moral concern for others as well as their ability to recognize their and others' fate is mutual and inextricably coordinate. Since both acts occur at some cost to the self, a naturally selfish child would not be expected to either equalize or repair. Still, some readers may want to point out that a kind of enlightened self-interest is being served by equalization. But morality itself is a recognition that human welfare is intertwined and that there is nothing inherently illegitimate about having one's self-interest served in a measure equal to others' self-interest. Only abstraction proposes that morality is selfless. In fact, an insight of modern psychiatry and psychology is that people give wholeheartedly only as they are given to. But we have been confused since we expected that the naturally selfish child was incapable of any giving. Therefore, his or her morally capable parents must do all the giving as well as provide all the limitations since the child simply lacks moral sensibility.

Two Examples of Equalization

In 85% of the dyads these four-year-olds acted to equalize at some point in the play, and overall, 32% of their plays were equalizations compared to 29% for the university students. Nevertheless, only 27% of the children never *verbalized* moral ideas—such as "We chose red because we each get the same amount" or, in protection of legitimate self-interest, "This game is not fair, you're winning too many pennies." Sixteen percent spontaneously verbalized these ideas before the staff leader did, while 57% used such words, usually immediately after the staff leader asked their opinions about fairness. Notice that although 27% of the children *never* articulated these ideas, only 15% *never* enacted these ideas. I present two examples of equalization.

Two girls have been continuously playing so that each has been receiving an equal number of pennies. But the staff leader, whom we designate by "SL," is not certain that they understand the contingencies or that they are deliberate about their choices:

SL: What would happen if you, Jackie, put down a blue card and Mary put down a red card?
Jackie: I would get pennies and she wouldn't.
SL: Would that be fair?
Jackie: Noooo. Because then I get pennies and she doesn't. (*pause*) It gets really kinda unhappy.
SL: Mary, how would you feel if you got some pennies and Jackie didn't?
Mary: (*biting her lip*) Sad.
SL: How come?
Mary: I don't like Jackie getting sad and we're friends and we always do the same thing.
SL: When you both put down red, how does that make you feel?
Both Girls: Happy!
Jackie: 'Cause then it's more like it, 'cause we both get something. (*Each will receive one penny.*)

A more complicated form of equalization also occurred: Two children agree that they will take turns winning pennies by alternately playing the blue-red combination. One child will play red; the other plays the blue; and then the pattern is reversed. In this next example, Betty and Mark have whispered to each other and devised such a plan which they decide not to tell to the staff leader (Mark is ahead by two pennies).

Mark: Come on, Betty, let's do it a different way.
Betty: No! You said, you said.
Mark: Oh, yeah, then I get to, then you get to put red down, right, yeah?
SL: What are you going to do?
Mark: *We* made a plan.
SL: What's your plan?
Mark: We can't tell it.
SL: Okay, but do you know what the plan is between yourselves?
Betty: Yeah.
Mark: Yeah.

SL: Ready: one, two, three. Chose. (*Both children quickly glance at each other and without hesitation put down their cards. Betty plays blue while Mark plays red.*) Excited by their mutual success, they are eager to implement the second part of their plan.

Mark: And there's another plan.

Betty: Yeah.

SL: Oh, we'll see what happens then.

Betty: Now this time I get to put down a . . .

Mark: (*interrupting*) Red.

SL: Is that what the plan was?

Both: Yeah!

SL: Okay, here we go. Ready, one, two, three, choose. (*This time Mark immediately puts down a blue and Betty, in keeping with the agreement plays her red card.*)

SL: So, Mark, you get two, and Betty doesn't get any. So does that seem fair?

Betty: (*quickly*) Yeah.

SL: Why?

Betty: 'Cause the other time I got pennies.

SL: I see. Since you got two pennies last time it's fair because . . .

Mark: (*interrupting*) And we're going to keep doing that over and over until we stop.

An Example of Reparation

The children frequently leaned over to examine both bowls and to count the total contents. They then sometimes worked out a plan to equalize the total number of pennies to repair inequalities, sometimes after the child who was ahead recognized the inequality. Although the "winners" were not always happy about making reparation, 60% of the pairs did so at some point.

In this example, Mimi, who has two pennies, proposes that they play so she can win more pennies, while Jane, who has six, will get none. Jane agrees with some reservation, but Mimi is energetic in protection of her own self-interest.

Mimi: Now this time you put down a red and I'll put down a blue. (*She turns to Jane as she speaks, gesturing with her finger in a forceful manner.*)

Jane: Yeah. (*Mimi smiles.*)

SL: You what, Jane?

Jane: If we both have to take a red . . . (*then, more decisively*) Okay, if we both do blue and red. (*She nods her head at this decision, smiles, and points to the cards on the board.*)
SL: Mimi, why don't you tell Jane your idea?
Jane: She wants to put down *blue*. Let's do that.
SL: Okay. Ready? One, two, three, choose. Okay, Mimi, you put down a blue; Jane, you put down a red, what happens?
Mimi: I get two and she gets none. (*She has a big grin on her face and giggles as she speaks. Jane is staring expressionless at the table, sucking on her hair.*)
SL: So this time, Jane, you put a red down but didn't win any pennies. How come you did that?
Jane: 'Cause Mimi wanted me to do it.
SL: 'Cause Mimi told you to?
Jane: I didn't mind. (*She begins picking her nose.*)

Although Jane played as Mimi asked (or demanded; Mimi is markedly forceful when she proposes this solution), she seemed to have some doubts at first, saying, "If we both have to take a red," as if she was considering the options, but she made up her mind. Later, she seemed a bit downcast. Her self-interest ran counter to her friend's, but still she repaired the inequity.

An Example of Default

Defaults occur when one partner plays competitively, while the other attempts to equalize. Some occasion of default occurred in 65% of the sessions. Although children's self-servingness sometimes seemed to outweigh concern for their friend, at other times they justified acting in their own behalf on account of their partner's previous violations.

In this example, Bobby played blue unrelentingly throughout, although Mike made him fully aware of the inequity. In the end Mike protects his self-interest—he copes—by quitting the game.

Mike: Can you put down red, Bobby?
Bobby: No, I'm going to put down blue.
Mike: Well, you're supposed to put down red.
SL: Bobby, why do you keep putting down blue?
Bobby: Because I want to.
SL: How many pennies do you want to win?
Bobby: (*with great emphasis*) A lot!

SL: What do you think is a fair way to play the game?

Bobby: Me get some and he get some.

SL: Is that's what's happening now?

Bobby: (*shakes his head, no*) I get some. Let's do it again.

Mike: Why can't I get red and you get red, so next time I get red and you get red so we both get red.

SL: Bobby, what do you think of his idea? Mike says why don't you both put down red.

Mike: And then I get as many as you do.

Bobby: I want to put down blue and he put down red.

SL: What happens then?

Bobby: I get some.

SL: And he doesn't get any.

Mike: Can I put down red and you put down red?

Bobby: That I won't (*with determination*).

Mike: Well, I feel like it.

SL: What can we do? Can we figure a way to work this out?

Mike: I don't know. I can skip playing if I can't get any.

SL: Well, should we keep playing the game?

Mike: I want to quit 'cause he'll get some and I won't.

Bobby's default seems to reflect insensitivity to his friends's feelings and wishes as well as a strong desire to fulfill his own needs. Although he acknowledges that the fairest way to play the game is to equalize, he disregards Mike's suggestions that they equalize; in other words, he defensively isolates these two sets of ideas from each other. After the game stops, he projects responsibility on the staff leader, demanding that Mike be given "some more pennies."

An Example of Betrayal

The final self-serving action is *betrayal,* which occurs when one child breaks an explicit or a tacit agreement. Betrayals occurred in 30% of the dyads. In this last example, Kate has four pennies and Sally has eight. Kate expresses her frustration at the inequality in strong moral terms. Sally responds not by proposing reparations but equalization. Although Kate readily agrees to the plan, it turns out that she had no intention of acting on her agreement.

Kate: Sally, this game is just not fair!

Sally: No, it isn't! It isn't fair! (*She says this with a big smile, punctuating her words with nods.*)

Kate: 'Cause I'm not getting so many pennies. (*She bangs her fists on the table to emphasize her words.*)

SL; Well, what could you do?

Kate: (*banging her fists again*) I don't know!

SL: Do you have an idea you can tell Sally?

Sally: (*suddenly coming to life*) I know! (*She cocks her head; Kate looks at her quizzically.*)

SL: What?

Sally: If we put down (*pointing to the board*) both red, we'll get one, two, three, four, five, six, seven, eight, and one more (*pointing to the board*) makes nine.

SL: Kate, what do you think about that? Do you think it would be fair? (*Kate nods her head. The girls play, but Kate puts down a blue card instead of the agreed-upon red.*)

Sally: Put down red! Uh oh. Put down red. (*She touches Kate's card.*)

Kate: (*She glances briefly at Sally.*) No, I don't want to (*emphatically*). (*The staff leader asks Kate why she played her blue card.*)

Kate: 'Cause I wanted to.

Sally: (*She looks at Kate, and then turns to SL with a pout.*) I don't.

SL: Wait. Kate, how come you think that's fair?

Kate: (*Looking down at her hands.*) 'Cause, Sally won so many but I didn't, so I tried to win.

Conclusions from This Study

The major conclusion to be drawn from these observations is that *these four-year-olds did not act as they should if they are cognitively unable to understand and coordinate their views with another's or if they are morally selfish. Although they were not consistently morally concerned nor were all the children equally concerned, any respectable evidence of concern for others in a conflictual situation like NeoPd is a challenge to the idea that small children are morally deficient.* One cannot do what one is incapable of doing. The four-year-olds adjusted their conduct and comments to accommodate to the wishes and needs of the other child, and their incidence of equalization and reparation at 38% of their plays was not radically different from the 31% for the university students whom we had previously tested with this same situation. Another comparison is that by the end of play, 60% of the four-year-olds were sustaining equalized play compared to 80% of the university students.

One reservation about this conclusion needs to be stated. Although NeoPd is a good situation for systematic observation of young children's actions in response to moral issues, the children may have sometimes acted to comply with what they assumed the adult wanted. We do not think they did. The staff leaders impartially accepted all solutions, but it was clearly necessary for them to encourage the children to confront the dilemma. If they had not, play would undoubtedly have been disrupted by early leave-taking, hyperactivity, or tears.

A second finding is that these four-year-olds acted in NeoPd as if they were having the same kind of experiences as the adolescents and young adults we studied earlier—in the kind of problems they generated, solutions they developed, and emotions that accompanied their acting. In other words, *they experienced the same moral impulses, uncertainties, outrages, and stresses.* They became emotional in the same ways—frustrated during stalemates, angry during defaults and betrayals, and relieved and happy when they arrived at a mutual solution. When they equalized, a satisfied glow of good conscience was sometimes evident. Like the young adults and adolescents, they first unthinkingly worked to get pennies just for themselves but changed their course of action when they recognized their partners' indignation. Like the older students, some victimized four-year-olds could not or did not make their indignation sufficiently open and functional so the other child could recognize it.

Both children and the older students took up defensive maneuvers to rationalize their defaults and quell their anxiety over being victimized. Preschoolers sometimes sucked their fingers or hair, picked their noses, wiggled in their chairs, or stared expressionless at the table; university and high school students became immobilized and repressive or alternatively, cocky and belligerent. When four-year-olds realized their wrongdoing, they sometimes denied their act by pleading ignorance: "I don't know the colors." The students justified themselves with another kind of denial, "I thought it was just a game." The four-year-olds projected responsibility on the staff leader's poor anticipation of their needs, and several said their mothers would give them "more pennies"; the university students accused the project staff of being cheap for not supplying more generous payoffs or belittled the amount of payoffs.

The clearest difference between the age groups is that the four-year-olds were not often verbally articulate or sophisticated about their positions and emotions. But we now have preliminary evidence that they "read" each other's emotions from facial and hand expressions and bodily set. The incidences of their moral solution from the first one-third of their play to the last third increased from 28% to 53% as their violations decreased from 31% to 19%. The four-year-olds' equalizations plainly could not have been in reaction to their partners' cognitive persuasions.

There is another difference. The children were not as adept as the older students in anticipating the effects of future plays, which meant that they were not as vigilant in protecting their self-interest. The older students quickly read the printed matrix and usually recognized the equalizing solution, but often they did not act accordingly because they were wary about equalizing since the simultaneity of each play leaves a partner open to default. In contrast, the young children showed little anticipatory mistrust, either because they did not clearly see that playing red left them vulnerable to a competitive response or because they did not expect to be violated.

Children of this age are constantly reminded of their relative lack of power and resources, and despite our support of their coping, some experienced NeoPd in this same way. But like adults do, they defensively sustained belief in their self-agency. Children who played to equalize but then fell victim to their friend's defaulting were chagrined. Contrary to their apparent emotional reactions, some still justified their choice, "I played red 'cause I wanted to." An important moral skill, which undoubtedly takes years to acquire, is knowing when it is foolish to trust and wise to be vigilant. Some current educational efforts to help children fend off sexual abuse seem to be telling children that they must be vigilant and that they have a moral right to protect themselves even against loved adults.

SPECULATIONS ABOUT DEVELOPMENT

Since this study and the work of the prosocial researchers suggest preschoolers have basic moral understanding, it seems that something other than morality has been taken to be moral development.

I suggest that the young gradually develop the skills that allow them to tolerate and resolve the conflict inevitably involved in moral exchange. Moreover, they acquire the knowledge, experience, and power that enable them to act in a wider range of complex situations. Our simplified version of NeoPd set up a conflict of legitimate self-interests that was cognitively and informationally within the grasp of these young children; they had all power to resolve this conflict; no one else was going to do it for them but their efforts were buttressed by the staff leader's support and encouragement. In other words, conditions were optimal for helping them to cope rather than defend or disintegrate. In situations that are beyond their cognitive grasp and less supportive of their coping, these children would have undoubtedly defaulted, or being very young, capitulated or attacked.

I suggest then that young children's understanding of basic human reciprocity is much the same as adults', but children lack knowledge, cognitive skills, objective power, responsibility, and material resources to empower their negotiations. Because children are readily stressed, moral violations only intensify the helplessness they already feel. Extending the work of Seligman (1975), I suggest that one reason why helplessness is traumatizing is that it is a moral outrage to humans' sensibility.

Clearly, moral functioning must also improve as children become sophisticated in talking about morality, although people of all ages seem to avoid moral words in action situations, perhaps because this seems accusatory. Articulation of a difficulty often serves to clarify its nature, an expected benefit of psychotherapy. The staff leader helped the children verbally articulate what they were doing and why, but only 16% of the children spontaneously used moral words or offered moral explanations before the staff leader asked for opinions about fairness and 75% seemed immediately to pick up on the staff leader's words. Although the adolescents and young adults more often called each other directly to account for moral violations, some were so caught up in the conflict that they, too, were unable to articulate their positions.

CLINICAL IMPLICATIONS

This view of children's morality has far-reaching implications for practice. Its interactional features place it at the heart of clinical interchange, and it may explain the vulnerability of some children whose environmental conditions are good and the resiliency of other children whose conditions are poor. Views of children's inherent moral nature probably do not vary with socioeconomic status, and we know, for instance, that child abuse occurs in all socioeconomic conditions. When parents or therapists deal with children about moral problems, adult attitudes and actions are surely affected by whether or not they think the child has moral understanding or is morally empty. If young children are empty, interacting with them in a moral conflict would be like trying to resolve an argument with someone who does not speak the language. Thus, the only logical, responsible, and even caring role for the adult is that of a loving, not overtaxing tutor who vigilantly prevents gross violation.

But if young children do possess moral understanding, then they are a different kind of human being. This person has moral sensibilities, motivations, and emotions about what's fair and what's not fair. As a sensitive father of a four-year-old in our study said, "Obviously, we have to come

down on her when she's wrong, as she often is, but she's got to walk away
from it with her moral honor intact." When children's moral understandings are not believed to exist, adults invite sullen or devious sabotage or
withdrawal as the morally indignant child works to protect his or her
integrity, irrespective of social cost. In other words, adults inadvertently
violate a child's moral honor when they think the child does not understand reciprocity. As a consequence, children's belief in good faith—that
moral issues are usually resolved, reasonably and fairly—can hardly be
forced. A child's commitment to good faith in moral negotiation has to
be based on intrinsic confidence; it cannot be trained or socialized.

The adult caretaker, then, has the problem of building the child's optimism that most moral conflicts can be resolvable in good faith. Given the
erratic quality of everybody's moral performance, children also need to
expect that everybody (not just kids) violates from time to time, so their
violations and parents' must be forgiven. Nevertheless, since young children are especially stress-vulnerable—as are all powerless, socially helpless people—adults need to help children cope with conflict so they need
not defend by denial, rationalization, and projection or regressively capitu-
late by crying, attack, or running away. Moral development in its essence,
then, may be increasing tolerance and persistence in the face of the conflict that is inevitably involved with all moral issues of any importance.

Morally conflicted people of all ages have difficulty understanding
their protagonist's position but equally important for vulnerable children,
whether they are hyperaggressive or hypertimid, is their need to learn
how they can reasonably protect their own legitimate self-interests. It
takes at least two to solve a moral conflict and if the victimized child does
not make his or her position known, it is not altogether clear that the other
child or person is always defaulting. Developmental psychologists have
gone to great lengths to learn how "selfish" children can learn concern for
others. This traditional curriculum follows the Judeo-Christian enjoinder
that we should turn the other cheek. Consequently, in our culture considerable guilt surrounds the open protection of even legitimate self-interest.
Equal effort needs to be devoted to trying to understand how children can
learn to reasonably protect their self-interests without guilt. Moral negotiation simply cannot work unless all involved make their positions known.

These research-based observations that indicate children are morally
aware and therefore necessarily partners in negotiation lead to recom-
mendations to parents that are a lot less guilt-provoking than the usually
implicit clinical message that their primary duty is to be loving, firm, and
consistent with their children.

Parental fairness is obviously important, not simply for the sake of

modeling but for the sake of fair treatment. But fairness requires equalization between two sets of self interests—the parents' and the child's;
otherwise, a morally corrupt relationship results. When parents do not
reasonably protect their own legitimate self-interests, they can stifle their
moral indignation with their child. Family interchanges become a subtle,
convoluted, and tedious war of all against all. Parents who do not protect
their own legitimate self-interests can only feel first morally outraged
and humiliated by their children; second, angry; third, guilty for their
anger.

Since usual and better living conditions—like higher incomes, education, intact families, nonpsychotic parents, healthy bodies—usually give
people more moral options, it is not surprising that childhood resiliency
is generally related to such positive features. But clinicians can do very
little about any of these factors. Furthermore, such benefits are not a
sufficient explanation since some children whose conditions are optimal
turn out to be vulnerable and some in deleterious conditions turn out to
be resilient. I suggest that childhood resiliency and vulnerability have
specific relationships to the moral climate of families that build children's
expectancies about the nature of moral interchanges. Resilient children
will have reason to be optimistic that moral difficulties can usually be
worked out: They will be heard; they will usually be able to protect their
legitimate self-interests; they will understand that no human is faultless,
that even adults morally violate, so they will "speak truth to power" and
be able to forgive themselves. Resilient children may be those who are
confident that most human interchanges make moral sense and those
who understand why some interchanges do not.

Vulnerable children may be those who expect to be ignored or used, so
in self-protection they must return the treatment—no matter how self-
defeating—with all the means at their disposal: They will refuse to
thrive; they will be chaotic; they will parody their adults; they will sabotage; they will evoke guilt; and so on. They will give up being heard and
move day to day in a desperate game of self-protection. Human beings
do not endure excessive, prolonged stress without searching for means
of reducing it whatever its social cost.

From the perspective of the interactional theory that I propose, moral
conflict is accepted as a central feature of life that everyone confronts
and must therefore engage. Moral conflict cannot be avoided even by
mature, highly sensitive, and morally adequate people. Still, most moral
systems promise that after some stage of moral maturity or state of
elitism is attained, tranquility will be the benefit. This illusion certainly
does not conform to clinical knowledge.

From the standpoint of common sense—as well as the interactional perspective that I propose—moral dialogue and conclusion ideally require that parties fully and accurately exchange views about the legitimacy of each other's claims. This is the essence of social coping. Moral dialogue is surely farcical when one or all parties defensively distort or negate critical aspects of their positions and mutual conflict. All social discourse is based on the moral assumption that we can generally depend on what people say. This common understanding is the keystone of my research and leads to the assertion that moral functioning is likely to be of higher quality when people and children are able to cope with the conflict and lower when they must defend.

Some psychological theorists do not agree with this distinction between coping and defending. They point out, correctly, that defensiveness reduces people's anxiety; presumably, then, they would have to argue that defensiveness improves moral performance. But when we consider moral-social interactions, this argument seems simplistic. No person is an island, especially when it comes to morality. Defensiveness may reduce personal anxiety *if* its distortions and negations are not exposed by others. However, exposing protagonists' distortions during a moral conflict is exactly what people want and need to do. When one discussant defensively distorts and negates, good faith suffers and the other party acquires a second problem of deciding whether to continue dialogue or not, as we saw in the example of Bobby and Mike. Furthermore, distortion and negation are often met in kind, which only further complicates the conflict. This moral underpinning of social reality means that defensive reactions almost always cost, no matter what relief they may temporarily allow. According to the interactional perspective, people commonly assume that parties to a moral dispute will be accountable to one another, that is, participants will, in good faith, mutually assess the real moral issues involved and then in good faith jointly create a plan that will rebalance their relations.

In this chapter I have offered a view of the beginnings of morality in young children that is profoundly different from the conventional wisdom most theories hold and if true, it leads to a different kind of interaction with children than is usually recommended. Nevertheless, not all adults, or even most adults, actually and consistently act in practical life as if real, small children are morally ignorant. But confusion and contradiction between solid practical knowledge and theoretical abstraction should not go uncorrected. If this view has worth, it would have the status of what Stephen Jay Gould (1983) has called a "nasty little fact" that challenges developmental and clinical theories and so, perforce, it would have to be accommodated.

REFERENCES

ANDERSON, N.H. (1980). Information integration theory in developmental psychology. In F. Wilkening, J. Becker, & T. Trebesso (Eds.), *Information Integration by Children.* Hillsdale, N.J.: Lawrence Erlbaum Associates.

BALES, J. (1984). Research traces altruism in toddlers. *APA Monitor, 15*(1), 20–22.

COLES, R. (1980). Ulster's children: Waiting for the Prince of Peace. *Atlantic, 246,* 33–34.

GOULD, S.J. (1983). False premises, good science. *Natural History, 92*(10), 20–28.

HAAN, N. (1982). An interactional theory of morality. In N. Haan, R. Bellah, P. Rabinow, & W. Sullivan (Eds.), *Social Science as Moral Inquiry.* New York: Columbia University Press.

HAAN, N. (1985). Processes of moral development: Cognitive or social disequilibrium? *Developmental Psychology, 21,* 996–1006.

HAAN, N. (1986). Systematic variability in the quality of moral action as defined by two formulations. *Journal of Personality and Social Psychology, 50,* 1271–1284.

HAAN, N. AERTS, E., & COOPER, B. (1985). *On Moral Grounds: The Search for Practical Morality.* New York: New York University Press.

LERNER, H. (1980). *The Belief in a Just World.* New York: Academic.

RADKE-YARROW, M., ZAHN-WAXLER, C., & CHAPMAN. M. (1983). Children's prosocial dispositions and behavior. In P.H. Mussen (Ed.), *Handbook of Child Psychology, Vol. IV: Socialization, Personality, and Social Development* (4th ed.). New York: Wiley.

SELIGMAN, M.E.P. (1975). *Helplessness.* San Francisco: Freeman.

Part II

RESILIENCY IN CONTEXT: CHILDREN COPING IN EXTREME CIRCUMSTANCES

3
Moral Energy in the Lives of Impoverished Children

ROBERT COLES

For over 25 years I have been trying to understand how poor and often quite vulnerable children manage to make do in the face of odds that seem, at times, hard to contemplate, even, never mind face down, every day, as facts of anyone's life. I do not wish to romanticize those young people, turn them into indomitable heroes who conquer anything and everything as they march triumphantly through life. These are, by and large, boys and girls of our American ghettoes, of Brazil's favelas, of South Africa's infamous, apartheid-mandated "homelands" or "townships"— and they are by no means without the "mark of oppression," a phrase Abram Kardiner and Lionel Oversey used a generation ago to describe the psychological consequences of political and economic and social and racial injustice. Still, child psychiatrists, like everyone else, must learn to live with ambiguities, even a paradox or two—and it is quite possible, one begins to realize after spending time in those sadly inadequate rural and urban slums of various nations, for a particular child to be penniless, malnourished, utterly uneducated, ailing as a consequence of a range of chronic diseases, with no future prospects of any significance—and never-

45

theless demonstrate certain qualities of mind and spirit which strike an observer from another world as astonishing.

I recall, for instance, one of the children I first came to know when I began working with migrant farm workers in the Southeastern part of the United States. She was a black girl of nine and already an experienced picker of whatever crops awaited the "crew" to which her mother and aunts and brothers and sisters and cousins belonged. When I met her in the mornings she smiled quickly and always wished me a "nice day." Her politeness was also evident when I would be preparing to leave: She would say goodbye, wish me well, ask me to send her regards to my wife, and express the hope that I would return soon. These were, admittedly, small gestures, and I fear that for all too long I ignored them, looking, of course, for the hurts, the worries and anxieties and fears this child was no doubt trying to keep under some control. But one day when I came visiting, she smiled her usual greeting and then told me that she had especially enjoyed seeing my wife on the last visit, and she remembered her dress—how "pretty" it was. A little later, as we talked about her present life, and what she saw ahead for herself, she remarked that she knew she would never be living a "rich life," but she did have her hopes, and one of them was that she, too, would be able to wear some pretty clothes, occasionally.

I nodded enthusiastically, though with a certain sadness, because I was reasonably sure how hard it would be for her to buy those clothes, given the wages migrants were then making, and still make. But she was aware of my undeclared train of thought. I now condense remarks made on that day and on several others in order to indicate just how aware, in fact, she could be, with respect to so many matters:

"My grandmother told us never to expect too much, and I know she's right. If you start believing your dreams will come true, then you're going to be in a lot of trouble, because you'll be disappointed real bad, and you'll feel sorry for yourself. We're not going to live like they do on the television programs, but we have our laughs, and we're all together here, and we can sit and laugh, and that's good.

"I asked your wife where she bought that pretty dress, that real pretty one, and she told me in Atlanta, and I told her I hoped to have a dress like that, and I'd feel real good to wear it. You need to have some pretty things! That dress has a beautiful yellow color, and the belt is thin, but it's strong, I can tell, and the collar is a nice collar, not too big, but you look at it, because it's got that 'design' on it, the white lines, and the belt is the same. Her shoes were nice, too—light-weight, I could tell. You mustn't keep thinking of what you're wearing when you wear it, though—then you behave like a 'big-shot,' and no one likes you. A pretty dress will lift your soul to God, my mum says, and He'll see you and give you a blessing! Then if you're blessed, you can help someone smile, who sees you, and that's spreading sunshine, and that's what we should try to do. God puts us here to try to give Him a hand. He's planted us, like we plant the crops—and He'll be harvesting us, too, that's for sure! You want to be one of his good crops! You want to be what He wants, and then you're what you're here to be!

"In church we'll pray to Him, and when I do I think of Him as a man with a smile, and He puts His arms out and wants you to go running until He can hold you close. God wants us to be near Him, and if we are, we're lucky! He wants us to look as pretty as we can, but not flashy. There's a difference! To look pretty is to think of Him, and the person who sees you. To look flashy, that's to think of yourself! If you're wrapped up in your own arms, the minister tells you, then you're all alone. If you're trying to go see someone else, and be nice, then you're joining up on His side, and He wants us to help each other, like we do when we pick the crops. My momma tells us that she'll get real tired a lot of times, and she wonders what the reason is, that we're here, and then she'll look at us, me and my sisters and brothers, and she knows the answer to her wondering, and it's not just us, who matter, no sir; it's God, He matters. He's the one who put us here, and we're His, and so He's our reason to hold on and do the best we can—that's what momma says.

"There will be days, I know, when momma isn't convinced; she'll be doubting even Him, she's so low. I feel low a lot of times, too! I lie there, and I look up at the sky, and I say I wish You'd come, dear God, and show us that You are paying us mind, and not spending Your time with all the rich folks! You mustn't have those bad thoughts, and even so, you do—and that's all right, because if you was perfect, then you'd not be here, that's for sure; you'd be a star up there, shining and inspiring us down here, a pretty star. I saw a dress once, and it had lots of stars, and I called it a 'sky-dress,' and my momma thought I was talking my strange talk, until she saw the dress one day herself, and she laughed and said I was right to say what I was saying!

"When our father got killed in an automobile accident we thought we'd all follow him right away. We thought he'd call us, and we'd be taken to Him. God would figure out how. But we're still here. Maybe we are supposed to be separated for a while, so that we'll really be glad to see him, our father. He used to drink a lot, but he was good to us. He gave my mother everything he made, except for his drinking money. We never were mad at him for holding those dollars to himself—no, never.

We thought he'd worked hard, and he told us if he couldn't have some beers, he'd want to die. Then that car hit him, when he was trying to cross the highway, and he didn't have a drop of beer in him. He'd just had his breakfast, a cup of coffee and a roll—and then he was struck and dragged and he was dead when they got to him.

"When he drank a beer or two he talked about all the funny times in his life—the grower's wife who paid him to sleep with her, and the time he won $50 in a Bingo game, and the cop who was the meanest one in the world, and one day he was shouting at our people, and he just stopped talking, and he turned blue, and he fell down, and my father ran over, and saw that he wasn't breathing, and he prayed to God to be nice to that cop, even if he was a bad, bad one—because you shouldn't be sore at someone after he's dead and gone! 'Pray for him,' our daddy said, when he told us what happened, and we did. But then daddy winked, and he said we shouldn't forget that God keeps His eyes on all of us, so no one is going to get away with anything. I was glad when I heard that, because I thought maybe with all the people the good Lord has to keep track of, there might be some who get away with a lot, and that cop was no good, and you don't want someone no good slipping by, and finding himself in God's place—the place He keeps for those who try their best, and their best isn't enough for this world, but it is for the next one, where there's a God to keep the records and not the growers and not the crew leaders."

True, these are scattered remarks, connected together by an observer and writer anxious to find a certain overall coherence in particular children, and too, make those general statements which are the essentials of a persuasive line of inquiry. Still, from a strictly phenomenological point of view, each of those observations by this child requires a listener to pay close heed, to acknowledge a sensibility at work. The longer I get to know a girl such as this one, the more attentive I am to the themes she pursues in our talks, the more evident it seems (to me, at least) that she is, in her own intermittent fashion, as morally alert and reflective as many of us would consider ourselves to be, or (more tentatively) hope we might end up being. This is a child who, after all, has seen a good deal of suffering herself, who has experienced loss, wanton cruelty, the meanness and harshness of a vulnerable, impoverished life, and yet, a child who, in that life, has stopped upon occasion to take stock, to wonder why, to look around and ask those questions it is in our nature as human beings to ask, each of us in our own ways: Where do we come from? What are we? Where are we going? Gauguin worked them into his great Tahiti testimonial tryptich (1897), and an obscure nine-year-old girl, who was already a migratory farm worker, was similarly inclined to ponder them.

Such moral energy may, actually, be encouraged by the grim circumstances those of us who are well-off call abstractly "poverty" or "marginal socioeconomic living." When I was a resident in psychiatry at the Massachusetts General Hospital (1956) I well remember the conversations I had with victims of severe (bulbar) poliomyelitis. We were witnessing and struggling against the last major outbreak of that once dreaded disease before the arrival of the Salk vaccine. We were working with young people, predominantly, who were confined to "iron lungs," the massive machines that meant the difference between life and death for those unfortunate youths. As I look back at my old "process notes," the records we trainees in psychiatry were encouraged to keep, I find that a similar moral energy was at work—perhaps a response of children faced with a medical tragedy which, in its own way, made for a kind of impoverishment, a continuing jeopardy which those children could not help noticing and trying to comprehend. A youth of 14, for instance, kept telling me that she was in a "prison." She was not delusional or paranoid, merely quite factual as she looked up at me, tried to talk, while noticing the big iron machine whose movements ensured her continuing life. "My body is in this big steel cage," she reminded me, and she went on to say this: "I guess I'm outside the machine—my head is—and I can't figure out why it has to be *me* who's been picked. What did I do to deserve this? That's all I keep asking myself!"

We had recently experienced a thunderstorm, and so she was especially sensitive to the newly personal meaning of electricity in her life. We (the doctors) had begun to notice such a developing "trend" in our patients and, indeed, we had already begun (what else to do?) formulating a psychological concept meant to "explain" what was happening—the "anxiety," the breakdown of "denial." We were right, of course, but maybe not as phenomenologically or existentially inclusive as we might have been. That youngster was not only reacting to a psychiatric crisis, secondary to a medical crisis, as we are wont to say. She was responding in the tradition of Job, asking the questions the Hebrew prophets put to God, put to themselves, also; she was asking the questions Jesus and His disciples asked, the questions people for centuries have asked in the midst of suffering hurt and injury. Another youth, a boy of about 13 or 14, visited her one day, and heard her ask her questions, and then asked me his question, the natural one an "expert" is likely to hear: "What should I say to her?" I mumbled and stumbled, and in the fashion of my kind (ping-pong players of sorts!) threw the answer back, asked him what he wanted to ask, to say. He lobbed the ball back, though, to my acute discomfort, by telling me that he had not known *what* to say, and so had said nothing. He wanted to "check out the right thing to do" with me, and so I had, yet again, my moment in that youth's sun, but alas, to no avail. I told him that "the patient" needed whatever "support" we could all muster and let the matter drop there, as did he (to my relief at the time).

I bring up this relatively obscure moment in one doctor's life not only because it may have some general significance—how often such times come to us physicians!—but because that small incident had a strong impact on me. I kept remembering the questions I was hearing from all those polio patients by concentrating on that one patient's particular questions on that particular day, and I kept remembering my own sense of helplessness and vulnerability (might I, too, get polio?) by remembering my difficulty in responding to that young visitor, who wanted me to be more concretely helpful (maybe, more honestly helpless!) than I was prepared to be (felt it proper for a doctor to be).

I also was beginning to wonder whether it was quite fair of me to consider these patients as *only* in medical and psychological distress. Was I not also being impressed, day after day, by some remarkable encounters—young people saying what was on their minds, as well as asking me questions? That same girl who had bulbar polio and feared she might suddenly die due to a power failure induced by an electrical storm told me a day or two later that she herself had an answer to the question she had been putting to herself and others. What was her answer, I wondered aloud with the pretended casual manner people like me learn to offer as evidence of our professional maturity, our "cool." She said this to me: "I've had a bad streak of luck, but I might turn it into a good streak down the line, I hope." I wrote that down, and mulled that over, and came up with words I had learned, such as "rationalization"; but I also kept thinking of George Eliot and *Middlemarch*—her enormously edifying effort to render through a story the endless complexities of this life, and not least, its continuing ironies and paradoxes, which no amount of abstract formulation can quite banish. Indeed, it can be argued that even as that young polio victim was "defending" herself against life's riddles, its seeming random nature, and even as poor children all over the world do likewise, so it is that we who are called doctors or social scientists also manage to mobilize our fair share of "defensive behavior"—our barrage of explanations (if not reifications) meant to give us the notion that there is a *sense* to this life, a meaning (albeit hidden from others).

Such a symmetry, such an irony, was not beyond George Eliot's comprehension—her awareness, as a matter of fact, that she herself, in her particular mode of inquiry and exposition, was heir to the very same human limitations, the blind spots and weaknesses which she so knowingly analyzed as a writer. Ultimately, she knew, the issue is moral as well as psychological and sociological: what we do with whatever much or little we have had given us by chance, by circumstance, by luck good or bad. Nor is such a realization, she knew, beyond the ken of those who lack intellectual refinement, or yes, the psychological sophistication she most certainly had, and some of us prize so highly today, hence her willingness to put in the mouths of her well-known "rustics" (Mr. Garth, for instance, in *Middlemarch*) some of her most edifying thoughts, that "wisdom" her readers and critics over the generations since her death have so continually mentioned and lauded. I dare say that she might not have been surprised, had she heard the youth I have mentioned knowing on a hospital ward, or the one I met later in the course of my research in that mysterious geographic entity called "the field" (and speaking of ironies, it was literally a "field," of course, where I talked with migrant farm children). Such is the stuff of life, she knew, that out of sorrow a redemptive moment or two might be rescued, even an entire life somehow redeemed.

Not that one rushes (one says again and again) to "romanticize" the suffering of people, turn any ghetto resident or desperately ill patient into a hero of sorts, a repository of all the psychological strengths and moral virtues the rest of us cannot seem to take for granted. People who are in pain (be it medically connected or a consequence of social and economic forces) can be as bitter and narrow and insensitive and mean-spirited as the rest of us manage to be, also including some of us who enjoy excellent health and are rather well-to-do. Even as suffering knows no color line, no barriers of class and caste, of race and nationality and educational attainment—we all fall sick, are "at risk" in the sense that at any moment that proverbial devastating "accident" can take place—so it is that some moments and more of moral dignity can, as it were, also be found in just about any human situation, even one that seems unpromising. Victor Frankl has reminded us that in the concentration camps, no less, there were those who would not surrender that most basic of human rights—the freedom to resist evil, to keep it at bay, no matter the threat, no matter the immediacy and power of a murderous devil, brute Nazi power. We know, so many of us, about the witness of Dietrich Bonhoeffer and Edith Stein, two religiously sensitive and philosophically accomplished victims of Hitler who perished in his death camps. Their personal and intellectual "stories" are legendary, and deservedly so; and in Bonhoeffer's case there are the unforgettably compelling and instructive "prison letters." But he was the first one to remind us (to remind himself and the correspondent he was addressing) that some very smart people are not necessarily good people, that the distinction Emerson made between "character" and "intellect" in his famous (1836) essay, delivered (of all places) at Harvard at a Phi Beta Kappa exercise, is an exceedingly important distinction, still.

In essence, Bonhoeffer, too, was a psychological "expert" who made a "speciality" of studying populations at risk. He lived for years in a death camp, died in it, even as he had chosen voluntarily (he was an Aryan of the upper class in Germany) to behave in such a way that he would end up in one: he fought the Nazis with all his might. Was he a "masochist," someone with one or another "problem"? After all, he was in America, studying at Union Theological Seminary when the Second World War broke out, and he need not have returned to Germany thereafter. He could even have fashioned a respectable moral career for himself as an anti-Nazi emigré, anxious to alert America to the evil abroad. As a matter of fact, I once heard Reinhold Niebuhr (1951), who taught at Union then and knew Bonhoeffer, recall the perplexity many felt, as they contemplated his departure for Germany. They even speculated that Bonhoeffer ought to go "talk" with someone, see a psychiatrist, lest he put himself in extreme jeopardy.

Yet, Bonhoeffer wanted it to be otherwise and saw his return as utterly necessary, and yes, as his chance at "health," though his notion of that state may not be the one all of us find congenial. For him "health" had distinct moral implications, even spiritual ones. I dare say he might have found not entirely uncongenial this statement, culled from the remarks made over time of a boy who lived (in 1975) atop a Rio de Janeiro favela: "We don't have much here, and when I look at the Copacabana people [while he begged from them] I know that we have *nothing*, and they have *everything*. But even with nothing you can laugh, and you can have your friends, and I see lots of them [the rich ones of Copacabana] and they look like they'll cut out anyone's heart if he steps in their way for a second, and they don't smile, even at the people they know. I wonder what He thinks of them, our Lord. [He points to the famous statue of Jesus Christ, atop a mountain, and dominating the city, a constant visual if not spiritual presence there.] I wonder if He isn't smiling—I mean, at them, those poor, poor people of Copacabana and Iponema, loaded, loaded as can be [in Portuguese, he said "piles of money in their hands"] and still they look as if God has struck them hard, and they are scared He'll never smile on them, and so they will never be able to smile back at

Him, and they're going to burn later in Hell, like the priest says will happen to a lot of us!

"My mother says that it is no good to be poor. She says she wishes we could be rich. She says that when she goes to Copacabana she dreams of living in one of those big, beautiful buildings. She says she wonders if she'd notice us herself, if she was one of 'them.' She's afraid she might not, that if she was one of 'them,' she'd not be one of 'us,' and that would mean she'd not notice 'us.' And *God forbid*, because Jesus never forgot us, He lived with us, and He died the way we die, and thank God that He sent Jesus to us, and there He is, looking at us all day, and He's lit up, so we see Him at night, and still, that doesn't mean we always remember Him, so we can end up in worse trouble, much worse trouble, than we're now in, because to forget God is worse than to be poor!

"What kind of trouble? [I'd asked.] I don't know. Let the priest answer. Maybe he doesn't know! He tells us that you can't know for sure what God thinks of you until you die, and there's always a chance to be saved. But He must be watching us, and even if He isn't, He'll figure us out when we show up! I look at people on the street [he begs, he hustles his various deals] and I figure them out, and I'm not wrong, usually. So, imagine what He can do—one look and the person's naked! I'd be shaking [before God] and I'd start spilling the beans ["pouring out the inside of me"] and I just hope He gives me the wink, and says it's okay, and we'll let you through the good side, and we can send some others to the bad side!

"If you are true to your family and your friends, He will forgive you all your sins, lots of them. I hope so! I have many sins for Him to forgive! But I love my family, my people here. We're all together; we're the skin and bones of this place, and even if the skin stinks and the bones are broken, we hold together, and I hope God will receive us and He'll make us better, a lot better. It won't be the perfume and the big cars and the jewels of the Copacabana that He'll give us. I ask you, can you imagine the Jesus of that statue with His arms out riding in a big car, a chauffeur driving Him? He'd walk, and He'd have sores on His feet; He wouldn't have shoes, maybe. He'd be covered with sores, like my brother. He'd bleed like my mother. He'd have a belly shouting for food, but no big deal. Just take the soda and a tortilla, and be glad you've got that! But He'd be the boss, and I think we'd get his wink; I hope so! I even pray so, every once in a while, though if you ask me, I have to tell you, I have to admit, a lot of time I get mad, as mad as the barking dog we killed the other day, so we wouldn't become mad hearing it. When I get mad I don't believe He'll ever come here, and I don't believe—I'll say it—He ever really was, not for us. Then I talk to Him—that statue! I say, hey, put up or shut up! Hey, You, stop with those arms stretched wide and lift them up and don't forget to lift us up. I mean make the arms work and give us a hand, give us both hands, because we need everything we can get; we need You! Do You exist? That's when I get no answer! Silence! I kick our dirt and say "enough," and I try not to look at Him, the statue, and I say never, never again will I fall for You! But there will be a time, later, sometime, and He gets me, He catches me looking, staring; and I smile, and tell him okay, we're in business again!"

There is more, so much more one can extract from all those months of watching and listening. As William Carlos Williams once put it, and I'll never forget the time, in that old jalopy of his: "We have to keep hoping against hope that we'll be rescued from our own deafness and dumbness by this one, that one—there must be someone!" He was, indeed, rescued, as one realizes when in the company of his marvelous beauty of language, its evocation and continual rendering of the ordinary, humble, often frail and wounded and ailing American experience, its sights and sounds, its textures and grain, its ups and downs and blind spots and impasses and blinding breakthroughs, the leaps from the immanent and everyday to the utterly compellingly universal and edifying. Again and again Williams tried to comprehend the down-and-out people he attended as a physician. He observed their cycles of eloquence and moral reflection, followed by their mute submission to a tyrannical and devouring everydayness. "The great suck of self," Walker Percy put it, and of course, the great and ever demanding press of "society," that "reality principle" some of us mention all too casually: bread and water if one is lucky, and not much more. For Williams, someone poor and destitute, as well as someone relatively rich and well educated, could be seen and heard demonstrating great moral power. For Williams it went like this— the thrust of a given writer's faith, and one only repeats, gratefully, what it was one's lucky privilege to get to hear time and again: "Wait for them to open the book—we all have one in us—and when they do, these kids, these poor folk, you'll be their student, and you'll learn, if you sign up with them. And don't forget, they'll help you with right and wrong, because they know they've got to figure out the difference; it's up to them, because God helps those who help themselves, and that includes those kids and you and me."

I have listened to those words in my head as I have listened to the voices of the children I have come to know—the moral energy of fellow human creatures: *there*, being expended; and on a good day, *there* spoken; on a really good day, *there*, respectfully attended and appreciated; on the best of all days, *there,* with its healing force upon one's mind and heart. The "themes" keep grabbing one: the struggle of boys and girls to figure out this life, sort out its various signals and portents, its accidents and incidents, its damn horrors, and its spell of sparkling glow, "the shine of someone you really can trust," as a boy, a Brazilian *favelado* once put it. He was "at risk." He will always be lucky and damn grateful to have made it from one sunrise to one sunset; and, of course, he prays in his many ways and words for more sunrises and sunsets, although he knows the "bad last day" will come when a judgment will be handed down inscrutably, so he often implies, says outright: he and Kafka, and maybe the young itinerant Moses or Jesus Himself, and many others whose nature it is to summon words to the task of moral reflection, any scrap and morsel of words under any (national, racial, regional, social, psychological) sun and moon. "I love their energy, the fights they have and the love they show, and I love hearing them try to figure—add and subtract—this life out." This moral arithmetic, William Carlos Williams never doubted, is each and every child's unnervingly particular, thoroughly idiosyncratic possession; and some men, women, and children have so little to take for granted that they have to use that moral arithmetic rather often, keep counting and counting, figuring and figuring, as they move along this earthly journey.

4

Risk and Resiliency in Childhood: The Lives of Street Children

J. KIRK FELSMAN

Historically, the streets of major cities have served as both theatre and battleground for the children of the poor. Nowhere is this more apparent than in the cities of present-day Colombia. Thousands of street children, so-called gamins, are, from an environmental perspective alone, at high risk for psychopathology. Darting in and out of traffic, begging in open-air restaurants, singing for change on city buses, bathing in public fountains, or sleeping together curled up among stray dogs, these young ragamuffins manage the often-tangled course of human growth and development with little or no support from the traditional institutions of family, school, church, or state.

Amidst such environmental adversity, the gamins represent a self-selecting group of children standing at the intersection of human strength and vulnerability. Much of their daily life is a display of endurance, resiliency and adaptation as it is witnessed in childhood. This chap-

The author would like to acknowledge a Frederick Sheldon Fellowship from Harvard University that supported the field work and also a Lyndhurst Prize that provided the time to write.

56

ter will place the Colombian phenomenon of street children in a broader historical and cross-cultural context, examine its etiology, and consider the adaptive, resilient elements of their daily lives in the face of stark environmental circumstance.

The word *gamin* comes from the French, meaning urchin. It is but one of the by now pejorative names with which these children have been labeled. Most regard it as *feo* or ugly. Other names such as *chinos de la calle* ("children of the street," from the Quechua chino, for "child") or *chinches* ("bedbugs") are used to refer to the smallest waifs, as young as age five. Ultimately they prefer their own names or nicknames for themselves. Collectively, most would rather be known by some variation of *muchachos* or *ninos de la calle* (boys, or children of the street). Their sensitivity to names reflects both a strength in a shared identity and a tenacious desire to be recognized individually.

The street urchin has become so much a part of Colombian society that the National Ballet Company has included a standard piece, entitled *Gamin*, while a popular T.V. soap opera on the same theme has been broadcast in the capital, Bogotá. Yet the gamins represent an enormously complex social problem that continues to be poorly understood. The formulation of social policy has not relied upon applied research, but has generally assumed the sympathetic stance of advocacy. The result has been an emphasis on weakness and pathology at the expense of recognizing equally evident signs of strength and healthy adaptation among these children.

CONTEXT

Most accounts of street children have been of narrow focus: a particular group of children, in a particular place, at a particular moment in history. The continuity of description linking one group with another has seldom been appreciated. Modern groups and those of earlier times have shown striking similarities. For example, their members are mostly male. Their peer relationships, group life, and survival strategies have been much the same, whatever their time and place.

With a street urchin population estimated at over 5,000, Bogotá has been referred to as the "capital of the abandoned child." Yet, street children are not unique to Colombia. Major cities in present-day Brazil, Mexico, Turkey, India, and elsewhere are facing problems on a similar scale. Srivastava (1963) has done substantial research in India, while Borrelli (1963) continues to work with the "scugnizzi" (spinning tops) of

Naples. Gage (1979) has reported on the street boys of Istanbul, and *Time's* (1978) initial coverage of street children in Brazil has now been more fully described by Tacon (1981). In Vietnam, there are the *Bui Doi* "dust children." Substantial numbers of street children are also reported in Thailand and the Philippines. More recently, there have been descriptions of street children in South Africa, Rawanda, and Zaire. As a result of the growing attention to this phenomenon, an International Program on street children was established in Geneva in 1982 and served as a clearing house for information. In October, 1983, it began publishing a quarterly notice, *The Street Newsletter*. More recently, an international project "Child Hope" has been headquartered in Guatemala City, and another organization, Streetwise International, is based in Cambridge, England.

Comparative cross-cultural studies of street children offer a rich matrix for future investigation. Equally important, however, is an appreciation of the continuity in description to be found in historical accounts. In *Les Miserables* (1931), Victor Hugo makes reference to the street children of Paris, just as Dickens drew upon London's street urchins in *Oliver Twist* (1921). Social/historical works of the late 19th and early 20th centuries include accounts of the Barnardo Homes of England (Bready, 1935), the gamins of Paris (Woods, 1895) and "vagrant" children in Russia (Miller, 1965; Zenzinov, 1975).

A vague but consistent misperception persists that such problems have existed only recently or "over there," in the "developing" countries. However, I first encountered the word gamin and a reference to "howling urchins" in Stephen Crane's *Maggie, A Girl of the Streets* (1893). In *How the Other Half Lives* (1890), the writer, photographer and social reformer, Jacob Riis, provides graphic portraits of street children among the urban poor in turn-of-the-century New York City. Campbell's *Darkness and Daylight* (1892), along with the work of Brace (1880) and Woods (1895), added significantly to such accounts, as did original articles in magazines of the day such as *McClure's*, *Everybody's* and *Contemporary Review*. Two more recently published historical accounts can be found in Leroy Ashby's *Saving the Waifs* (1984) and David Nasaw's *Children of the City* (1985).

In 1852, according to official police records, there were an estimated 10,000 "vagrant children" adrift in the streets of New York. Other estimates placed the number as high as 30,000. What stands out most among these portraits of New York's inner-city life are the vivid descriptions of the children referred to as "Street Arabs" (Campbell, 1892; Riis, 1957; Woods, 1895). They were also commonly referred to as "canawl-boys" and "street rats." Sleeping in tangled heaps, they could be found in doorways, under staircases, in privies, on rooftops, or inside discarded packing boxes; the most prized sleeping spots were on the hay barges or over the warm air grates of the bakeries. According to Riis, although there were orphans and abandoned children among them, most of the boys slept out by choice, having gradually abandoned their families. He cited hunger, split families, and beatings from fathers as the three main causes underlying their flight.

The boys' group/gang life is loosely described, but their interdependence is clear. Most worked as bootblacks, newspaper boys, and night messengers. Theft was certainly not beyond them, and they relied on a "flash" language for privacy and to give each other warning. Some served as "feelers," employed by older rogues to work in the best pickpocket locations—reminiscent of Fagin as described in Dicken's *Oliver Twist* (1921). The boys' pastimes included swimming, shooting craps, smoking, drinking, and hopping rides on passing wagons.

While Riis may be faulted for his at times romantic, paternalistic, and ethnocentric attitudes, he was one of the first observers to focus on the healthy, adaptive traits in these boys. Resisting an often pejorative public viewpoint, he wrote of the urchin:

> Vagabond that he is, acknowledging no authority and owing no allegiance to anybody or anything, with his grimy fist raised against a society whenever it tries to coerce him; his sturdy independence, love of freedom and absolute self-reliance, together with his rude sense of justice enables him to govern his little community. Not always in accordance with municipal law or city ordinances, but often a good deal closer to the saving line of "doing to others as one would be done by" (Riis, 1957, p. 148).

In a later book (*Boys in Men's Shoes*, 1944), Burroughs echoed Riis' words when he described the street boys of Boston as "ambitious, energetic, industrious and independent." Both observers respected and gave credit to the street children for their ability to survive against great odds, while at the same time pointing out the "dangers" and "growing temptations" of the street. In summary, their accounts witness the resiliency in children who were managing to get along in a "high risk" environment.

METHOD

This research is based upon 10 months of fieldwork, completed primarily in Cali, Colombia, with two additional months spent in Bogotá and Cartagena. My initial sample of Cali's street children included 300 semistructured interviews with children randomly encountered in the streets in a cross-section of Cali's barrios. Three criteria were used to determine a "street child." First, he must be under 16 years of age and thus still a minor by Colombian law. Second, he could not be under direct parental supervision at the work site. Finally, he had to be engaged in "street work" as distinguished from a contractual form of official employment. The basic information sought concerned age, sex, formal education, time spent in the streets, type of work, place of sleep and indication of family ties.

At the time of my initial work, most street children were described as "abandoned." UNICEF has estimated that there are some 40 million street children in Latin America, with numbers projected as high as 20 million in Brazil alone. Similarly, a recent UNICEF publication suggests that "these forty million little people are living in the streets entirely or virtually without families" (Tacon, 1981, p. 37). The implicit assumption in these figures and statements is that these children are all very much alike, that is, that they are living in the streets in the same way and for similar reasons. In sharp contrast to these assumptions, my work suggests a marked diversity among these children, with significant differences in both the etiology of their condition and the nature and rhythm of their daily street life.

Based on this sample (see Table 1), it appears that Cali's street children fall into three rather broad, distinct groups: those children orphaned or abandoned; those who maintain active contact with home; and those who have left home. It is important to note, however, that all of these street children interact and overlap to some degree.

The first group, comprised of children who have actually been orphaned or abandoned, is often mistakenly assumed to be the largest. Indeed, it is actually the smallest group, representing roughly 7% of the overall population. This misperception has been partly fostered by superficial writing about street life, generally based upon quick, one-shot interviews. Street children often describe themselves as orphans, both because good storytelling is basic to successful begging and because denial may be one of the most effective defenses against inner pain and conflict.

The abandoned child may often be one the family is least able to care for, perhaps suffering from some physical deformity or neurological impairment. Although such factors may initially be an asset in a street-begging situation, the disability gradually becomes burdensome and possibly unbearable. Four of seven abandoned children in the initial sample had severe physical and neurological disabilities. Such children are least

TABLE 1
Initial Sample

Initial Sample: 300				
			Total	%
1.	Orphaned		14	4.5
	Abandoned by parents		7	2.5
2.	Abandoned home		96	32.
3.	Relations with home		183	61.
		Total	300	100

equipped to face life in the streets, but with the lack of adequate care facilities they are seldom afforded alternative care. There are no reliable statistics regarding abandoned children in Colombia, but there is no doubt that many simply perish. This demographic representation of abandoned and orphaned children is generally consistent with the findings of Pineda (1978), as well as the historical descriptions of street children in New York City and Naples (Borrelli, 1963; Riis, 1957).

The second and largest category of Cali's street children consists of those who maintain family connections. Making regular or sporadic contact with home, they circulate, often spending the majority of their time in the streets. The amount of time spent at home may be tied to variability in the family situation. Some spend the day in pursuit of money or goods to be brought home after nightfall. Others are involved in a wider street life, returning home only around religious holidays or when driven by an inner need to make contact. Coming and going with different levels of intensity and visibility, this group adds to the confounding of statistics.

Carmen (age six), Elena (age five) and Maria ("*la nina*"—the baby) are sisters who continue to beg together within a circumscribed number of blocks in downtown Cali, appearing at the same restaurant every morning. Initially, I was struck by the contrast between their joyful, spontaneous play with one another outside, and the sad story and presentation they made together while "working." Coached by her elder sisters, cowering a little and with outstretched hands, Maria was always the first to approach a stranger and begin to tell their story, which included a mother in a home for the destitute. It was apparent that they were not really interested in handouts of food, but would continue to press for small change. Over the months I came to know them as well as their mother, who was around the corner only a few blocks away, selling fresh fruit from a vending cart (not her own) on the edge of a street busy with pedestrian traffic. Daily, they made the trip in from a nearby squatter settlement and the girls would beg together, checking in with their mother periodically during the day and returning home with her at night.

The children comprising the final group (32%) of this sample exist at an extreme. They are abandoning children who, having *chosen* to leave home, are essentially responsible for their own physical and emotional survival. The transition to full-time street life appears variable, ranging from a gradual drifting away from home to dramatic, absolute breaks in contact. To the knowing eye, this final group, the gamins, displays recognizable qualities including physical appearance and movement, patterns of peer relations, and survival strategies that distinctly set it apart from other groups of street children. A core group of 25 was randomly selected from the gamin subsample, determined by the following criteria: 1) that they were essentially responsible for their own immediate emotional and physical well-being; 2) that they did not have regular or sustained contact with their natural families; 3) that they currently or had initially lived in the streets. Table 2 provides data concerning this core group of gamins who became the focus of the study and with whom this chapter is primarily concerned.

Before turning to a descriptive analysis of the gamin's daily life, there are two issues that warrant particular emphasis. First, the most observable element in the gamin population is predominately male, which is consistent with current and historical descriptions of street children in other countries. Second, it is important to clarify the misconception that the gamins represent a unique, wholly separate subculture. At this point, one can only speculate as to the reasons for this overt lack of girls in the gamin population. Culturally, it can be argued that in Colombia young girls are more needed and accepted within the family. The care of younger siblings and house chores are expected of them as "women's work," whereas a more aggressive, independent role is prescribed for young boys. In short, girls are socialized to remain within the home. The Whitings' (1975) research has indicated that children who are responsible for other children are generally more nurturant and less egoistic, and that sibling caretaking promotes development of prosocial, responsible nurturant behavior. Kagan (1962) states that in children the fundamental determinant of continuity in behavior is the degree to which it is congruent with cultural sex role standards. The work of Witkin and Berry (1975) offers evidence that young girls tend to be more field-dependent than boys, especially when reinforced by the culture. Chodorow (1974) indicates that, because of early social environment, "the feminine personality comes to define itself in relation and connection to other people" (p. 44). Gilligan (1977,

TABLE 2
Profile of Core Sample

Core Sample: 25 gamins

			Total	%
1. Ages	5–6 years		2	8
	7–9 years		7	28
	10–12 years		10	40
	13–16 years		6	24
		Total	25	100
2. Ages at which they left home	4–6 years		4	16
	7–12 years		15	60
	13–16 years		6	24
		Total	25	100
3. Time in the streets	< 12 months		11	44
	1–2 years		6	24
	2–4 years		4	16
	> 4 years		4	16
		Total	25	100
4. Place of birth	Cali		14	56
	Other		11	44
		Total	25	100
5. Number of siblings at time of departing home	< 2		0	0
	2–3		5	20
	4–5		9	36
	6–7		8	32
	> 7		3	12
		Total	25	100
6. Parental presence/absence at time of departing home	Biological father:			
	Present		7	28
	Absent*		18	72
	Biological mother:			
	Present		21	84
	Absent		4	16
		Total	25	100
7. Education	0 years		9	36
	1–2 years		10	40
	3–4 years		4	16
	5+ years		2	8
		Total	25	100

* Stepfather (*padrasto*) present: 15 (60%)

1979, 1982) echoes Chodorow's views in her observations that women tend to think and act relationally or contextually, and that the concerns of obligations to others take precedent over individual rights.

From a more psychoanalytic perspective, the high incidence of father absence in the gamins' families may serve to heighten oedipal conflicts and increase the boys' need for separation from their mothers. Also, the coming and going of *padrastos* (stepfathers) may alter the dynamics of the family situation, creating more conflict for young boys than young girls. Resentment, competition over the mother, and factors of power and responsibility within the home would be at issue. It is commonly reported that *padrastos* simply refuse to support another man's children, male children in particular.

Another consideration is the possible interaction of biology and psychosocial stage of development with culture. We know that young boys in Western societies appear to be more vulnerable to behavior problems than are girls. Certainly, the referral rate of boys over girls to United States child guidance clinics supports this viewpoint. Rutter (1970) suggests that, indeed, young boys may be especially sensitive to problems of family stress and discord. Such factors may converge at a time when more aggressive behavior is culturally sanctioned for boys, leading to an active, independent response over a more passive, reflective course. In addition, it appears that young Colombian girls who live independently of their families are drawn into domestic work or organized prostitution, a fact reflected in the number of preadolescent girls found working the streets, accepting refuge and shelter of the most exploitative kind.

Articles in the Colombian press, as well as the limited body of research on the gamin population, often mistakenly make reference to them as a separate subculture. Such a narrow conceptualization ignores the degree to which the gamins interact with, and are dependent upon, the larger culture. They are an integral part of the urban street poor. Their lives are intertwined with, not separated from, the flow of everyday street life. Virtually every form of work these children pursue is also engaged in by the adult street population. At times, this interaction is cooperative, and gamins can be found working alongside the "*zaranderos*" (the ragpickers, "those who sift the common from the precious"), who pull their wooden carts through Cali's streets, seeking and separating anything collectible—cloth, cardboard, glass, plastic, and wood—all of which is then sold back to particular artisans or industrial users. Yet there is also direct competition with adults whose survival strategies rely upon begging, or the provision of services such as shoeshining, or selling cigarettes, gum, or lottery tickets.

Etiology

Recent social policy literature regarding street children (Hollnsteiner & Tacon, 1983; Tacon, 1981) suggests environmental circumstances as the sole etiological source of their condition. Without question, factors such as poverty, rural to urban migration, civil strife, family violence, and physical and sexual abuse play a central role in the genesis of street children. However, such a limited view does not account for those children who have been exposed to similar fate and circumstances and are not in the streets. Not all "poor," "broken" homes, even those with the stereotyped *padrasto,* produce gamins. The vast majority of children living under such conditions remain at home.

Clinical experience with children has revealed the complex nature of abusive environments, and in the most pathological cases, we see children who will go to any extreme to conceal and protect such a relationship. How, then, are we to understand why one or two children choose to leave such a home while the larger number of siblings remain? I would argue that environmental circumstance may be a necessary condition, but it is not sufficient to explain the phenomenon of street children. What is required is an interactionist perspective, one that gives equal weight to intrinsic factors within the individual child. Thus, the etiology of this particular group of street children rests upon environmental circumstance as it interacts with such individual differences as temperament, intelligence, and character (i.e., personality), along with such factors as physiological predisposition, locus of control, cognitive style, and level of cognitive and psychosocial development.

Moreover, there is a need to consider the manner in which these children left home. Although a few reported a dramatic break or expulsion following an extreme incident (e.g., a severe beating), most stories portrayed a very different evolution, a gradual drifting away—a night away from home became a few days, and then a week. This pattern suggests a "testing of the waters," a cognitive as well as affective appraisal of street life. This often included some prior consolidation of supports, including a particular kind of "work" and the firm establishment of peer relationships. In these cases, the child was not simply impulsive and "running away"; indeed, he knew a good deal about where he was going. These particular children actively set out with the intent of shaping a different kind of life for themselves, and it is possible that, for some of them, the departure from home was a move toward both physical and psychological health.

PEER RELATIONSHIPS

While peer groups are to be found in almost all societies, their formation, organization, and influence on members vary considerably. Street life is unprotected and open to exploitation. Thus, for the gamin, peer relationships take on altered significance. Peer support is directly tied to survival itself.

The gamins are most commonly found in two types of groups—the *gallada* (literally, a roost) and *camada* (brood or litter). The gallada is found predominantly in Bogotá and is clearly distinguished from the camada by aspects of leadership, organization, and territoriality. Typically composed of eight to 15 children, the gallada may include adolescents of up to 15 or 16 years of age, as well as children as young as seven and eight. Membership is enduring and numbers do not fluctuate radically from week to week. Galladas tend to have *jefes* or leaders, usually an older boy respected for such attributes as size, strength, athletic ability, intelligence, and street sense. His judgments are generally accepted and adhered to.

Galladas may carry specific names, and rules of both membership and conduct are practiced. Members regularly split up during the day to pursue specific tasks or duties, having earlier agreed upon a fixed spot at which to regroup later in the day. The younger boys continue to be the most successful beggars and in this respect remain quite important to the group, commanding a degree of equality with the older boys.

Although regarded as little more than gangs of delinquent thieves by much of the Colombian public, galladas do offer their members some degree of protection against the constant vulnerability to violence and abuse in the streets. The real or perceived threats of physical and sexual exploitation by older street people, the unsympathetic, even abusive treatment by the police, and the competition for control of scarce resources (e.g., a preferred location for sleeping, access to a particular river or fountain for bathing, or to restaurants and movie theatres for begging) all contribute to the problems of territoriality, and fighting between rival galladas is not unknown. Although the gallada's involvements in crime and violence must be recognized and contended with, it must first be realized that these children do not band together to fight and steal; rather, they band together to meet primary physical and emotional needs not being addressed elsewhere.

Camadas represent small groups of children, as few as four or five and seldom more than 10 or 12 in number. On the whole, they tend to be younger than those children in galladas. With an average age of 10, they may range from five to 15 years. Their organization is relatively loose, with no rigid requirement of membership. Importantly, there is seldom a *jefe* or designated leader and, while some boys may have stronger, more dominant personalities, much of the decision making is collective in nature. Such flexibility should not be mistaken as a lack of cohesion.

So, too, one must not underestimate the amount of strength and support generated within the camada, as the daily *lucha* (battle or fight) is shared. Again and again, gamins stated that they "are not alone—there are all the other boys of the street." Their own histories, pains, and sorrows receive substantial validation, and to some extent this shared knowledge adds both cognitive and emotional leverage. Even the experience of poverty is altered by this sharing, especially as the majority of the gamins do quite well in contrast to other urban street poor. Overall, the peer group may, through collective effort, allow a child to begin to feel more hope for his future.

DAILY LIFE

Street children are often referred to as "vagrant," a term implying a random, purposeless wandering, attributed to individual failure. On the contrary, the behavior of street children is neither haphazard nor purposeless, but quite goal-directed, a coherent, combined effort to meet the pressing survival needs of food, clothing, and shelter, as well as everpresent emotional needs. Their daily lives may be more accurately described as a form of "urban hunting and gathering" (Peattie, 1982), one in which even their forms of entertainment reveal a mixture of necessity with pleasure.

Street life revolves around the scarcity and pursuit of work. Women and children make up over half of Cali's street labor force, yet they are consistently paid less than men for their efforts. Working with the least security and under the worst conditions, they are at the bottom of the labor chain. It is estimated that over 30% of the children in the "popular classes" work at least eight hours a day, seven days a week, with a daily yield of less than three dollars (Birkbeck, 1978). In many families there is no single breadwinner, and thus most resources are pooled.

The gamins are an integral part of this labor force, and their survival strategies reveal a very creative, adaptive fit to the immediate environment. Many gamins are involved in some form of service work such as carrying goods around a marketplace or providing menial labor for shop owners. Guarding parked cars is a common practice, especially in front of the post office or stores in the main commercial district. In Bogotá, unlike Cali, it is said that to refuse such service is to ensure theft—one pays for protection. Other gamins stand on islands in busy intersections and rapidly wipe the windows of cars stopped at lights, in hopes of tips.

Some pursuits require capital. Those who work as *lustrabotas* (shoeshine boys) not only need money for the initial purchase of a box, polish, and brushes, but also must continue to acquire diverse colors of polish and replenish their stock. A younger boy will often buy the used kit of an older boy who is "doing well." Selling newspapers also requires initial capital, as the papers must often be paid for when they are picked up. The child then keeps the profits from his sales. Newspapers are given out between 3 a.m. and 7 a.m., forcing these children to sleep near the distribution points. Selling cigarettes (individually from the pack), gum, or lottery tickets also requires capital. Maintaining a specific street corner or building entrance can become crucial to business success and, while territoriality may be respected due to consistent occupation, it is by no means assured. The prized locations outside the lobbies of private buildings are often reserved for adults, and most gamins are forced to move along the streets in search of customers.

Regardless of other work, most gamins' daily existence is tied to begging in one of its myriad forms. Moving in small groups or in pairs, they comb Cali's commercial districts, lined with open-air restaurants, shops, and moviehouses. Augmented with a mask and a drum (tin can and a stick), requests become performances, the creative solicitation of leftover food and spare change. Receiving acknowledgment that a customer's leftovers are free to be taken, the child may eat a single scrap on the spot or quickly scrape the remains into a small can or box, usually to be distributed among companions rather than hoarded for later consumption in private.

Another form of begging takes place on city buses. Allowed to crawl over the turnstyle by sympathetic drivers, young boys (often in pairs) will move up and down the aisle singing of their plight, sometimes chorusing, "for I am the child of no one." Here again, they must compete with adults (particularly those with an obvious physical handicap) who, with a captive audience, will make a speech, then move between the seats with outstretched hands.

Gamins are adept at singling out sympathetic tourists. Remarkably charming and entertaining, these children are capable of producing a quick skit or telling a heartwrenching story at a moment's notice. Although they generally dislike being photographed, gamins will often clown it up and pose for a fee—swimming in a fountain or diving for coins, and so forth. Occasionally, tourists will be moved to take a child into a store and buy new shoes or another article of obviously needed clothing. Regardless of the setting, begging is highly competitive, requiring stamina, intelligence, and imagination.

At the extreme, work becomes crime. The gamins are involved in petty theft. Due to their success in begging, the younger boys of the camadas are seldom forced to turn to theft. Still, an unguarded purse or bag, windshield wipers from a car, or food from an inattentive shopkeeper or street vendor can fall prey to the swift movements and fleetfootedness of these children.

In sum, like all of Colombia's urban street poor, the gamins rely on a diverse range of survival strategies to meet their daily material needs. Some of these activities are truly service-oriented and are more than marginally important to the city's daily functioning. Begging and petty theft can be regarded as "parasitic," but only this final category of work ever involves criminal or antisocial behavior.

Assessments of "cognitive" or "psychosocial" development must necessarily be contextual. We are bound to struggle with what behavior means and represents within the particular environment in which it occurs. Considered from this perspective, the gamins' daily life is largely self-starting and self-managed. To steal a set of windshield wipers, travel across town to the black market, successfully negotiate a price with a fence, and then purchase a T-shirt require a complex range of visual–perceptual, analytic, and social skills. Begging in open-air restaurants requires equally complicated skills—assessing and choosing an audience, gaining access to them, and creating and producing a successful performance. These survival strategies reveal levels of ego development (cognitive, moral, psychosocial) that might remain unacknowledged by quantitative assessments not attuned to the contextual factors of the environment.

ENTERTAINMENT

Much of the gamins' daily life is purposeful and largely conducted "on the move." The bounding, unrestrained energy of these children roving through the streets projects a romantic, carefree, adventurous image. Most possess a good sense of humor and easily engage in spontaneous physical play. Yet even their play reveals a clear mixture of pleasure and necessity. The swimming and horseplay so commonly observed in public fountains and the River Cali serve equally as a means of bathing and washing clothing. These resources are also used by poor adults, but more often at odd hours that ensure some degree of privacy and less chance of official harassment. The gamins, however, sweep in at will, sometimes displaying showmanship that may lead to the pitching of coins by tourists or sympathetic passersby. Each incident may serve largely one purpose or a combination of them all.

Hopping rides on the backs of moving trucks and buses takes on a competitive air. It is a skill that requires practice and concentration. Although a dangerous pastime, it also serves as direct transportation, and the proficient child can travel from one end of the city to the other. For entertainment, vehicles are selected at random, but for transportation, specifically numbered buses are chosen that will pass the desired destination.

Gambling by pitching of small stones or coins is common. More often than not, play is for keeps, and each child must judge what he can risk. Gambling requires skill and concentration, as well as constant wagering, assessment, and risk-taking.

Group drug use appears to vary enormously with age and group association. Though sometimes a source of entertainment in a harsher physical climate like Bogotá, drugs may stave off cold and hunger and thereby enable sleep. Drug abuse was not a widespread and serious problem in the gamin population I studied in Cali.

Athletics is a natural form of entertainment, one that serves the same purposes in many other cultures. The push of physical growth, the mastery of a changing, developing body, and the competition with peers remain central. Expanding proficiency can increase self-esteem and help develop the social skills necessary for managing in group life. Soccer is a favorite pastime, a sport at which many gamins are quite skilled. The lack of proper equipment is of little consequence. Most boys lack street shoes and simply play barefoot. Where no ball is available, they manage with a number of rags tied tightly together, with stones serving as goal posts. Many know the names of Colombia's soccer heroes and make the same remarks of identification that are typically expressed by school-aged children in the United States.

The movies are perhaps the all-time favorite source of entertainment for street children. Occasionally, the boys' conflict about the absence of significant people is handled through the unconscious use of fantasy, as is revealed through particular stories or their identified aspirations for the future. But the demands of day-to-day survival leave little room for broad, creative role-playing. I witnessed very little of such self-generated "as if" drama that taps into a safe, free-flowing imagination. Thus, the movies serve a variety of needs. It may provide a ready-made internal escape from a harsh actuality, as well as protection from the damp physical cold. If allowed, many gamins will sit through the repeat of a double feature, taking full advantage of the shelter. In addition, the lines of waiting moviegoers are a viable source of income. The youngest gamin of the group is often posted by the ticket office, making a play for the change being returned to customers. At the final feature's conclusion, the theatre is cleared and the covered bay of a moviehouse may serve as the night's shelter, cardboard bedding spread over ceramic tile. The theatre offers a physical and psychological respite from the streets.

RESILIENCY

Given the harshness of their environment, much of the gamins' daily life is an irony. Most appear to be in better physical health than many same age peers in the squatter settlements. While they are not free of emotional problems, the lack of overt, severe psychopathology in the gamin population is striking. When viewed contextually, their daily survival strategies and the nature of their group life demonstrates a range of adaptive resilient behavior. As a group, the gamins are particularly adept at seeking out, identifying, engaging, and drawing upon the supports that do exist, even in a bleak environment.

In examining the sources of the gamins' resiliency, the temptation to isolate a single necessary , sufficient factor must be overcome. It is more likely that a variety of internal and external factors coalesce to differing degrees within each child. Internal predisposing factors interact with specific external forces to ameliorate risk, allowing for the emergence of individual and collective adaptive behaviors of varying levels of intensity.

Internal Factors

The gamins' observed physical strength, agility, and coordination possibly have a physiological component. The ability to bring focused physical energy to bear on a specific task, physical endurance, resistance to exhaustion, and the quick recovery of physical equilibrium all contribute to their active mastery of the street environment. In addition, a significant percentage of the gamins were observed to be active, inquisitive, and assertive. These clinical observations were reinforced in the interviews with their mothers and prompt a consideration of temperamental predisposition.

In describing the delinquent boys in their original study, the Gluecks (1968) observed that "such characteristics as a tendency to act out their difficulties (extroversion), greater freedom from fear of failure and defeat, and less dependence on others, might under proper circumstances and influential guidance, be assets rather than liabilities" (p. 27). Thus, while such traits may prove extremely maladaptive and contribute to a child's risk factor in environments, such as the school classroom or a large, difficult family setting, at a different chronological age and in a different setting (such as the streets) they may prove to be quite adaptive, contributing to the child's ability to survive.

Related to the factors of physiology and temperament is a necessary consideration of both cognitive and psychosocial levels of development. The average age of the core sample was 11 +1 years (Table 2), and by self-report the gamins first left home between the ages of seven and twelve. This age range approximates the psychosocial demands and struggles characterized by Erikson's (1950) fourth stage conceptualization "industry vs. inferiority." In Erikson's words: "Industriousness involves doing things beside and with others, a first sense of the division of labor. Competence, then, is the free exercise of dexterity and intelligence in the completion of serious tasks. It is the basis of cooperative participation in some segment of the culture" (p. 282). In Robert White's (1959) early writings, the term competence is used in an almost biological sense. For White, competent behavior is selective, directed, and persistent, satisfying an inner need to interact with the environment. He employs the term "effectance motivation" to describe the underlying process. The aim of this interaction is the *feeling* of "efficacy," a subjective, affective pleasure derived from competent involvement with one's environment. Kagan (1984) cites the desire to predict and control the environment, as well as to match behavior to a standard, as major motives in developing a sense of efficacy at this age. These self-starting, self-directing capacities complement Piaget's interactionist conceptualization of cognitive development as it hinges upon the workings of internal maturation and the external force of experience.

Effectance is tied to self-esteem, a quality that encourages what Grinker (1963) referred to as "expecting well." For the gamin, tasks, goals, and challenges in the environment are immediate and abundantly clear. Success is tangible and provides its own reward and satisfaction. It does not rest upon the hollow praise children so easily see through when being showered with compliments for success at tasks that were of no major challenge. Thus, Hartmann's phrase (1958), "the average expectable environment," takes on a different form and meaning in these children's lives. For the gamin, the stakes riding upon competent, effective behavior are sometimes quite high. "Task failure" has serious risks and may result in pain, nagging hunger and cold, or worse, physical punishment and abuse.

Intelligence and competence must be assessed in the economic, political, and sociocultural context in which it occurs. It is not always measurable by standardized psychological instruments. Nerlove and Roberts (1975) have reported on the "natural indicators" of cognitive development observed in their sample of Guatemalan children. They focus upon the structural features rather than the content of behavior (e.g., the extent of adult supervision and degree of self-managed activity, the complexity of an activity measured by the number of separate action sequences involved, the rate and distance traveled from home and the degree to which activities are self-starting and elaborated). For example, the gamins' use of language to keep a conversation private in a public setting is not representative of "bad Spanish" or "poor verbal skills." On the contrary, it can be viewed as creative, intelligent, and adaptive to the demands of the environment. Other examples abound. The sequence of behavior required to conceptualize suspended political banners of cloth as a potential source of bedding material, to scan and scale the buildings from which to retrieve them, and to acquire the needles and thread necessary to sew up the sides into a crude but efficient sleeping bag, demonstrates a convergence of cognitive, analytical, social, and physical abilities. On weekends, various gamins regularly traveled to the beach in Buenaventura, some three to five hours away by automobile. To reach the edge of Cali, negotiate a ride on a freight truck, raise enough money by shining shoes and begging to feed himself, swim at the beach, and successfully negotiate transportation back to Cali within a set time frame is no small accomplishment for an unsupervised 10-year-old.

For Loevinger (1976), "the striving to master, to integrate, to make sense of experience is not one ego function among many but the essence of the ego" (p. 85). The spirit of the gamins and their demonstrated resiliency are embodied in a quote from Robert Coles (1964) in reference to a young black boy. Coles described this boy's ego as "the tough side of his personality, the stubborn, crafty, inventive qualities that poor and persecuted people often develop simply to survive, found an event, a challenge that could draw upon them—make them qualities that could guarantee success rather than, as before, keep chaos at arm's length" (p. 122).

Although the stress of the environment places the gamins at high risk and may prove overwhelming, the press of reality may simultaneously operate in another way. Forced to meet the actuality of their situation, the gamins find that many tasks are within their grasp. As Kris (1950) points out in his discussion of "optimal stress," manageable stress may serve to promote development of cognitive and social skills. Repeated competent, effective behavior has positive implications for self-esteem. It works against the crushing, paralyzing sense of helplessness generated by repeated failure at tasks too difficult to master.

The concepts of "psychological differentiation" and "locus of control" also enter in a consideration of the gamins' resiliency. Goodenough and Witkin (1977), among others, have suggested that people reflect individual "cognitive styles," most commonly measured along dimensions of "field-dependence" and "field-independence." According to Witkin & Berry (1979) field-independence is typified by the ability to differentiate parts of a field from their context, experiencing them as discrete from the organized background. In general, these people function more autonomously, have a more articulated body concept, and have a stronger sense of separate identity. Witkin and Berry (1975) have also observed that in Western societies, hunter-gatherers and nomadic peoples are far more field-independent than are peoples of sedentary, agrarian societies. Thus, field-independence is considered the more adaptive style for smaller, less organized social units that are necessarily attuned to immediate changes in the environment.

These notions of cognitive style may aid in conceptualizing the gamins' entry into the streets and their adaptive, resilient behavior in a high-risk environment. Although a strongly field-independent style might be maladaptive within a difficult home situation in the squatter settlements, it is quite adaptive in the environment of the streets; moreover, the demands of the street would reinforce such a predisposition. Almost without exception, the gamins have been observed to operate on the field-independent side of psychological differentiation. Their visual/perceptual organization is highly developed. Observing them moving through the streets, one is struck by their attentiveness to all that is going on around them; they cannot afford to walk along blindly. Their sensitivity to the environment is self-protective. Opportunities to acquire the basic necessities of daily life must be recognized and seized.

Phares (1976) describes "locus of control" as both a situation-specific and a broad, generalized expectancy. For "internals" the source of change is located within the self, while for "externals" outside forces predominate in the course of events. Internals are rated as more independent and self-reliant, seeking out more information when facing a difficult task. They are better in cognitive processing, thus enhancing their coping efforts, and are regarded as more persistent and better able to master their environments.

Active debate continues as to whether locus of control is a belief and attitudinal variable or is a determined predisposition with an internal logic (Rotter, 1966; Witkin & Berry, 1979). Regardless, the amount of fatalism in a person's outlook on life clearly affects the degree of passivity or initiative taken in response to adversity. One hears at times a strong and understandable fatalism in the lives of the materially poor in Latin America, often expressed in the phrase "Quien Sabes? Solamente de Dios" (Who knows? Only God). The sense of resignation that may accompany such a statement was uniformly absent in the gamins' posture toward their daily life as well as in their notions of what the future might hold. For many, the active determination to leave home reflects this stance in the extreme.

Anthony (1974) has suggested that when parental or family psychopathology is present, vulnerability becomes a function of involvement. Thus, field-independence, an internal locus of control and the capacity to maintain one's sense of self, would contribute to healthy, adaptive behavior in the midst of family psychopathology. The avoidance of helplessness and the belief in one's ability to initiate change contributes to self-esteem, the capacity to expect well and ultimately to develop an *internal* image of oneself as a survivor, or "one who recovers" (Murphy, 1976).

External Factors

The synthesis of internal qualities and attributes that contribute to an individual child's healthy adaptive behavior also draws upon external supports provided by the environment. Climate, city size, and racial diversity are external factors that affect the nature of the gamins' daily struggle. However, the most direct impact on how these children regard themselves results from the nature of their social supports, their relationships with peers and members of their community. Their lack of a traditional family magnifies the importance of these relations.

Rutter (1978) concludes that disturbed interpersonal relationships are strongly associated with psychiatric disorder in both children and adults. Garmezy (1974) includes strong peer relations as a major sign of competence in disadvantaged youth, while others have pointed out the possible ameliorating effects of peer associations for children at risk. Potential "corrective emotional experiences" (Sullivan, 1953) to be found within peer relations of the juvenile and preadolescent era have been echoed by Biller (1974), whose work on paternal deprivation points at peer relations as a major source of support in the case of fatherless boys.

Younger gamins often work and travel in pairs during the day. Such friendships become reminiscent of the "chumship" so well described by the late psychiatrist Harry Stack Sullivan (1953). In general, boys of about the same age and physical size begin, over time, to resemble each other in word and act. The child comes to know himself through another who is similar—the other child indeed may become what George Eliot (1872) called "an equivalent center of self." These boys exhibit tremendous loyalty, often transcending that owed to the camada itself. Shared food will first be offered to this friend, and clothing, etc., become interchangeable. If a transition is made from the street into a program, it may become a mutual journey. Such relationships provide a wealth of emotional as well as physical support. In describing each other as brothers or as a *"nero"* ("one who accompanies me"), they share the daily struggle and find strength in each other, realizing the phrase from Proverbs, "Brother beside brother is a fortress."

The strength and resiliency within groups of unattached children have repeatedly been witnessed and commented upon. Visiting Makarenko's youth program, Maxim Gorky remarked, "The striking thing is the presence of gifted children in this noisy crowd of vagabonds. One feels sure that many of them will become remarkable men" (in Zenzinov, 1975, p. 194). Riis' (1957) similar observations on New York's Street Arabs have already been quoted. Anna Freud and Dann's (1951) work with a small group of three- and four-year-olds brought into a residential home from the concentration camp of Tereszin is also of note. Describing elements of abnormal development and the children's difficulty in being separated from one another to work with adults, they proceeded to point out the positive, healthy elements of the children's "precocious bonding": a strong mutuality, the sharing of food, toys, and clothing, all accompanied by intense displays of emotional support.

The camada and its position within the population of the urban street poor is a central reference point for the individual gamin. The gamins repeatedly made comments like, "We are not alone"; "It's not only me"; "There are all the others." Thus, each child's reality is affected by the "actuality" of the situation and expressed "reality" or interpretations of those with whom he shares it. According to Kagan (1984), children of the gamins' age set standards and make cognitive judgments about their position vis-à-vis the others around them. For many children in the United States, the socialization of the peer group is secondary to that of the nuclear family. Thus, a young boy might arrive at a guidance clinic with a feeling of isolation, sensing he is different or that this "problem" (as defined by others) is his alone. For the gamins, the peer group is primary and serves the additional purpose of reality testing. They know each other's stories, the hows and whys of their being in the streets. Along with emotional support, this knowledge provides cognitive understanding and better perspective taking.

By and large, the gamins in the core sample externalized the *causes* for their difficult situations, but internalized the active *choice* to be in the streets. Their sharing of each other's stories acknowledged and re-inforced the interpretation that their situation was due to unjust circumstances beyond their control and not because of anything intrinsically wrong within themselves. Causality was rooted in such factors as over-crowded rooms, empty dinner plates, and abusive parents, rather than in their own "badness." Such a stance has enormous internal significance. The majority of the gamins state their difficulties are undeserved. The tendency to feel singled out for such a burden is tempered by the company of so many others who share it.

Equally important, the gamins are able to witness, express, and thereby bear the pain of their actuality. Although looked down upon and discriminated against by segments of Colombian society, the gamins draw strength from their acceptance by, and position among, the other urban street poor. Common expressions such as *"la lucha en la calle"* (the fight or battle in the street) acknowledges that one must participate in the shared struggle. Campbell (1892) reported that the New York Street Arabs used the slogan "to carry the banner" to indicate this shared condition.

The gamins also acknowledge their predicament in their songs, both popular and individual. Again, Campbell stated that the Street Arabs cherished the song, "There is Rest for the Weary." Songs are also individual and testimonial. In Cali, the gamins' favorite collective song was *"La Hija de Nadie"* ("The Child of No One"). It is a powerful ballad that holds special meaning for them. The words refer to fate and circumstance, "by criminal error of destiny," and to "brothers" who, through a "pact," will help sustain each other. The song acknowledges the vulnerability of their situation.

These observations on the resilient, adaptive behavior of the gamins has focused largely on the years of "middle childhood" (ages 7–12). During adolescence the struggle for gamins becomes increasingly complicated by both internal development and external environmental pressures. The physiological changes brought on by puberty are compounded by changing social demands in the environment. Surviving through begging and petty theft becomes ever more difficult, and the opportunities for solid employment remain equally restricted. The group/gang life of the camada becomes less adaptive, and the work of the streets, especially its criminal temptations, becomes difficult to avoid.

An inevitable question raised by this inquiry is what becomes of gamins. Since prospective, longitudinal work on the gamin population has never been completed, the answer resides largely in the realm of speculation. As Garmezy (1974) points out, the greatest period of vulnerability to developing psychopathology is between 15 and 45 years of age. Thus, the gamins' resiliency and the natural history of his evolution over the life cycle remains unknown, but an older Colombian man, who had been a gamin, provided me with what to him was a tempered, commonsense answer. Smiling about my naivete and persistence, he responded: "Well, it depends. What becomes of any man? You're right, the gamins are smart and strong; they survive. But it still depends on where you go, what you find, who you meet."

CONCLUSIONS

The intent of this chapter has been to offer a few observations on a specific group of children living in a high-risk environment and to extend those observations to a more general consideration of adaptive, resilient behavior as it is witnessed in childhood.

It appears that the existence of street children is both a modern and historical phenomenon, with familiar features that are seen in various cultures. There are relatively distinct subgroups among street children, with marked diversity in the rhythms and nature of their daily street life. Finally, the etiology of these particular street children, the gamins, does not appear to rest solely upon environmental circumstances, but is also a matter of internal factors such as physiology, temperament, and character; in short, personality. It follows, then, that the study of high-risk children necessitates an interactionist effort. Disciplined attention must be given to the unique matrix of internal and external factors at work in the individual child.

Garmezy (1980) has drawn upon a quote attributed to Robert Louis Stevenson as an analogy for stress-resistence: "Life is not a matter of holding good cards, but of playing a poor hand well (p. 249). Certainly, the randomness of cards dealt is reflective of the awesome arbitrariness that marks every child's entry into this world. We all must work with what fate and circumstance continue to provide or deny us. Yet the "cards dealt" (as innate capacities) are critically important, as is the specific game (environmental context) being "played." It is the unique coalescence of the two that constitutes the individual's "playing." Yet, it must be emphasized that the living of a life is not realized in the playing of a single hand. On the contrary, the weight and value of cards change as do both the ability *and* opportunity to play and replay them.

Adaptation is a function of the individual's unique strengths, capacities, vulnerabilities, and "goodness of fit" with the demands and opportunities of the environment. Indeed, "it does depend . . . where you go, what you find, and who you meet." All play a significant role throughout the life cycle.

REFERENCES

APTEKAR, L. (1988). *The Street Children of Cali*. Durham, NC: Duke University Press.

ASHBY, L. (1984). *Saving the Waifs*. Philadelphia: Temple University Press.

ANTHONY, E.J. (1974). The syndrome of the psychologically vulnerable child. In E.J. Anthony & C. Koupernik (Eds.), *The Child in His Family: Children at Psychiatric Risk, Vol. 3*. New York: J. Wiley & Sons.

BILLER, H. (1974). *Paternal Deprivation*. Lexington, MA: Lexington Books.

BIRKBECK, C. (1978). *Niños en la calle: Problemao solucion?* SENA, Cali, Colombia.

BORRELLI M., WITH THORNE, A. (1963). *A Street Lamp and the Stars*. London: P. Davies.

BRACE, C.L. (1880). *The Dangerous Classes of New York*. New York: Wynkoop & Hallenback.

BRAZIL'S WASTED GENERATION. (1978). *Time Magazine*, p. 32, September 11.

BREADY, J. (1935). *Doctor Barnardo*. London: Allen & Unwin Ltd.

BURROUGHS, H. (1944). *Boys in Men's Shoes*. New York: Macmillan.

CAMPBELL, H. (1892). *Darkness and Daylight*. Hartford, CT: A. D. Worthington.

CHODOROW, N. (1974). Family structure and feminine personality. In M. Rosaldo & L. Lamphere (Eds.), *Women, Culture and Society*. Stanford, CA: Stanford University Press.

COLES, R. (1964). *Children of Crisis, Vol. 1*. Boston: Little, Brown.

CRANE, S. (1893). *Maggie, A Girl of the Streets*. In *The Complete Short Stories*. New York: Doubleday.

DICKENS, C. (1921). *Oliver Twist*. New York: Macmillan.

ELIOT, G. (1872). *Middlemarch*. Cambridge, MA: Riverside Press, 1956.

ERIKSON, E. (1950). *Childhood and Society*. New York: Norton.

FELSMAN, J.K. (1985a). Street children: A selected bibliography. *ERIC*, October, CG–01907.

FELSMAN, J.K. (1985b). Abandoned children reconsidered: Prevention, social policy and the trouble with sympathy. *ERIC*, October CG–01906.

FELSMAN, J.K. (May-June, 1984). Abandoned children: A reconsideration. *Children Today*, *13* (3): 13–18.

FELSMAN, J.K. (1981). Street urchins of Cali: On risk, resiliency and adaptation in childhood. Unpublished doctoral dissertation, Harvard University.

FELSMAN, J.K. (April, 1981). Street urchins of Colombia. *Natural History*, pp. 41–49.

FREUD, A. WITH DANN, S. (1951). An experiment in group upbringing. *Psychoanalytic Study of the Child, 6:* 127.

GAGE, N. (1979). Too many boys, Istanbul Streets are home. *New York Times*, June 28.

GARMEZY, N. (1974). The study of competence in children at risk for severe psychopathology. In E.J. Anthony & C. Koupernik (Eds.), *The Child in His Family, Vol. 3*. New York: J. Wiley & Sons.

GARMEZY, N. (1980). Children under stress: Perspectives or antecedents and correlates of vulnerability and resistance to psychopathology. In A. Robin, J. Arnoff, A. Barclay, & R. Zucker (Eds.), *Further Explorations in Personality*. New York: Wiley.

GILLIGAN, C. (1977). In a different voice: Women's conceptions of the self and morality. *Harvard Educational Review, 47* (4).

GILLIGAN, C. (1979). Woman's place in a man's life cycle. *Harvard Educational Review, 49* (4).

GILLIGAN, C. (1982). *In a Different Voice*. Cambridge, MA: Harvard University Press.

GLUECK, S., & GLUECK, E. (1968). *Delinquents and Nondelinquents in Perspective*. Cambridge: Harvard University Press.

GOODENOUGH, D.R., & WITKIN, H. (July, 1977). *Educational Testing Service.* Princeton, NJ, NIMH Report ETS-RB-77-9.
GRINKER, R. (1963). Self-esteem and adaptation. *Archives of General Psychiatry, 9:*414–418.
HARTMANN, H. (1958). *Ego Psychology and the Problem of Adaptation.* New York: International Universities Press.
HODGE, W. (1981). Bogotá school reclaims waifs from the street. *New York Times,* August 16.
HOLLNSTEINER, M.R., & TACON, P. (1983). Urban migration in developing countries: Consequences for families and their children. Child development and international development: Research-policy interfaces. In D.A. Wagner (Ed.), *New Directions for Child Development, No. 20.* San Francisco: Jossey-Bass.
HUGO, V. (1931). *Les Miserables.* New York: Modern Library.
INTERNATIONAL CATHOLIC CHILD BUREAU. (October, 1983). Inter-Ngo Programme on Street Children and Street Youth. *The Street Newsletter,* Nos. 1–4.
KAGAN, J. (1962). *Birth to Maturity.* New York: John Wiley & Sons.
KAGAN, J. (1984). *The Nature of the Child.* New York: Basic Books.
KRIS, E. (1950). Notes on the development and on some current problems of psychoanalytic child psychology. *The Psychoanalytic Study of the Child, 5:*24–26. New York: International Universities Press.
LOEVINGER, J. (1976). *Ego Development.* San Francisco: Jossey-Bass.
MCPHERSON, H. (1979). Children of the streets. *Washington Post,* 1, January 14, p. 1.
MILLER, F. (1965). *Wild Children of the Urals.* New York: E.P. Dutton.
MURPHY, L. (1976). *Vulnerability, Coping and Growth.* New Haven, CT: Yale University Press.
NASAW, D. (1985). *Children of the City.* New York: Anchor Press, Doubleday.
NEEDHAM, G. (1884). *Street Arabs and Gutter Snipes.* Boston: D.L. Gurnsey.
NERLOVE, S., & ROBERTS, J. (1975). Natural indicators of cognitive development: An observational study of rural Guatemalan children. *Ethos,* (3): 265–295.
PEATTIE, L. (June, 1982). Personal communication.
PHARES, E.J. (1976). *Locus of Control in Personality.* Morristown, NJ: Learning Press.
PINEDA, V.B. (1978). *El Gamins Su Alberque Social Y Su Familia, Vols. 1–2.* Bogotá, Colombia: UNICEF and Institute Colombiano Bien Estar Familiar.
POOLE, E. (1903). Waifs of the street. *McClures', 21* (1): 40–48.
RIIS, J. (1957). *How the Other Half Lives.* New York: Hill and Wang.
ROTTER, J. (1966). Generalized expectancies for internal versus external control of reinforcement. *Psychological Monographs, 80* (1): 1–28.
RUTTER, M. (1970). Sex differences in children's response to family stress. In E.J. Anthony & C. Koupernik (Eds.), *The Child in His Family Vol. 1.* New York: John Wiley & Sons.
RUTTER, M. (1978). Early sources of security and competence. In J. Bruner & A. Garton (Eds.), *Human Growth and Development.* Oxford: Clarendon Press.
SRIVASTAVA, S. (1963). *Juvenile Vagrancy,* Bombay, India: Asia Publishing House.
SULLIVAN, H.S. (1953). *Interpersonal Theory of Psychiatry,* New York: Norton.
TACON, P. (1981). *My Child Minus One.* New York: UNICEF.
WHITE, R. (1959). Motivation reconsidered: The concept of competence. *Psychological Review, 66* (5):297–333.
WHITING, J., & WHITING, B. (1975). *Children of Six Cultures.* Cambridge: Harvard University Press.
WILLIAMSON, E.E. (1898). The street Arab. *National Conference on Charities and Correction. XXV:* 358–361.
WITKIN, H., & BERRY, J. (1975). Psychological differentiation in cross-cultural perspective. *Journal of Cross-Cultural Psychology, 6:*4–87.
WITKIN, H., & BERRY, J. (July, 1979). Psychological differentiation: Current status. *Journal of Personality and Social Psychology, 37,* July, 1979.
WOODS, R. (1895). *The Poor in Great Cities.* New York: Arno Press, 1971.
ZENZINOV, V. (1975). *Deserted: The Story of Children Abandoned in the Soviet Union.* New Haven: Hyperion.

5

Children from Alcoholic Families: Vulnerability and Resilience

RICHARD BERLIN and RUTH B. DAVIS

The theme of this volume is the resiliency and vulnerability of children and how these matters apply to our clinical practice. It is probably not overstating the case to say that nowhere are the issues of resiliency and vulnerability of children more inextricably interwoven nor more pressing for our clinical sensitivities and interventions than in the children of alcoholic families. Children growing up in alcoholic families constitute a population of over 20 million individuals in this country who must adapt to one sort or another of chronically disordered environment. It has been claimed that these children, as a group, are at risk for a variety of problems including poor school performance, troubled interpersonal relationships, delinquency, hyperactivity, physical/sexual abuse, and the development of alcoholism itself (O'Gorman, 1981). And yet, as caregivers working for the past several years with the children of Somerville, Massachusetts, we have been witness not only to the damage associated with family alcoholism, but also to the resourcefulness, patience, and courage of children and adolescents who are coping day to day with the effects of alcoholism on themselves and on their families.

RISKS AND VULNERABILITIES

What are the risks for children associated with parental alcoholism?

Prenatal

Fetal Alcohol Syndrome. The work of Lemoine and colleagues in France in 1968 and Jones and colleagues in the U.S. in 1973 identified a syndrome characterized by CNS dysfunctions, mental retardation, growth deficiencies, facial abnormalities, and other major and minor malformations. These infants were irritable, tremulous, with poor suck and decreased adipose tissue; they were frequently evaluated for failure to thrive. As expressed in one article, "Maternal abuse of ethanol during gestation produces a readily identifiable dysmorphic condition and appears to be the most frequent known teratogenic cause of mental deficiency in the Western World" (Clarren & Smith, 1978, p. 1066).

Preschool

Parental alcoholism may adversely affect the preschooler to the extent that 1) it is such a frequent cause of marital conflict, separation, divorce, or desertion, 2) it is associated with physical violence and the increased likelihood of physical or sexual abuse, or 3) it exposes the preschool child to toxic doses of shame or terror which lead to increased abandonment anxieties, increased dependency/clinging behavior or a defensive pseudomaturity which undermine the separation-individuation process and the formation of a cohesive self. In essence, preschoolers living with alcoholism are at risk for breakthroughs of the "protective shield" provided by adequate parenting which fosters the development of the earliest experiences of competence and mastery. Wallerstein and Kelly (1980) have documented in the three-to-five-year-olds they have studied the fear, bewilderment, global self-accusations, macabre fantasies, and intensified or inhibited aggression associated with marital disruption. When marital disruption is further complicated by the alcoholism of one or both parents, the preschooler is even more stressed. As for the connection between alcoholism and violence, the Booz-Allen and Hamilton study (1974) cites the presence of physical violence as an increased risk factor for children in these families. Even if the child is not the actual target of the abuse but simply there when the violence occurs, this study suggests the results are comparable. Depression, poor relationship with the opposite sex, confusion in sexual identity, and poor impulse control are all outcomes associated with physical violence.

Here are brief vignettes of two preschool boys from alcoholic families seen in psychotherapy, one who could not stop playing the same theme over and over and over again, and another who could not play at all.

Bobby, a four-year-old boy, was brought to the clinic by his mother who was worried about his restless sleep, recurrent nightmares, and frequent crying spells. His preoccupation in his dreams, in his talk, and in his play was with monsters; he was constantly on the lookout for them and constantly doing battle with great hordes of them. Every night at bedtime several monster stories had to be read before Bobby would consider going to sleep. Bobby's parents had separated 18 months prior to his visits to the clinic after 10 years of marriage, increasingly disrupted by the father's alcoholism. The actual separation had been tumultuous, with the father returning drunk to the house and smashing several windows. During this time the father was hospitalized for a suicide attempt and then the mother was hospitalized for a month for a "nervous breakdown." According to the mother's report, when Bobby would see his father following the separation, he would say, "Beer makes you a monster." Once, after not seeing his father for six months, Bobby asked him after the first few minutes of sitting down together at a restaurant, "Are you not a monster anymore?" In play sessions with his therapist, Bobby would stage endless, breathtaking battles with monsters and, with characteristic bravado, show off how invincible he was as a monster-fighter.

Teddy was a five-year-old boy who lived with his alcoholic mother, older brother and sister, and his mother's alcoholic and abusive boyfriend. Teddy and his sibs had been removed from their home several times by the Department of Social Service during periods of particularly heavy drinking by the mother or when the mother went into detox. Teddy was described as highly distractible, hyperactive, and easily angered. He has set several small fires in the house. The DSS worker reported that he often told her of vivid nightmares in which he was threatened or hurt by monsters. When Teddy was three, his father was killed in an automobile accident.

When Teddy entered the playroom for the first time, he sat stiffly in his chair and warily surveyed the surroundings. He held himself back but stared vigilantly at each successive toy his glance fell on. He did not play with any of the toys but instead asked where they came from and how much they cost. He was finally persuaded to draw a picture and he hastily scribbled out a picture of a monster with a baby in its mouth. After drawing this, he appeared increasingly anxious and avoided the interviewer's looks and questions for several minutes. Then the interviewer asked him about his dreams and, in particular, if he ever had any scary ones. After a moment's hesitation, the floodgates gave way: Teddy now spoke very rapidly and related in vivid detail a nightmare about being pursued by a monster with enormous teeth who could find Teddy no matter where he was hiding. As the narrative of the nightmare progressed, there emerged another story, this one about his father's fatal automobile accident. The two stories intertwined and eventually blurred as Teddy heaped more and more terrifying and gruesome details into this telling of his fantasied and actual horrors. His anxiety grew and grew until suddenly in the midst of his recounting, he bolted from the room.

Middle Childhood

Parental alcoholism may adversely affect the grade-school child in ways that show up in the areas of 1) school performance, 2) peer relationships, and 3) regulation of mood and self-esteem. At school, some of these children will be compulsive overachievers who cannot tolerate less than perfection 100% of the time. Others will start missing school on a regular basis or be identified by teachers as troublemakers, poorly motivated, and poorly attentive. Some of these motivation/attention problems will be due to attention deficit disorder. In 1971, Morrison and Stewart reported on a study of 59 hyperactive children in the St. Louis area in which they found that the hyperactive children were twice as likely as controls to have a first or second degree relative with alcoholism. Cantwell reported similar findings in a study in the Los Angeles area in 1972, noting an increased prevalence of alcoholism among the parents, especially the fathers, of hyperactive children. Less frequently identified by teachers or school personnel are the children who manage to keep up their studies but are quietly forlorn and empty.

Dorothy was eight years old and in third grade. She was the oldest of three, with two brothers, ages four and two. She usually kept her eyes downcast and spoke softly. Her mother said that Dorothy had a wonderful smile that could brighten up the room, but it seemed less and less often that Dorothy became enthusiastic about anything. She was doing very well in all her subjects at school, but her teacher noticed that Dorothy was constantly worrying that she was not doing well enough, and when a mistake was pointed out to her she became self-critical and angry. Dorothy's father was alcoholic and had been living in a different town since the parents separated about two years previously. He saw his children very infrequently. When Dorothy was asked about how her father treated her when he lived with the family, she said with angry tears in her eyes, "He treated me like I was a wall. He didn't see me."

In terms of peer relationships, various studies have mentioned problems in handling aggression and controlling impulses. Fine et al.'s study (1975) of 8–12-year-olds from alcoholic families in Philadelphia emphasized the social isolation, lack of autonomy, and fearfulness of those children. It is in middle childhood that the social stigma of having an alcoholic parent may begin to influence the child and thus reinforce the family's pact of denial. The child is often embarrassed or fearful at the prospect that a friend might see how "weird" his father or mother act when they have been drinking. Thus, friends may simply not be invited over. Resentment at the parent who does not keep promises or meet responsibilities is also a common emotion in the grade-school child; the child is on a teeter-totter of hope and disappointment. In the area of mood regulation and self-esteem, these children as a group are at risk for feelings of helplessness and worthlessness, and may be more prone to self-criticism and actual depression. Several studies have indicated a disruption in the process of identification with or role learning from the alcoholic parent (Barnes, 1977). The opportunity to idealize the same-sex parent before the inevitable disillusionments of adolescence is one of the bastions of middle childhood. When alcoholism in the family creates intense ambivalence about this process of idealization and identification, the child may be more vulnerable to the development of problems with self-esteem, especially if nothing changes for the family by the time the child enters adolescence.

Karen was nine years old, in fourth grade, and lived with her mother, who was alcoholic, and her younger sister, age three. She began psychotherapy at the Clinic following her mother's suicide attempt and hospitalization. For several months Karen missed most of her appointments with her female therapist; when she did show up, she would attempt to wait on her therapist, offering to brush her hair or inquiring with concern about her cold or her fatigued look. After the therapist began meeting Karen at school and bringing her to their appointments, her attendance became very regular. It was soon apparent that Karen was a child who very much enjoyed using fantasy and make-believe. Karen had created an imaginary planet called Mahawaii, which was a world where nothing went wrong. There were always kind people and lots of food, and there was a completely different calendar from the one on Earth, so that Karen could see her therapist even during the time her therapist would be on vacation. In a spaceship made out of a chair Karen would fly off to

Mahawaii through a dark and treacherous zone in outer space where collisions and other disasters were avoided in the nick of time. After playing at this fantasy for some time, quite abruptly Karen stopped and instead used her sessions to make various gifts for her mother. These gifts, which were usually cards or drawings, would be done exactingly, with Karen pausing to consider what her mother's favorite color was or how much glitter to put on the paper. Only after this alternating sequence of either flights to the delightful Mahawaii or the worrying out of the perfect gift for her mother had been repeated a few times did it become clear to the therapist that these shifts in Karen's use of the sessions reflected the shifts in her mother's struggle with alcoholism. When her mother was in better control, Karen could delight in her abilities to use fantasy in the increasingly protective atmosphere of the therapy. When her mother was drinking heavily and out of control, Karen was earthbound and stuck with her feeling of responsibility to make the perfect offering that might make a difference.

Adolescence

The adolescent in the alcoholic family is at risk for: 1) impulse control problems, acting out, delinquency, promiscuity, running away; 2) depression and suicidal behavior; and 3) drug and alcohol abuse. Adolescents who are estranged from their families due to the emotional neglect or behavioral conflict associated with family alcoholism and who have already been experiencing failures and disappointments in school and in interpersonal relationships are often headed for trouble. Their behavior often makes people angry and tends to push others away. These children are a study in loneliness and isolation.

Adolescents living in families with parental alcoholism are often stuck in an impossible situation. Intense loyalty binds are often at the center of the drama of separation they enact with their parents. Both the alcoholic and the nonalcoholic parent may rely heavily upon the adolescent to fulfill their needs: needs for nurturance, for vindication, for the day-to-day running of the family. Stierlin (1974) describes "binding" as one of the three major modes of transactions between adolescents and their parents, the other two being "delegating" and "expelling." We see binding as a significant feature in the separation dramas of adolescents from alcoholic families. Leaving home is fraught with what Stierlin calls "breakaway guilt, a guilt that operates mainly unconsciously and gives rise to acts either of massive self-destruction or of heroic atonement" (Stierlin, 1974, p. 50). Leaving home is also fraught with realistic fears about what might happen to parents and younger siblings, all of whom have been looked after by the departing adolescent. Many of our adolescents stay on, feeling trapped, angry, and helpless. One girl described how she sat down her alcoholic mother a few months prior to high school graduation and said, "I'll be leaving soon and Welfare will cut off your checks for me so let's plan how you're going to have enough money to live on after I'm gone." This mother settled the issue by running away from home first, before the daughter could leave.

Actually, running away is a frequent occurrence for adolescents dealing with parental alcoholism. While the act of running away may appear to be an impulsive expelling of the child by indifferent parents, more often it is the planned, reasoned decision of a bound adolescent who is struggling with massive breakaway guilt. Such youths are commonly misunderstood by those charged with the responsibility for helping them, since they are too often perceived as spoiled, ungrateful children having a temper tantrum, while the painful bind of their intense loyalty conflict is ignored.

Carol, an attractive 17-year-old high school senior and the only child of divorced alcoholic parents, described her life at home as increasingly unbearable. Her father's drinking constantly disrupted her life, yet she was unable to "hurt him by running away." She was failing school and in danger of not graduating because of sleepless nights and an inability to concentrate. At times she felt that the only choice that made any sense was to kill herself. She impulsively enlisted for four years in the Army but then felt much confusion and self-doubt about this choice. She vacillated for weeks in the throes of this dilemma and finally decided that she was better off staying at home, even though she continued to express intense feelings of being trapped.

Impulse control problems, in general, are well documented in this group. Action serves to relieve internal distress while at the same time diverting family attention from the alcoholic parent to the "troubled child." Adolescents in trouble with the law are now known to suffer, at a higher rate than the general population, from learning disabilities, often undiagnosed. It is also becoming increasingly clear that an extremely high number of juvenile offenders are children of alcoholic parents.

Depression and suicidal behavior are further risks for adolescents living with parental alcoholism. Feelings of hatred and preoccupations with revenge, which are common when family alcoholism is compounded by physical violence, only increase this already considerable risk. The isolation of the adolescent in a family that denies the parental alcoholism serves to exacerbate the normative experience of being misunderstood, of not feeling heard. Increased abandonment fears, heightened vulnerability to shame experiences, impaired ego ideal, all contribute to the frequency of depression and suicidal behavior in adolescents from alcoholic families.

The third main risk category for adolescents from alcoholic families is the development of substance abuse and alcoholism problems. Here, Erikson's notion (1956) of negative identity choice is apt, that is, "an identity perversely based on all those identifications and roles which, at critical stages of development, had been presented to the individual as most undesirable or dangerous, and yet, also as most real" (p. 87). The adolescent living with parental alcoholism probably has, as he or she begins to experiment with alcohol, similar thoughts and feelings to those of Jerry, whose experience is described with remarkable clarity by Deutsch in his book, *Broken Bottles, Broken Dreams* (1982):

> After years of watching the bottle disrupt his home and his happiness; after endless images of drunkenness and nothing to suggest any other style of drinking; with a daily accumulation of a sense of his impotence to control that bottle and what happens once it appears; and with the fascination that made him wonder as a child just what was in there that his father loved so much; Jerry drinks. Jerry cannot lift a beer to his lips without somewhere inside associating his act with every incident of drunkenness he's suffered from; he cannot grimace at the bitterness of the beer without the internalized understanding that one drinks in spite of the taste, for the power of the alcohol. With his poor self-concept, poorer now because he is indulging in the greatest of evils, what chance does he have to feel control over the magic of alcohol? (p. 86)

FAMILY FACTORS

Garmezy (1977) has emphasized the usefulness of thinking about two pieces of the puzzle as clearly separable: the development of risk and the maintenance of risk. It is within the context of the family that the development and maintenance of risk for the particular child gets played out and inextricably knotted. How is one best to begin considering the distortions of family process associated with parental alcoholism? Clearly, there is no prototypical "alcoholic family." In fact, there is great variability in the effect of alcoholism on the family. Wilson and Orford in their 1978 article on children of alcoholics mention a number of important considerations in regard to the diversity of the problem: 1) the variability in drinking patterns of different alcoholics as well as the differing effects of alcohol on behavior and mood, i.e., bingeing versus daily drinking, drinking in the home versus outside the home, "hot" effects on behavior and mood (abuse, threats, expansiveness, contact seeking) versus "cold" effects (withdrawal, melancholia, contact avoiding); 2) differences in the duration of the drinking as well as differences in the age of the child at the onset of the parent's drinking problem; and 3) differences in the effects of an alcoholic father versus an alcoholic mother in terms of different drinking patterns, but also in terms of the differing effects on family roles and tasks. One might add to this list the difference between living with a single parent who is alcoholic versus living with an alcoholic parent plus a nonalcoholic parent versus living with two alcoholic parents.

But, despite the great variability from one alcoholic family to another, are there some common impasses or risks for families with parental alcoholism? In their book, *No Single Thread: Psychological Health in Family Systems* (1976), Lewis et al. use a model for assessing level of family functioning based on five categories: 1) power structure; 2) degree of individuation; 3) acceptance of separation and loss; 4) perception of reality; and 5) affect. Let us attempt to sketch out some of the common impasses for the family with parental alcoholism against the background of the successful mastery of the tasks necessary for family competence and flexibility as described by Lewis's model.

Power Structure

Each family has its own organizational rules as to how power is held and wielded. In the healthiest families, there is a clear hierarchy in which the parents are in charge and have a stable coalition with one another, which does not weaken generational boundaries and in which the children are less powerful than the adults but are sure of their influence in family decisions. A spirit of cooperativeness, negotiation, and compromise characterizes these families, and effective planning and decision making is the result. As one moves along the continuum from family health to disturbance, one sees a shift in the direction of both increasing coercion and confusion in regard to parental authority, weaker parenting coalitions, blurring of generational boundaries, and less creative planning and decision making.

Power issues in the family with an alcoholic parent revolve around the dual actuality, either acknowledged or denied, of the powerlessness of the alcoholic to control his or her drinking and the powerlessness of the nonalcoholic to control the alcoholic. In our cases with the best out-comes, the nonalcoholic spouse "hits bottom" fairly quickly and there occurs the crisis described by Joan Jackson (1954) (stage IV in her seven-stage model of the family's evolving adjustment to alcoholism over time), in which the nonalcoholic spouse takes over more and more control and responsibility for the running of the family and the alcoholic becomes more and more peripheral. Power issues become clearer after the crisis of extruding the alcoholic. On the other hand, some families seem to remain stuck in Jackson's stages I through III, characterized by denial, isolation, futile attempts to control or placate the alcoholic, and increas-ingly intense affects of fear, resentment, and despair. In these latter families, there is a shared experience of helplessness in which the nonal-coholic parent condones and/or is unable to prevent repetitive scenarios organized around the power of the drunk experience. The drunk experi-ence becomes the stronger reality which alters or dominates other family members' perspectives. Children are encouraged or ordered to do or not do certain things in order that some aspect of the drunk experience for the family will be changed. They are thus offered the bitter illusion of power or effectiveness as they are delegated to accomplish "mission im-possible." "Walking-on-eggs" or "tiptoeing past the ogre's den" are de-scriptions used to convey the fact that the central feature of these interac-tions is intimidation, the bracing of the self for the next onslaught. Where the nonalcoholic spouse abdicates certain other parental duties, the children, often the oldest, become drawn into assuming more and more responsibilities for keeping things running smoothly.

This situation is even more apparent in the family with a single parent, usually the mother, who is alcoholic. Here the weight of responsibilities for basic survival issues becomes heaped upon one child, again usually the oldest. It is not uncommon to see seven- and eight-year-olds with major caretaking duties for younger siblings in the power vacuum cre-ated by the single parent's alcoholism.

Ronnie, aged nine, was one of the most affable, cooperative members of our alcohol education group. He usually kept the peace when others in the group started to wind up. But on one occasion, as group was about to begin, he simply could not settle down. He paced back and forth in the room with an increasingly panicked look. He finally revealed what he was so distressed about: his younger brother and sister, also group mem-bers, had not yet arrived and Ronnie was berating himself for entrusting their care to another child so that he could go to his team's baseball practice. He was essentially inconsolable until he saw his brother and sister walk in the door.

Degree of Family Individuation

The issue here is the capacity of the family to tolerate autonomy in its members, encourage clear ego boundaries and identities, and respect the differing thoughts, feelings, and actions of one another. In the healthier families there is the members' ability "to express themselves clearly as feeling, thinking, acting, valuable, and separate individuals" (Lewis et al. 1976, p. 57) as well as the receptiveness or permeability to others' experience.

Here again, as in the area of family power structure, our families doing the best are the ones in which the nonalcoholic spouse can take a stable "I" position and teach/support the children to do likewise. One mother, who was 18 months into reorganizing her family without an alcoholic father, expressed it this way, "I'm just getting my head on straight after all the craziness. Now I can start to see that these kids have been going through the same thing as I have, only they understand it even less than I do. I've got to help them understand it, but before I couldn't because I was just lost in it, too."

One of the most frequently mentioned impasses in alcoholic families is the power of the addicted individual to dominate interactions, galvanize attention, and generate highly reactive and repetitive scenarios. As a teenager in one of our groups said in describing his family's response to his alcoholic father: "We all dance to his tune." Our colleague, Deutsch (1982), has referred to this impasse as "the centricity of the alcoholic and alcohol-related behavior" (p. 31). "The obsession of the mind" compelling the alcoholic to drink becomes the obsession of the family. Family members all lock into the runaway escalation of a "symmetrical struggle" (Bateson, 1972, p. 324) in which all share a pervasive experience of powerlessness.

One can readily perceive that the power of alcoholism as family obsession stands in the way of acceptance of autonomy and separateness in the children. Furthermore, when the alcoholic is obsessed with his or her illness and the nonalcoholic spouse is obsessed with the alcoholic, there is a heightened impermeability to the children's experience. This is exemplified in the John Cheever (1978) short story, "The Sorrows of Gin." Amy Lawton is a lonely fourth-grader whom we first meet as she is reading *Black Beauty* in her room, while her parents entertain their friends downstairs in another endless round of "social" drinking. It is soon apparent that Amy is surrounded by adults, including her father, who drink too much and who are constantly shooing her away. When the cook, Rosemary, who has been her only confidante, is dismissed for drunkenness, Amy starts the regular practice of pouring out bottles of gin into the pantry sink. One night her father accuses a babysitter of drinking an entire bottle of gin which in fact Amy has disposed of, and in the ensuing battle, the angry voices wake her up. Cheever (1978) describes her thoughts at this moment in this way: "Lying in her bed, she perceived vaguely the pitiful corruption of the adult world; how crude and frail it was, like a piece of worn burlap, patched with stupidities and mistakes, useless and ugly, and yet they never saw its worthlessness, and when you pointed it out to them, they were indignant" (pp. 207–208). Full of guilt and self-contempt, Amy decides to run away the very next day. In the last scene of the story, her father goes to retrieve Amy from the train station after the stationmaster has tipped him off that she is there. When Mr. Lawton sees her on the bench with her cardboard suitcase covered with decals, he is touched "as it was in her power to touch him only when she seemed helpless or when she was very sick" (p. 209). A moment for empathy, for taking in his child's experience, is upon him but it is short-lived and the storyteller reveals to us the full poignancy and terrible banality of this missed chance: "The power of her figure to trouble him was ended; his gooseflesh vanished. He was himself. Oh, why should she want to run away? Travel, and who knew better than a man who spent three days of every fortnight on the road, was a world of overheated plane cabins and repetitious magazines, where even the coffee, even the champagne, tasted of plastics. How could he teach her that home sweet home was the best place of all?" (p. 209).

Acceptance of Separation and Loss

The third category has to do with the ability of the family "to acknowledge and adapt to the great changes brought about by growth and development, aging and death" (Lewis, 1976, p. 68). Each family moves through time and must deal with the inevitable transformations of its members: children grow older, leave home; parents age, become sick, die. Rituals are used to highlight important moments in the family's time trajectory. What is the impact of parental alcoholism in this area of acceptance of change and the creation of rituals and values to guide the family? First of all, there is likely to be, as with other chronic illnesses, a protracted grief response in the family to the loss of functioning of one parent. Unlike other chronic illnesses, however, alcoholism with its cycles of denial and shame, its overresponsible/underresponsible dichotomy, and its Jekyll-Hyde transformations makes for high static and ambivalence in this protracted grief response. Here again, the family that has achieved a greater degree of distancing from the centricity experience is in a better position to acknowledge the loss and thus to mourn it more fully. Furthermore, the adaptively distancing family can preserve important rituals and values from being adversely affected by the alcoholism. Wolin et al. (1980) found that in alcoholic families that were able to maintain their rituals there was less risk for developing alcoholism in the children than in alcoholic families with disrupted rituals.

The sense of the family as a group moving through time is also affected by parental alcoholism. Steinglass (1980) describes the alcoholic family's life history as cyclical rather than progressive, with predictable transitions between "wet" and "dry" periods creating what he terms an "inflexible stability" (p. 211). Or, as Kellermann (1973) puts it, in using the metaphor of a play with the title "A Merry-Go-Round Named Denial" to characterize the alcoholic family: "The play continues to run year after year. The characters get older but there is little, if any, change in the script or the action" (p. 11).

Perception of Reality

Each family creates a context of shared meanings which has been referred to as the family "mythology." Families will differ in the major themes of their mythologies as well as in the congruence between the family mythology and the family reality as observed by others. In the most disturbed families, there is the most incongruence between myth and reality, with the likelihood that the reality of the perception of the child may be sacrificed to accommodate a rigidly held but rarely acknowledged myth. In healthier families, myth corroborates behavior; there is sufficient flexibility in the myth to allow for change as family realities change.

Alcoholism has frequently been referred to as an illness of denial. A child who participates in a system of denial over years develops a distorted perception of reality. One learns to blur fact and fiction or, as Woititz (1981) puts it, "These youngsters lose a sense of truth" (p. 190). In a situation where one night a full-scale battle can rage through the house and the next morning everyone acts as if nothing happened, it is understandable how the process of meaning making in the family gets significantly skewed. Both adults and children in the alcoholic family often mention their fear of going crazy. This fear is directly related to the chronic experience of lack of validation of one's perceptions in a highly oscillating system. For the child growing up with denial and mystification, there also may develop a blunting of interest and curiosity as

well as heightened shame responses and a belief in one's own helplessness. The child loses her or his vitality as a meaning maker.

The importance of having someone clarify what alcoholism is to these
children cannot be underestimated. Several studies have pointed to the
fact that children in alcoholic families do not know how to ask for help
because they don't really know what the matter is (Whitfield, 1981). The
problem has been labeled "parental fighting" or "my misbehavior" but
not alcoholism. In our elementary-school alcoholism education groups,
39% of children of alcoholics agree with the statement, "When children
do something bad, it makes their parents drink" in comparison with 13%
of other children. A fourth-grade boy from an alcoholic family was
fascinated by the story of *Pepper,* which we use in our alcohol education
groups. In the story, Pepper, the dog, eventually understands that his
master, who has been forgetting to feed him or take him out for walks, is
an alcoholic and is sick but has not stopped loving him. When the group
was asked what made Pepper feel better, this child responded, "Knowing
what the matter was."

Affect

The last category to consider is affect. What is the predominant mood
or feeling tone in the family? Where is the emotional thermostat set?
What are the possibilities and limits for emotional expressiveness and
empathy? One would expect the best functioning families to have a
prevalence of the positive affects: joy, curiosity/interest, and so forth,
and to have a warmth to their feeling tone. Clarity in expressing one's
feelings would be valued and empathy would be in clear evidence.

In the alcoholic family there is likely to be a dearth of the positive
affects of joy, excitement, and so on, and much more prominence of the
negative affects of anger, resentment, fear, hatred, and shame. If there
is violence and abuse, the intensity of the negative affects is even higher.
In the Jekyll-Hyde world of "now you see it—now you don't," there is the
alternation of affect suppression with periodic affect explosions: "The
way I lived was like one of those tornado or nuclear war drills we used to
have in elementary school. Dad would start acting crazy and it would be
time to tuck and duck" (Porterfield, 1984, p. 33). There is a great emphasis on being able to read the warning signs for the next affect escalation.
There is an effort to make the next outburst as predictable as possible, to
build in safety signals. The real danger is to share a collective belief in
helplessness if the family loses the ability to anticipate or predict the
alcoholic's behavior. Seligman's work on learned helplessness is ex-

tremely relevant here (Seligman, 1975). Predictable shock is consistently preferred over unpredictable shock; in predictable shock, the negative affects are time-limited and containable. When shock is unpredictable, there is a chronic fear response which lasts as long as one is uncertain of the uncontrollability of the situation.

Besides fear, another significant negative affect in the alcoholic family is shame. Shame for the young child involves the experience of having the parent who is expected to be familiar and approached with interest, excitement, or joy suddenly turn into the stranger, the unfamiliar one. The young child right from birth spends much time in focused staring as he or she reads off meaning from the face of the parent. One study found that one- and two-year-olds spent an average of 22% of their entire day "staring at a person or thing with intensity, as if to study its features" (Pines, 1969). The sudden transformation of the parent and the parent's features from familiar to strange associated with the intoxicated state is likely to interfere with the child's process of reading off meaning from the face of the parent and to lead to more frequent and intense shame experiences. In the school-age child, shame is frequently experienced, as the child's growing sense of social expectations of cooperation, compromise, and fair play is violated by the alcoholic parent's outrageous disregard for the "rules." In adolescence, it is not uncommon to see a countershame position taken by the teenager, who sees the threat of humiliation everywhere and strikes back with a "Damn your eyes" attitude.

Another powerfully disruptive affect that alcoholic families struggle with is hate. Deutsch (1982), in his work with adolescents from Somerville, frequently encountered children who shared with him what he called "the murder fantasy": "All the time I used to lay in bed at night and plot how to kill her without getting caught and stuff. I was a mean kid" (p. 47). In the Booz-Allen and Hamilton study interviewing adults who had grown up in alcoholic families, there is mention of one woman who "became aware of her hatred when she felt surprise that, when her mother died in a drunken stupor, no one asked if she had killed her" (Booz-Allen & Hamilton, 1974, p. 33).

PROTECTIVE FACTORS

In our work with the children and families of alcoholics we have begun to view the crucial task that they must master, if they are to cope successfully with the dilemmas of alcoholism, as the task of adaptive distancing.

By adaptive distancing, we mean the process of breaking away from the centricity experience in which the parent's alcoholism is the "stronger reality" for all family members, and being able to move to more nonreactive positions from which the actuality of the alcoholism can be dealt with in less totalistic ways. In focusing on adaptive distancing as a key protective process in our families, we have been influenced by the work of two outstanding clinician/researchers, Stella Chess and Judith Wallerstein. Chess, in her contribution to this volume, describes one of the children followed in the New York Longitudinal Study whose status in early adulthood "defied the voice of doom," which would have predicted a much poorer adjustment based on high-risk factors present at age three. She writes, "Stanley is one of a number of our subjects who were able to *distance* (our italics) themselves from an extremely stressful home environment. Such distancing provided a buffer that was protective of developmental course, of self-esteem, and of ability to acquire constructive goals" (see p. 195, this volume).

In a similar way, Wallerstein (1983), in an article on the psychological tasks facing children who must cope with divorce, lists as one of these tasks that of "disengaging from parental conflict and distress and resuming customary pursuits" (p. 234). Her description of this task of disengagement is worth quoting at length:

> At a time of family disequilibrium, when one or both parents may be troubled, depressed, or very angry, when the household is likely to be in disarray, the child needs to find, establish and maintain some measure of psychological distance and separation from the adults. In order to achieve this distance, the child needs actively and very painfully to disengage from the parental distress or conflict, despite what may be the intense need of one or both parents for nurturance and support from the child. In effect, with little or no expectable parental help, the child needs to take appropriate steps to safeguard his or her individual identity and separate life course.
>
> The second part of this task requires that the child remove the family crisis from its commanding position in his or her inner world . . . only by mastery of both aspects of this task, namely that which faces outward toward the family and involves relative disengagement from the parental orbit, and that which faces inward, namely toward the child's inner thoughts and feelings and involves relative mastery of anxiety and depression, can the child maintain his or her development unimpaired by the family crisis and make his or her way back to the world of children or adolescents. (p. 235)

Both Chess and Wallerstein are pointing to a process which we think has been too little studied in the literature on risk, vulnerability, and resilience. Wallerstein, in particular, is emphasizing that the task of adaptive distancing involves two challenges: to disengage enough from the centrifugal pull of parental distress to maintain pursuits and satisfactions in the outside world of peers, school, and community, but equally as crucial, to be able to "remove the family crisis from its commanding position" in the child's inner world. Thus, a reactive or defensive distancing in which the child or adolescent resorts to flight or isolation might appear to lead to increased disengagement from the parental distress but without any progress made on the other half of the task, namely, the handling of the anxiety, depression, and other negative affects which are the inner burden of the child from an alcoholic family. The distinction between defensive and adaptive distancing is important, especially in adolescence, because the most common coping strategies used by these children are flight or isolation. The reactive or defensive distancer appears to have removed himself or herself from the parental orbit, but in denying or minimizing his or her own distress may not be able to connect up with new relationships with peers or other adults that require open and honest give-and-take. The reactive distancer is more likely, on the one hand, to shun relationships, thus taking an isolated or solitary course through adolescence, or, on the other hand, to choose a more delinquent, impulsive, substance-abusing group as his or her most frequent contacts.

Peter had fled from his home at 17 when the constant fighting, both physical and verbal, between himself and his mother and stepfather, who were both alcoholic, had reached an intolerable level. He was living in cars or basements in the neighborhood. His arrogant and exploitive treatment of others was well-known and no one offered to take him in. Eventually, he sought out his older sister who lived on her own, and she was willing to let him stay with her. But after several incidents of stealing there, she threw him out. When seen at the clinic, he talked grandly about how he was going to make it big in California with the help of his father whom he had not seen in over 10 years. He ridiculed the therapist for suggesting that he might be in any distress and said that all he needed was "some wine and weed." On his way out, he stole some money off the receptionist's desk.

The adaptive distancer also tends to use some form of flight away from the pull of the parental alcoholism but, unlike the reactive child, the adaptive one is more likely to flee toward activities and relationships that allow some breathing room for reparative work and acknowledgment of the effects of the family alcoholism on the adolescent's sense of self. The adaptive distancer tends to be able to develop relationships with others based on reciprocity and not on categorical compliance or defiance like the reactive distancer. In the adaptive children, there is less likely to be the overanticipation of humiliation or shaming which, of course, then perpetuates those very painful experiences that interfere with genuine autonomy and limit the ability to use others in a helpful way.

Billy at 17 was a person we had known for almost 10 years. We first saw him at age eight when his parents' marriage was starting to dissolve because of father's alcoholism and violence. In addition to all the family problems, Billy was a very active, distractible fellow who was diagnosed as having attention deficit disorder and placed on medication. The breakup of the marriage actually lasted several years, with much bitterness, threats, and counterthreats. Billy sought refuge with his grandparents and maiden aunt who lived next door and often he would refuse to leave there when things got too "hot" at home. At 15 he had found a girlfriend in the neighborhood. The two were inseparable, and Billy especially liked to hang out at her house and became quite attached to his girlfriend's mother. At the alternative high school, he had his characteristically hard time settling down to his studies and was often in trouble for roller skating in the halls. But, despite his rambunctious ways he was well liked by teachers and other students. He planned to join the Army after finishing high school.

As we have focused more in our work upon the task of adaptive distancing, we have tried to identify more clearly those factors in the individual child, the family, and the community that either facilitate or impede the successful completion of this task. In the Booz-Allen and Hamilton report prepared for NIAAA in 1974, four areas were mentioned as affecting the degree of risk for the children in alcoholic families: 1) socioeconomic status; 2) presence of physical abuse; 3) age and ordinal position of the child as well as size of the family; and 4) supportiveness of other family members. Let us look more carefully at their findings in each of these areas and, in particular, at how those findings would influence the resolution of the task of adaptive distancing.

Socioeconomic Status

The findings here were that the children most likely to "escape through success . . . are most often those who have been provided certain economic advantages. For example, children identified as high achievers were predominantly middle and upper class; underachievers were predominantly lower class. Similarly, children from blue collar families express a lack of self-confidence twice as frequently as children of other backgrounds" (Booz-Allen & Hamilton, 1974, p. 55). The report goes on to state that this does not mean that children from upper income groups do not experience great difficulties: "In fact, children from professional and managerial families experienced the following problems with greater frequency than any other groups: depression, suicidal tendencies, confusion in sexual identity, poor relationships with the opposite sex" (p. 56).

While self-confidence and achievement orientation are certainly complex and multiply determined attitudes, we have seen in our families how economic hardships, diverting of the child's attention to matters of survival, and lack of opportunities for mastery or success experiences are major obstacles in developing a sense of freedom in the child to work on his or her own projects or inclinations instead of contributing to the ongoing family struggle to make ends meet. The effects of parental alcoholism on the finances of the families we work with are not easily buffered, and it is often the child's or adolescent's business to cook, clean, mind the younger children, and bring in money when they are old enough. This is especially the case in the single-parent alcoholic family. All of these efforts directly or indirectly interfere with the task of adaptive distancing where "the child needs to take appropriate steps to safeguard his or her individual identity and separate life course" (Wallerstein, 1983, p. 235).

Physical Abuse

The findings here are that parental violence and abusive behavior dramatically increase the risk for children from alcoholic families. The outcome data also suggest that no matter whether the child is the actual target of the abuse or simply there when the violence occurs, the impact is similar. Significant difficulties with interpersonal relationships were reported as well as high rates of serious depression and drug and alcohol abuse. We think a critical factor impeding the task of adaptive distancing in children from alcoholic as well as violent families is the affect of hatred. Hate is a powerful bond; strong hate, like strong love, involves an exclusive focus on the object of the intense emotion. And this exclusive focus makes it extremely difficult for the child or adolescent to diminish the "commanding position in his or her inner world," which the negative affects occupy. An adult woman who had been both physically and sexually abused by her alcoholic father throughout her childhood and adolescence described in psychotherapy a recurrent daydream in which her head was in a vise, and she could not take her eyes, which were full of vengeance and hate, off her father's face.

Age, Ordinal Position, and Family Size

Increased risk is associated with being 1) six years old or younger at the onset of parental alcoholism, 2) an only child, or 3) the oldest child. The child six years old or younger at the onset of parental alcoholism is at greater risk for several reasons: 1) it is more likely that intense shame or terror experiences will interfere with the formation of a cohesive self; 2) the preschooler is less able than the older child to understand the nature of alcoholism without significant cognitive/affective distortion; and 3) the number of years exposed to alcoholism, which is a chronic, progressive illness, is highest for the preschooler.

It can be argued that the only child and the oldest child are more vulnerable to the expectations and needs of the parents in any given family system. Certainly, the only child in an alcoholic family has fewer places to turn when the going gets tough, in contrast to the child with several brothers and sisters.

A 15-year-old boy, an only child who lived alone with his divorced alcoholic mother, described his dilemma about what to do when his mother was drunk and then decided to drive her car. Should he go with her to protect her? Could he dare to confront her about her intoxicated condition and risk her abusing him and then storming out to drive anyway? He had already on several occasions, while his mother was driving, snatched control of the steering wheel to avoid collisions or going off the road.

The oldest child in an alcoholic family often must assume many parental responsibilities and put aside individual pursuits or preferences for the sake of maintaining stability and order. Labeled in various studies as the "super-coper" (Booz-Allen & Hamilton, 1974), the "family hero" (Wegscheider, 1979), or the "responsible one" (Black, 1982), the oldest child in the alcoholic family takes on a task which directly interferes with the task of adaptive distancing, namely, the task of protecting the status quo.

Supportiveness of Other Family Members

Several studies, including that of Booz-Allen and Hamilton (1974), agree that the supportiveness of the nonalcoholic spouse is the most crucial variable in the degree of impact of alcoholism on the family. The more supportive the nonalcoholic spouse, the more likely there is available the nurturance, protection, guidance, and encouragement of individuation which children need for optimal development. In addition, a supportive nonalcoholic spouse can create a positive family atmosphere in which siblings are able and willing to look out for one another and validate each other's experience rather than be a group of isolates or a constantly warring band. The supportive nonalcoholic spouse can maintain enough openness of the family's boundaries to include other members of the extended family who can provide positive models and compensatory parenting to the children. The broader the base of supportive adults in the nuclear and extended families, the less powerful is the pull of the centricity of the alcoholic parent.

On the other hand, when the nonalcoholic spouse is not adequately supportive of the children but instead becomes locked into a reactive, resigned, embittered position or is caught up in the obsession of the alcoholic, then the opportunities for adaptive distancing become scarcer and the task of disengagement that much harder for the child. The family operates as a closed system which disregards the needs of its individual members and pursues a course marked by progressive isolation, estrangement, and despair. The Booz-Allen and Hamilton study found that children from nonsupportive alcoholic families reported depression and fear of going crazy twice as often, and suicidal tendencies three times as often, as did children from alcoholic families with a supportive nonalcoholic spouse, sibs, or extended family. As that study puts it: "The child whose nuclear family is nonsupportive, and who either has no other relatives or has nonsupportive extended family, begins to understand what being alone is all about" (p. 78). That terrible sense of aloneness is a reality one often encounters in work with such a child: "Everybody knew what my mother was doing to herself and me. Nobody would even talk to me about it. They were a sea of blank faces, like united in an adult conspiracy" (Booz-Allen & Hamilton, 1974, p. 78).

✳ Intervention Issues and Strategies

Over the past 10 years a strong, well-documented case has been made for the vulnerability of children living in alcoholic families. It is our intention in this chapter to highlight one particular life task for members of alcoholic families—"the task of adaptive distancing"—and to begin to view both vulnerability and resilience in terms of the relative success or failure the individual family member has in handling the various aspects of this task. Since we are clinicians working with children, it follows then that the focus of our interventions is on helping to develop or to reinforce the child's ability to adaptively distance from his or her alcoholic family. Let us look briefly at how we approach this clinical work.

The crucial reality we confront as helpers is the centricity experience. Children are dominated by the central role of alcohol in their family and are often caught up in a reactive pattern. Feeling responsible for the drinking, they try whatever they can think of to stop the alcoholic from drinking, and thereby put an end to the family's problems (or so their fantasy goes). Because the drinking does not respond to their valiant attempts to control it, they feel they have failed and are left with deep feelings of helplessness. Unpredictability and uncontrollability—two conditions that are extremely common in alcoholic families—play a key role in the development of the child's sense of helplessness. Interventions with these children must therefore effectively address their feelings of helplessness.

Successful treatment strategies have, at their heart, three core messages which need to be communicated: 1) children need to have the unpredictable made more predictable by understanding alcoholism, especially the confusing transformations in mood and behavior of the alcoholic parent; 2) children need to be helped to absolve themselves of the responsibility to control the uncontrollable (the important messages here are: alcoholism is an illness, it is not your fault, you cannot control your parents' behavior); and 3) children need to learn how to help themselves, how to protect their own separate life course.

Working in various settings in the community—a mental health clinic, an alcohol abuse prevention program, the schools—we prefer time-limited groups as our method of treatment with these children and adolescents. Groups provide a unique opportunity for members to learn that they are not alone, that it is safe to share their thoughts and feelings with others, and that they no longer have to keep the "family secret." Group members teach each other how to avoid "loyalty traps" and most important, how to love their parents yet not continue to feed into a family interactional pattern that perpetuates the centricity of alcohol. Our groups meet for eight to 10 weeks, and considerable time is spent on separation/termination issues. Given the protracted, unresolved grief response to family alcoholism and the interference with autonomy needs, children and adolescents in our groups usually lack the opportunity to handle positive separation experiences. The time-limited nature of the group gives them the chance. Once group has ended, children who desire or whom group leaders feel need another group can then be encouraged to re-enroll and are willingly accepted into another group.

The group format includes structured activities designed to provide information about alcohol and alcoholism, correct misconceptions, teach decision-making strategies, and elicit feelings and ideas about coping while also allowing ample time for free discussion of important issues. Our latency-aged children are involved in intensive groups in both school and clinic settings. Adolescents receive services primarily in intensive, peer-led psychoeducational groups or, when indicated, individually at the mental health clinic. (For further descriptions of our programs, see Davis et al., 1985; Deutsch, 1982; DiCicco et al., 1984.)

Of course, all of our work with children and adolescents goes on in a society that is tremendously ambivalent about alcohol. Advertisements blare forth that drinking alcohol means attaining status, sophistication, intimacy, and camaraderie. With few widely accepted rites of passage for our adolescents, drinking alcohol becomes a focal "power ritual" of teenage life. Ambivalence also runs high as to the causes of alcoholism, with some viewing it as a disease while others steadfastly maintain it is a moral failing. Even within the same community, drinking practices may range from strict abstinence to overly permissive attitudes and behaviors toward alcohol.

Alcoholism deeply and painfully touches the lives of many people. As clinicians, before we can work effectively with children from alcoholic families, we must be aware of our own personal attitudes toward alcoholism. We must confront our own feelings of helplessness, anger, or denial. Also, we must be clear about what we mean by *helping* these children. As Deutsch (1982) has put it, "Help is not necessarily a dialogue" (p. 120). Many of the children we work with need to hear what we say and how we say it many times before they can open up. Further, if help is defined solely as getting the alcoholic to stop drinking, then we are not hearing the needs of other family members. In our work we experience again and again the power of listening, of allowing children to share their secret, of helping them to make sense of the disruptive events happening in their families. Making connections in the group enhances coping skills and fosters the child's hope and feelings of competence. A note given to us by one of our latency-aged group members at the end of her group experience illustrates the power of the group to reinforce her courage and patience:

Dear Rich and Ruth,

I really don't want to leave because I still have some problems that I can't get rid of. But these ones I don't think you can cure. But I guess I can get rid of them myself. Well, I just want you to know that I appreciate you helping me.

REFERENCES

BARNES, G. (1977). The development of adolescent drinking behavior: An evaluative review of the impact of the socialization process within the family. *Adolescence, 12*(48): 571–591.

BATESON, G. (1972). The cybernetics of self: A theory of alcoholism. In *Steps to an Ecology of Mind*, (pp. 309–337). New York: Ballantine Books.

BLACK, C. (1982). *It Will Never Happen to Me*. Denver: M.A.C. Publications.

BOOZ-ALLEN AND HAMILTON, INC. (1974). *An Assessment of the Needs of and Resources for Children of Alcoholic Parents*. NIAAA Rockville, MD.

CANTWELL, D. (1972). Psychiatric illness in the families of hyperactive children. *Archives of General Psychiatry, 27:* 414–417.

CHAFETZ, M. (1979). Children of alcoholics. *New York University Education Quarterly, 10*(3): 23–29.

CHEEVER, J. (1978). *The Stories of John Cheever*. New York: Alfred Knopf.

CLARREN, S., & SMITH, D. (1978). The fetal alcohol syndrome. *New England Journal of Medicine, 298:* 1063–1067.

DAVIS, R., JOHNSTON, P.D., DiCICCO, L., & ORENSTEIN, A. (1985). Helping children of alcoholic parents, an elementary school program. *The School Counselor, 32*(5): 357–363.

DEUTSCH, C. (1982). *Broken Bottles, Broken Dreams*. New York: Teachers College Press.

DiCICCO, L., DAVIS, R.B., HOGAN, J., MacLEAN, A., & ORENSTEIN, A. (Summer, 1984). Group experiences for children of alcoholics. *Alcohol Health and Research World, 8*(4): 20–25.

EL-GUEBALY, N., & OFFORD, D. (1977). The offspring of alcoholics: A critical review. *American Journal of Psychiatry, 134:*4.

ERIKSON, E. (1956). The problems of ego identity. *Journal of the American Psychoanalytic Association, 4:*56.

FINE, E., YUDEN, L., HOLMES, H., & HEINEMAN, S. (April, 1975). Behavior disorders in children with parental alcoholism. Paper presented at the annual meeting of the National Council on Alcoholism, Milwaukee, WI.

GARMEZY, N. (1977). Observations on research with children at risk for child and adult psychopathology. In M. McMillan & S. Henao (Eds.), *Child Psychiatry: Treatment and Research*. New York: Brunner/Mazel.

JACKSON, J. (December, 1954). The adjustment of the family to the crisis of alcoholism. *Quarterly Journal of Studies on Alcohol, 15*(4): 562–586.

JONES, K., SMITH, D.W., STREISSGUTH, A.P., & MYRIANTHOPOULOS, N.C. (1973). Pattern of malformation in offspring of chronic alcoholic mothers. *Lancet, I:*1267–1271.

KELLERMANN, J. (1973). *Alcoholism, A Merry-Go-Round Named Denial*. Center City, MN: Hazelden.

LEMOINE, P., HAROUSSEAU, H., BORTEYRU, J.P., & MENUET, J.C. (1968). Les enfants de parents alcooliques: Anomalies observées. *Quest. Med., 25:*476–482.

LEWIS, J., BEAVERS, W., GOSSETT, J., & PHILLIPS, V. (1976). *No Single Thread: Psychological Health in Family Systems*. New York: Brunner/Mazel.

MORRISON, J.R., & STEWART, M.A. (1971). A family study of the hyperactive child syndrome, *Biological Psychiatry, 3:*189–195.

O'GORMAN, P. (1981). Prevention issues involving children of alcoholics. In *Services for*

Children of Alcoholics, Research Monograph No. 4, NIAAA. Washington, D.C.: U.S. Government Printing Office, pp. 81–100.
PINES, M. (1969). A review of growth studies at Harvard. *New York Times Magazine*, July 6.
PORTERFIELD, K. (1984). *Familiar Strangers*. Center City, MN: Hazelden.
SELIGMAN, M. (1975). *Helplessness*. San Francisco: W.H. Freeman & Co.
STEINGLASS. P. (September, 1980). A life-history model of the alcoholic family. *Family Process, 19:*211–226.
STIERLIN, H. (1959). The adaptation to the "stronger" person's reality. *Psychiatry, 22:*143–152.
STIERLIN, H. (1974). *Separating Parents and Adolescents*. New York: Quadrangle.
THOMAS, A., & CHESS, S. (1980). *The Dynamics of Psychological Development*. New York: Brunner/Mazel.
WALLERSTEIN, J. (1983). Children of divorce: The psychological tasks of the child. *American Journal of Orthopsychiatry, 53*(2): 230–243.
WALLERSTEIN, J., & KELLY, J. (1980). *Surviving the Breakup*. New York: Basic Books.
WEGSCHEIDER, S. (May-June, 1979). Children of alcoholics caught in family trap. *Focus on Alcohol and Drug Issues, 2:*8.
WHITFIELD, C. (1981). Children of alcoholics: Treatment issues. In *Services for Children of Alcoholics*, Research Monograph No. 4, NIAAA. Washington, D.C.: U.S. Government Printing Office, pp. 66–80.
WILSON, C., & ORFORD, J. (1978). Children of alcoholics. *Journal of Studies on Alcohol, 39*(1): 121–142.
WOITITZ, J. (1981). The educational aspects of servicing the children of alcoholics. In *Services for Children of Alcoholics* Research Monograph No. 4, NIAAA. Washington, D.C.: U.S. Government Printing Office, pp. 186–191.
WOLIN, S.J., BENNETT, L.A., NOONAN, D.L., & TEITELBAUM, M.A. (1980). Disrupted family rituals: A factor in the intergenerational transmission of alcoholism. *Journal of Studies on Alcohol, 41*(3):199–214.

Part III

ADOLESCENCE: DEVELOPMENTAL STRESS AND ADAPTATION

6

Family Aspects of Vulnerability and Resilience in Adolescence: A Theoretical Perspective

STUART T. HAUSER, MARIE ANNE B. VIEYRA,
ALAN M. JACOBSON, and DONALD WERTLIEB

Psychosocial development from early childhood, through adolescence, and into adulthood is shaped by a myriad of specific events, ongoing circumstances, and inherent strengths and vulnerabilities of the individual. Certain events and circumstances are especially likely to adversely affect this development. These situations vary widely. They include prenatal and birth complications (Field, 1980), poverty (Garmezy, 1983), a poor home environment (Werner & Smith, 1977), child abuse, severe family discord, parental psychosis (Wynne, Jones, & Al-Khayyal, 1982, Mishler & Wexler, 1968), loss and separation (Rutter, 1972), and chronic

This is an expanded version of the paper, Vulnerability and resilience in adolescence: Views from the family, first published in *Journal of Early Adolescence*, 1985, *5*, 81–100. Reprinted by permission of the publisher, H.E.L.P. Books, Inc., Tucson, Arizona.

illness (Whitt, 1984). Children exposed to such conditions are thought to be "at risk" for poor developmental outcomes.

The manifestations of problematic development in vulnerable children are as varied as the risk factors to which they are exposed. Poor outcome may refer to delinquency and behavior problems, psychological maladjustment, academic difficulties, and physical complications. Related to the topic of impaired development is that of resilience, or stress resistance. There are children who, despite exposure to significant risk factors, show few or no signs of developmental impairment. These children are thought to be "invulnerable" or resilient. A burgeoning literature deals with such varying developmental outcomes. Especially important are those studies examining specific risk factors, and processes mediating pathological as well as more favorable consequences.

In this chapter, we focus upon three relatively new topics within the risk and resiliency literature: *adolescent outcomes; chronic illness* as a risk factor; and the influence of *families* upon the impact of chronic illness in adolescence. By restricting ourselves to a specific developmental era (adolescence) and then examining—from conceptual and empirical vantage points—interfaces between developmental processes, an important stressor (chronic illness), and a key psychosocial environment (the family), we look in some detail at three basic questions: 1) How does childhood chronic illness affect adolescent development? 2) How do developmental processes influence the impact of chronic illness in adolescence? and 3) How does the family function to magnify, diminish, or otherwise transform the impact of chronic illness upon adolescent development?* These broad questions are threaded through the following sections, which move from review of risk and resiliency research, to more specific discussion of what is known of vulnerability and risk in diabetic adolescents and their families. Finally, we describe a program of research focused on diabetic adolescent development within the family.**

RISK AND RESILIENCE

Researchers who study children at risk have repeatedly observed that, despite the burdens of stress in their everyday lives, there are many

---

*There is a fourth logical question, namely, what are the effects of the illness upon the family? For example, how do diagnosis, course of illness, and complications influence family process? This important area is not taken up in this review since it would be distracting from foci upon development, risk, and resiliency. The question is reviewed, however, in Hauser et al. (1985), and Drotar, Crawford, and Bush (1984).

**Co-principal investigators of this research program are Drs. Alan Jacobson and Stuart Hauser.

children who manifest competency and autonomy in their behavior compared to others who, exposed to similar stresses, develop serious coping problems (Garmezy, 1981, 1984; Werner & Smith, 1982). Until recently, this important observation has been posed as an intriguing yet unexplored question. For example, Werner and Smith (1977), in their longitudinal study of children at risk in Hawaii, note:

> Thoughtful developmental psychologists and clinicians are left to ponder this: Why are there, among the children and youth in this community, . . . some who learned to cope, unaided, with great biological and environmental handicaps? Are they anomalies or invincibles who, in the words of Lillian Smith, "taught the terrors of their nature and their world to sing?" (p. 218)

A close examination of the "risk" literature provides evidence that such children are not "anomalies." Werner and Smith (1977) themselves state that although their focus is on vulnerability, "we could not help being deeply impressed by the resiliency of the overwhelming majority of children and youth and by their potential for positive change and personal growth" (p. 210). It is, in fact, only a minority of children at risk who experience serious difficulties in their personality development (Bleuler, 1974; Garmezy, 1981; Rutter, 1979). The majority of children exposed to various forms of adversity grow up to enjoy productive, "normal" lives.

For years, nested within an "illness model" of psychology, researchers have searched for the sources or antecedents of negative outcomes. There has been a neglect of the roots of the field of psychology—normative behavioral processes. Only recently have we turned toward a model based more on health than on illness, and only recently have we recognized that in order to effectively study deviations in behavior, or abnormality, we must also have a more clearly defined concept of what normal or healthy means (Garmezy, 1981) and understand the origins of health—"salutogenesis" (Antonovsky, 1979). Accompanying this focus upon health-related processes has been the conceptualization of "resiliency" or "invulnerability," together with new investigations of antecedents and correlates of resilient development (e.g., Garmezy & Rutter, 1983; Garmezy, Masters, & Tellegen, 1984; Werner & Smith, 1982).

What has alternately been termed "invulnerability," "resiliency," and "stress resistance" has been operationalized in various ways. The definitions converge to describe a single construct, stimulated by the repeated observation that there are those who do well despite adversity. Garmezy (1983) outlines five essential elements in the research on vulnerability:

Whatever its identity tag, the identification of such research will probably be marked by . . . these elements: (1) an emphasis on prospective developmental studies of children who (2) have been exposed to stressors of marked gravity (3) which can be accentuated by specific biological predispositions, familial and/or environmental deprivations (4) typically associated with a heightened probability of present or future maladaptive outcomes but (5) which are not actualized in some children whose behavior instead is marked by patterns of behavioral adaptation and manifest competence. (p. 73)

For Garmezy (1983), competence in social, school, and cognitive realms is a marker of and a requisite for resiliency. The search for resiliency factors is, for him, a search for the antecedents or components of this competence. Much of Garmezy's extensive research program is directed toward identification and assessment of competence manifestations (cf. Garmezy, Masters, & Tellegen, 1984). Werner and Smith (1982) define resilience as "the capacity to cope effectively with the internal stress of [their] vulnerabilities (such as labile patterns of autonomic reactivity, developmental imbalances, unusual sensitivities) and external stresses (such as illness, major losses, and dissolution of the family)" (p. 4). They illustrate the construct through a subset of adolescents (42 girls and 30 boys) drawn from their larger study (Werner, Bierman, & French, 1971; Werner & Smith, 1977). These subjects had encountered at least four risk factors by the age of two years (poverty, family distress, etc.), but had not developed any serious psychological, behavioral, or learning problems by the age of 18. Similarly, Rutter (1979) views resilience as evidenced in "individuals who overcome adversity, who survive stress, and who rise above disadvantage" (p. 3). *Protective factors* are identified in his work as those variables that discriminate between those who develop behavioral and psychological problems and those who do not.

Finally, Block and Block (1980) refer to stress resistance in children as "ego resiliency," in contrast to those children who are "ego brittle." The two constructs are seen as two ends of one continuum. Ego resiliency refers to the ability to adapt flexibly and with "elasticity" to changing circumstances. Ego-resilient children were selected in the Blocks' research, on the basis of 1) their scores on a series of experimental tasks measuring areas such as the ability to change preferred tempo under instruction, ability to process two sorts of information simultaneously, ability to profit from feedback and to perceive communalities among diverse stimuli, and resourcefulness under frustration; and 2) teacher's assessments of the child's functioning.

Several bodies of research (e.g., Garmezy, 1983, 1984) point to variables that are likely related to coping and resiliency. These dimensions include several domains: 1) the child's personality attributes or dispositions; 2) family characteristics, including individual parent strengths and vulnerabilities; and 3) properties of the surrounding community, such as social supports and strains. Our perspective is that the family is of critical importance, since besides its direct influence on resiliency (e.g., competency skills), the family also affects related personality and social milieu dimensions, thereby exerting an *indirect* influence on stress resistance as well. We most fully consider family dimensions in this chapter, through review of current knowledge and presentation of an ongoing program of empirical studies directed toward investigating the influences of family factors in the development of chronically ill children (Hauser et al., 1984a; Jacobson et al., 1985). However, in light of the relevance of personality and the broader social factors (e.g., social supports), we first turn to briefly survey the contribution of these processes to resiliency.

PERSONALITY

Cognitive skills and styles are consistently reported as associated with stress-resistant outcomes. Werner and Smith (1982) found resilient adolescents to have better verbal communication skills than those who succumb to stress. Garmezy (1981), in a literature review of studies on competent black children in urban ghettos exposed to poverty and prejudice, noted that in resilient children, reflectiveness and "impulse control" were dominant cognitive styles. In more recent work, Garmezy's group describes significant correlations between measures of intelligence and manifestations of competence (Garmezy, Masters, & Tellegen, 1984). *Competence*, a requisite for resiliency (Anthony, 1974; Garmezy, Masters, & Tellegen, 1984), includes the ability to construct an internal representation of an event, or the ability to conceptualize and order the incoming data so that they can become sufficiently meaningful to be acted upon (Anthony, 1974). Not surprisingly, such competence is viewed as a function of intelligence.

Various other personality factors have been cited as linked with resiliency. Werner and Smith (1982) found that resilient adolescents, compared to a group of adolescents who had developed learning or behavioral problems, scored higher on California Personality Inventory (CPI) scales as *Responsibility, Socialization, Achievement via Conformance,* and *Communality* (which have indicated the degree to which a person's responses correspond to the common pattern established on the CPI). Similar CPI scores were noted in Benjamin's (1970) description of academically successful high school students from a midwestern ghetto and the Blocks' (1980) of "ego resilient" white males during the Great Depression.

Other personality variables associated with stress resistance are self-esteem and locus of control. In his study of 10-year-olds in inner London, Rutter et al. (1975) found that good scholastic attainment (which he previously found to be related to higher self-esteem) seemed to have a protective effect for disadvantaged children. Werner and Smith (1982) report that both positive self-esteem and internal locus of control were among the variables that discriminated between good and poor outcomes *only* with the occurrence of much stress. In a group of youths who had not experienced a great deal of stress in their lives, these factors did not discriminate the resilient from those with poor outcomes. In this way, Werner and Smith identified positive self-concept and internal locus of control as two ameliorative or protective factors important in counterbalancing the risk associated with stress. Garmezy (1981) identified a positive sense of self, a sense of personal power rather than powerlessness, an internal locus of control, and a belief in the capacity to exercise a degree of control over their environment as factors in the resiliency of disadvantaged Black children. These qualities were also found by Garmezy (1981) in resilient offspring of psychotic parents.

Superior social skills and coping styles are cited as contributors to superior psychological outcomes in those exposed to stressful circumstances. Garmezy (1981) notes that teachers and clinicians rated previously identified competent children as possessing particular social skills—they were friendly and well-liked by peers and adults, interpersonally sensitive, socially responsive and more "cooperative," "participatory," and "emotionally stable." Linked with these social skills were the adaptive copings that appear to be used by children who overcome the risk of severe stress. Stress-resistant children had the ability to regulate impulsive drives and to delay gratification, as well as to maintain future orientation. Murphy and Moriarty (1976), in their longitudinal study of children in Topeka, Kansas, describe resilient children as having such coping skills as an ability to count on "inner resources," being highly sensitive, and showing strong curiosity about people, things, and ideas. Rutter and colleagues (1975) cited adaptability and malleability among the chief characteristics that protect against psychiatric disorder in childhood.

The Social Milieu

Rutter (1979) underscores the importance of influences outside the home in the development of resiliency. Seen as particularly important is the school environment and the quality of the school as a social institution. In a study of the behavior and attainments of a cohort of 10-year-old children, begun one year before they were transferred to secondary school and followed over a seven-year-period, substantial variations in children's outcomes among schools were found, even after controlling for differences at admission (Rutter, 1979). Some secondary schools that had a high proportion who had demonstrated behavioral deviance in primary school, nevertheless had low rates of delinquency. The reverse was also true. Rutter uses this data to support the notion that "good schools can and do exert an important protective effect" (p. 60).

Also in the social realm, Rutter (1979) notes the possible importance of the scope of opportunities for the child. Evidence for this is mostly anecdotal, including observations that ultimate better adjustment is made by those deprived individuals who manage to avoid pregnancy or fathering a child in their teens, who had more education, and who married someone from a more favored background. These decisions help to break the cycle of disadvantage and to broaden the range of possibilities open to the youth. Greater opportunities, however, may simply be the by-product of resiliency. Work is needed to elucidate what mechanisms permit this greater range, both in terms of situational factors and individual differences.

Werner and Smith (1982), Garmezy (1983), and Rutter (1979) emphasize the ameliorative role of social support systems in the community. Werner and Smith found that resilient adolescents made extensive use of the informal assistance of peers, older friends, ministers, and teachers. Murphy and Moriarty (1976) also found this to be true in their observations and conceptualize the observation in terms of the importance of "identification with resilient models."

The number of life stresses to which an adolescent is exposed also relates to resiliency. Werner and Smith (1982) report that the resilient youths in their study were exposed to significantly fewer stressful life events than those children who developed serious problems. The interactive effects among stresses has been elegantly demonstrated by Rutter (1979). Six chronic family stress variables that were strongly associated with child psychiatric disorder included: low social status; overcrowding; severe marital discord; paternal criminality; maternal psychiatric disorder; and admission into care of a local authority. Families were divided according to how many stressors each had been subject to. In terms of psychiatric disorder in the children, these stressors potentiated each other. A combination of chronic stresses was associated with significantly poorer outcome than a summation of the effects of the individual stressors considered singly.

THE FAMILY: DIRECT EFFECTS

With the growing influence of family systems theory and research, the family has received increasing attention as a major influence in the protection of children and adolescents from psychopathology or poor developmental outcomes. Two different levels of analysis have been used in examining these familial influences. The first and more extensively studied approach may be considered to be on a "macro" level. Unlike the sociological definition of the term, which refers to broad societal influences, we view all studies that examine the family as a global entity to be operating on this level. This includes study of household composition and family structure, as well as the examination of general familial attitudes such as supportiveness and discipline. Less common is work on a "micro" level, looking in detail at how aspects of family communication and interaction may be linked with child or adolescent vulnerability and resilience. The unit of analysis here is the individual family member, in relation to, and in interaction with, the other members of the family. The existing literature on the "macro" level falls into two general categories: 1) influence of family structure and home environment; and 2) influences of parental attitude and support.

In terms of home environment, Werner and Smith (1982) and Garmezy (1983) both found less physical crowding to be associated with better outcome. Achieving lower-class Black children were described as having households which were less cluttered, less crowded, and cleaner. On the other hand, there is no consistent correlation between two-parent homes and outcome. Garmezy points out that in father-absent homes, the mother's style of coping and compensating was a powerful redemptive variable. Werner and Smith (1982) identified the number and type of additional caretakers (e.g., siblings, extended family) as essential in mediating the effects of the stress of single parenting on the offspring.

Parental attitudes have a major influence on the psychological well-being of the child. Werner and Smith (1982) report that resilient adolescents often leave from homes where there were consistently enforced rules. Rutter (1979) concludes that good supervision and well-balanced discipline may protect a child from high-risk background. Support for this conclusion comes from findings by Wilson (1974) that in conditions of chronic poverty, strict parental supervision was more effective than a happy family atmosphere in preventing delinquency.

Block and Block (1980) characterize the parents of ego-resilient children as competent, loving, and having shared values; in contrast to parents of "ego-brittle" children who were exposed to conflict and discord at home. A good relationship with and between parents, who were described as more understanding and supportive, discriminated resilient from troubled adolescents in Werner and Smith's study (1982). They found, as did Murphy and Moriarity (1976), that these families expressed closeness and respect for individual autonomy. In cases of an extremely troubled home environment, Rutter (1979) observes that a "good relationship" with one parent (defined in terms of presence of high warmth and absence of severe criticism) provides a substantial protective effect. Only one-quarter of the children in troubled families studied by Rutter showed signs of conduct disorder if they had a single good relationship with parents, compared to three-quarters of the children who lacked such a relationship. Garmezy (1981) describes an "adequate identification figure" as present in the families of achieving lower-class children. Lower-class parents whose children showed signs of competence more clearly defined their own role in the family, as well as the child's, and were more concerned and willing to help in their child's education and gave their child more opportunity for self-direction. In more recent work, Garmezy, Masters, and Tellegen (1984) found positive family attributes (e.g., good family communication, high degree of parental perceptiveness about their child) to be associated with competence and more adaptive behavior under stress. Still other parental features are elucidated by Anthony (1974), who observed that parents of invulnerable children were less possessive and anxious than the "average" child and more likely to allow the child his own autonomy.

While a fair amount of thought and research has been devoted to the identification and examination of protective factors in the home and family, few researchers have concentrated on "micro" level factors. A limited number of studies explore specific ways in which parents and children may interact so as to promote resilient outcomes. Among the works dealing with familial communication patterns as protective factors are those of Lieber (1977) and Wynne, Jones, and Al-Khayyal (1982). Wynne and his colleagues (1982) hypothesize that there is "healthy communication" in families that may provide the high-risk child with the

resources and coping strategies underlying resiliency and healthy functioning. These may be among the more important "antecedents to
health." Three family interaction variables are tentatively identified as
being associated with greater competence in high-risk children. These
are maternal warmth (Kauffman et al., 1979), a warm, active, and bal-
anced family interaction (Cole et al., 1980), and healthy and benign
parental attributions toward the child (Yu, 1979).

Four domains of healthy communication are summarized in Wynne et
al.'s broad discussion: cognitive/attentional, affective/relational, structur-
al/contextual and family subculture, values and myths. The greatest emphasis is upon the cognitive domain, in light of the authors' view that most
communication between the parents serves as a model for the child's
developing such cognitive capacities as attention, focusing, and sustaining
task orientation. In a study of high-risk 10-year-olds (one of whom had
been in a psychiatric hospital) measuring these four domains, communication patterns were assessed using direct observation of a family task. High
healthy communication scores (measured by clarity, accuracy, and com-
pleteness of instructions, parental structuring/orienting statements and
questions, presentation of percepts by the parents, parental statements
assessing progress, and closure) in the parents were consistently predictive of their child's cognitive and social-emotional competence in teacher
and peer ratings. Thus, when surrounded by focused, flexible, well-
structured, and task-appropriate communications, the 10-year-old sons
functioned in more academically and socially competent ways.

Using Wynne and colleagues approach (Wynne, 1967; Wynne et al.,
1977) to studying family communication, Lieber (1977) observed that
"positive focusing behaviors" (one parent taking a leadership role, clarify-
ing, and encouraging further exploration) were associated with familial
"low-risk" status. This status is derived from independent projective
analyses of families' "positive" behavior that predicted risk status more
strongly than the absence of disturbance in communication. Lieber concluded that parental facilitation of communication was worthy of further
exploration.

The notion of parental "facilitation" is one component within our own
recently constructed approach (the Constraining and Enabling Coding
System) to analyzing family interactions of chronically ill and nonpatient
adolescents (Hauser et al., 1982; Hauser et al., 1984a). Stierlin's (1974)
analysis of the impact of parental interactions upon adolescent maturation is our point of departure. The major theme in Stierlin's perspective
is that the families of disturbed adolescents can often be distinguished by
their prominent attempts to interfere with the autonomous and differen-

tiated functioning of their children. Among these impediments to independent perceptions and actions are "binding" (constraining) interactions through which parents actively resist the differentiation of their children.* We have substantially expanded this theory to account for forms of *enabling* interactions, through which family members encourage or support the expression of more independent perceptions or thoughts. Besides a detailed study of constraining (e.g., distracting, devaluing) and enabling (e.g., focusing, explaining, accepting), our work emphasizes bi-directionality, as we examine interactions from adolescent to parent, as well as those from parent to adolescent. At this point, we have found greater prevalence of enabling interactions in families whose adolescents function at higher levels of ego development (another possible marker of psychosocial competence), as contrasted with the increased frequency of constraining within those families whose adolescents are at lower ego levels (Hauser et al., 1984a).

Until now, we have not applied this model to the study of *stress-resistant* adolescents. Given its conceptualization of facilitating behaviors and linkage to ego development, there are certainly sound theoretical reasons to expect that this family assessment framework will be relevant to investigating such adolescents. Indeed, this envisioned relevance underlies the incorporation of this family assessment in our ongoing study of chronically ill adolescents and their families (Hauser et al., 1985; Jacobson, Rand, & Hauser, 1984), a project more fully considered in a later section.

The Family: Indirect Effects

Besides the direct influences of such variables as parental attitudes and supports, the family system affects personality and social milieu processes that are linked with resiliency. As with direct influences, these indirect effects of the family on the child may be viewed from both a "macro" and a "micro" perspective. On a more global level, one may examine personality factors of the child that are related to parental characteristics and attitudes. Given the possibility that a child's personal attributes and styles are, in part, influenced by parental factors, the family becomes implicated in another way in the resiliency of the offspring. For example, children's IQ has been shown to be related to that of their parents (Bouchard & McGue, 1981). Internal locus of control,

---

*Stierlin also describes two other modes of responding to separation: delegating and expulsion.

viewed by many as an important factor in resiliency, is correlated with a warm, praising, protective, and supportive family environment (Garmezy, 1983). High self-esteem in children is linked with high self-esteem and emotional stability in mothers, mothers' positive conception of their maternal role, low parental tension and conflict, the making of major decisions by either the mother *or* the father (*not* shared decision making), and shared everyday decision making between the parents (Coopersmith, 1967). Parents are also likely to influence, in part, their child's social milieu and support network. While questions of direction of influence and causality remain, it is apparent that parents and the family probably exert a substantial indirect effect on the resiliency of their children as well as an impact that can be measured more directly.

Indirect influences of the family work on a "micro" level as well. For example, "good" or "easy" temperament on the part of the child has been seen as a protective factor against stress (Rutter, 1979). The likelihood that parental behavior can be conditioned by a child's temperament (Bell, 1968) implicates the family in this protective factor. In a discordant home, the temperamentally easy child might avoid negative interchange and potentially promote positive parent-child interaction (Rutter, 1979). Such reciprocal effects between parent and child are likely pervasive in families and essential to clarify when analyzing the family's role in resiliency.

It is evident that the three domains of protective factors—personality, social, and familial—frequently interact as determinants of resilient developmental outcomes. Also affecting this favorable outcome is the amount of stress experienced and the existing or original amount of "risk." Werner and Smith (1982) have suggested that the balance among these factors accounts for the range of outcomes. Garmezy and colleagues (1984) detail a series of possibilities regarding how personal attributes and stressful events may interact to determine the quality of adaptation. Stress factors and personal attributes may combine additively in the prediction of outcome. Stress (if not excessive) may enhance competence; this is the "challenge" model. Or an alternative perspective suggests that personal attributes may modulate, buffer, or exacerbate the impact of stress. As the preceding discussion argues, the situation or event is even more complex, given the evidence for the importance of specific *family* and *social* factors that influence resiliency.

Research about resiliency in children and adolescents spans a wide range of populations and risk groups. The personality, social milieu, and familial correlates of stress resistance reviewed above have been found consistently across high-risk groups of children such as those exposed to extreme poverty, child abuse, parental psychosis, severe family discord, and chronic illness. In order to gain a clearer understanding of the mechanisms involved in healthy adaptation, and further, to learn how to best assist those children at risk, a careful and detailed examination of particular risk groups is necessary.

In the next sections we continue our intensive consideration of protective factors through focusing upon a special population of adolescents at risk—those with the chronic illness of diabetes. We give particular emphasis to how families may contribute to the development of resiliency in their diabetic offspring.

DIABETIC ADOLESCENTS:
FAMILY CONTRIBUTIONS TO RISK AND RESILIENCY

Diabetes mellitus is a chronic disease characterized by an insufficiency or lack of insulin production by the pancreas. This results in an impaired ability to metabolize glucose, and in high blood sugar levels. In type 1 diabetes ("juvenile diabetes") the pancreas ceases to produce insulin, rendering the individual dependent upon daily injections of insulin and extensive diet modifications. This form of diabetes most often occurs in childhood.

Even with careful treatment, diabetes can lead to serious physical complications. The National Commission on Diabetes has established that people with diabetes are 25 times more prone to blindness, 17 times more prone to kidney disease, five times more prone to gangrene and lower extremity amputations, and twice as prone to heart disease (Hanson & Henggeler, 1984). Although some controversy does exist, there is evidence that good metabolic control can delay or reduce these long-term complications (Hanson & Henggeler, 1984). Short-term consequences of low (hypoglycemia) or high (hyperglycemia) blood glucose levels can be, themselves, very unpleasant and dangerous. Low blood sugar levels can cause impaired cognitive and motor functioning, weakness, irritability, and anxiety; and if left untreated, loss of consciousness and death can occur. Hyperglycemia can lead to ketoacidosis, which may result in coma or death. For these multiple reasons, good metabolic control is a primary goal in the treatment of diabetes (Hanson & Henggeler, 1984).

In addition to such physiological risk factors, diabetes presents psychological risks, especially to the afflicted child and adolescent. These risks include a range of stresses and demands placed on the diabetic adolescent—physical pain, forced role changes, heightened uncertainty, changes in physical appearance, periodic separation from family and friends (Jacobson & Hauser, 1983), and a sense of isolation, of "feeling different." While studies using broad measures of psychological status show little difference between diabetic children and controls (Kellerman et al., 1980; Simonds, 1977; Zeltzer et al., 1980), several investigations do show personality differences. Swift and Seidman (1969) found diabetics to be overdependent, more anxious, and to be having more difficulties with peer relationships. Besides differences from normal children, there are data indicating important differences among diabetic patients. Several reports point to the fact that adolescents and children in poor control of their diabetes have more psychological symptoms than those in good control (Simonds, 1977; Sterky, 1963; Swift & Seidman, 1969). Any comprehensive assessment of adaptation in the diabetic child must take into account many areas (e.g., social, emotional, and physical [Shouval, Ber, & Galatzer, 1982]). Yet the physical and psychological importance of optimal blood glucose level control leads many researchers to use metabolic control as a major index of diabetic adjustment (Anderson & Kornblum, 1984).

Family processes may increase the risk of occurrence of these physical and psychological symptoms. On the other hand, aspects of the family environment may serve a *protective* function, enhancing physical and psychological outcomes. The family is intricately involved in the daily life of a diabetic child (Shouval, Ber, & Galatzer, 1982). With the onset of diabetes, patterns of eating and activity must change; and in many cases, parents initially assume much of the child's care. Drash and Becker (1978) cite two key reasons why the family is so critical for the diabetic child: 1) family members are constantly required to make clinical judgments concerning management of the disease; and 2) the regimen of diabetes overlaps with and often restricts many ongoing family routines.

The role of the family of the diabetic child has been studied primarily from a disease or pathology point of view (Anderson & Kornblum, 1984). These studies have often attempted to discover how parent variables contribute to the child's psychopathology (Hauser & Pollets, 1981; Hauser & Solomon, 1984). In contrast, the work of Minuchin and his colleagues (1978) on "psychosomatic" families of superlabile diabetic children emphasizes reciprocal influences of parents and children, and identifies types of family interaction—enmeshment and rigidity—which can lead to poor outcomes. While these observations regarding bi-directional influences are important, pathology is again highlighted. An alternative approach is to study family variables contributing to minimal or no psychosocial difficulties in diabetic adolescents (Johnson, 1980). In a plea to concentrate on these resiliency factors, Anderson and Auslander (1980) write:

> Most studies of diabetic management are based on an implicit "deficit model," as evidenced by the inordinate attention given to negative parental attitudes and problematic child behaviors. Yet, this focus on pathology has been carried out at the expense of identifying family strengths and successful strategies for coping with the treatment regimen at home. (p. 700)

Garmezy has encouraged the study of competence and stress resistance in chronically ill children, noting that in chronic illness, as in schizophrenia, there seems to be a combination of genetic predisposition and potentiating stress (Garmezy, 1979). Resiliency in diabetic adolescents is likely to be a function of the three areas we have been reviewing (personality, social milieu, family). Yet the evidence for the direct and indirect effects of the family and the importance of this environment in diabetes management suggests that family factors are likely to be key ones for understanding adaptation of diabetic adolescents. In parallel with the resiliency literature, two levels of family studies may be distinguished: a "macro" level (household composition, overall familial attitudes and roles, family environment); and a "micro" level (family interaction, family communication). Once again, it is the macro level that has been more intensively studied. These analyses of family functioning include the topics of: 1) family structure and home environment; 2) parental attitudes and roles; and 3) family "atmosphere."

Socioeconomic status, one aspect of household environment, may have a substantial impact on metabolic control and psychosocial functioning (Hanson & Henggeler, 1984). Gardner and colleagues (1983) found the family's social class to be directly related to the frequency of home glucose monitoring, which then influences metabolic control (Hanson & Henggeler, 1984). Another influence of social class is reported by Galatzer and Laron (1982), who found low socioeconomic level to be correlated with less knowledge in the child and parents. They suggest the implementation of a different approach with these families to strengthen their knowledge of the disease. Specific household composition factors have an impact on the family's initial response to their child's diabetes. These cover the composition of the family; the presence of significant others; the family's ethnic background; and finally, the educational level of family members (Wishner & O'Brien, 1978).

Parental attitudes have also been studied in terms of their relationship to metabolic control and adjustment. In a review of the early studies in this area, Anderson and Auslander (1980) identified several pathological maternal attitudes which were seen as "causing" poor control, including overprotection, overindulgence, perfectionism, and rejection. In contrast, mothers who were described as tolerant, consistent, and flexible were reported to have children who were in good control and well adjusted. Marrero and colleagues (1982) are among the few researchers to explore the role of paternal attitudes in promoting successful adaptation by the diabetic child. Studying the adolescent's perception of parental attitudes, this research team found that those in good control described their fathers as supportive, encouraging of autonomy, and nonpunitive.

Koski (1969) interviewed the parents of 60 diabetic children. She found significant correlations between metabolic control and maternal competence. Parents of the children in good control dealt more "constructively" with their feelings. In a follow-up study five years later (Koski, 1976), families and children with the highest level of control were described as having: 1) stable family composition; 2) clear, distinct boundaries between generations recognized by all family members; 3) realistic and cooperative attitude of family members in implementing treatment; 4) low marital conflict; and 5) the presence of two parents or a competent single parent. Similarly, Swift and his colleagues (1969) found that in families of diabetics in good control, there were: 1) fewer conflicts; 2) lower level of stress between the parents and diabetic child; and 3) satisfactory home adjustment by the child. Through intensive case studies of 13 diabetic children and adolescents, Quint (1970) found that the families of those with good control tended to incorporate the treatment regimen into the ongoing family routine. Also associated with good outcomes was parental congruence or consensus on treatment requirements. Quint concluded that parental style and family and cooperation were the two most critical influences on the diabetic child's self-esteem and adherence to treatment. Self-esteem has been noted by several writers in this area as clearly linked with resiliency (cf. preceding sections).

Another active research area is that of family "atmosphere" (shared family values and beliefs) and its impact upon diabetic adolescents. Anderson and colleagues (1981) obtained the family atmosphere perceptions of diabetic adolescents and their parents using the Moos Family Environment Scale (Moos, 1974). In addition, they assessed adolescent self-esteem (Piers, 1969). Metabolic control was tapped using measures of blood sugar. Parents of children in optimal metabolic control described their families as valuing independence, self-sufficiency, and open expression of feelings more than those of adolescents in poor control.

Shouval, Ber, and Galatzer (1982) found that for 30 Israeli diabetic children adherence to a medical regimen (based on optimal control and on reports from the psychosocial staff of the medical unit) was associated with a family atmosphere depicted as supportive, organized, and discouraging of expressiveness. Supportiveness, not independence, correlated with better outcome. The differences between these findings and those of Anderson et al. (1981) might be explained by cross-cultural variation, but further work is needed to clarify these results. Cederbland and colleagues (1982) also report findings regarding family norms and diabetic control. Parents of diabetic children and adolescents rated their families in terms of adaptability and cohesion (FACES) (Olson, Portner & Bell, 1982). Better metabolic control correlated with high adaptability and low rigidity scores for mothers, indicating that flexibility might be an important protective factor for diabetic adolescents.

Our own group (Hauser et al., 1984a; Jacobson et al., 1982) is studying relationships between family atmosphere and aspects of diabetic adolescent adjustment. Besides Moos's assessment, we include measures of perceived competence (Harter, 1982) and adjustment to diabetes (Sullivan, 1979a,b). Perceived competence refers to adolescents' perceptions of themselves in three domains: *cognitive* (school competence); *social* (peer competence); and *physical* (skills at sports and outside games). Diabetes adjustment includes the adolescent's views of diabetes, its treatment, and its influence on daily functioning. We have found that family orientations toward independence, participation in social/recreational activities, and organization are strongly associated with the diabetic adolescents' perceived competence. These dimensions, as well as a family orientation toward achievement, predicted aspects of diabetic adjustment. Such family atmosphere components were different from those that predicted perceived competence in a matched group of acutely ill adolescents, suggesting that perceptions of competence (or self-esteem) for the diabetic adolescents may involve family norms or beliefs that clearly differ from those underlying self-esteem for adolescents in other medical (e.g., acutely ill) groups.

Familial protective factors on a "micro" level for diabetic adolescents have been almost ignored in the literature. Until now, only one research group has reported analyses of data gathered by direct observation of diabetic families (Minuchin et al., 1978). As mentioned above, while drawing needed attention to reciprocal influences in the family and to family constructs such as enmeshment and rigidity, these researchers concentrate on the identification of pathological interaction in families. In addition to observing family atmosphere dimensions, our research program also follows family interaction dimensions and their relationship to the adjustment of diabetic adolescents. Family interaction processes are measured with the Constraining and Enabling Coding System (CECS) described earlier in this review. A pilot study with three diabetic adolescents, (Hauser et al., 1982) found enabling or facilitating interactions to be most prevalent in the families of those patients at higher stages of ego development. A second type of family process is assessed through our Family Coping Codes (Hauser et al., 1984b), which rate how family members appraise and manage stressful events (e.g., illness, losses) occurring to the family. In the next section, we look more fully at this research program devoted to multiple aspects of objectively observing diabetic adolescents and their families. Besides describing this project, we consider its potential contributions to elucidation of familial antecedents to resiliency.

THE HEALTH AND ILLNESS STUDY

Through our prospective projects (Hauser et al., 1982, 1984a,b, 1985, 1988; Jacobson et al., 1982, 1984, 1985), we are currently investigating influences between families and: 1) the psychosocial development of adolescent diabetic patients and 2) the metabolic status and overall "diabetic adjustment" of these patients. The current investigation, The Adolescent Health and Illness Project, is a multidimensional one, intensively following a cohort of newly diagnosed adolescent diabetic patients and their parents. A second sample consists of adolescents with a newly diagnosed acute illness, which is neither trivial nor life-threatening. These acutely ill adolescents and their parents, observed through the same psychosocial measures as the diabetic group, are used as a comparison group in order to clarify the specific impact of diabetes as a chronic illness.

The Health and Illness Project provides a special opportunity to identify protective factors contributing to resiliency in diabetic and "normal" adolescents. Garmezy (1984) speaks of three stages in the investigation of protective factors: 1) identification of resilient children; 2) a search for the correlates of such adaptive behavior in the child, family, and situational contexts; and 3) the systematic search for the processes and mechanisms that underlie this stress resistance. Our project is in a position to shed light on each of these three stages. It is distinctive in several ways.

First, it has a prospective design. In all of the above noted work on the family and diabetes, with the exception of Koski (1969, 1976), the design used was cross-sectional, making it impossible to discover causal influences. Several researchers have emphasized the critical need for longitudinal research in this area (Anderson et al., 1981; Hauser et al., 1982; Jacobson et al., 1982; Johnson, 1980). Through this longitudinal design, following over 60 newly diagnosed diabetics and their families through the first four years of the illness (and a group of 60 acutely ill children and their families), we hope to unravel questions of causality between individual and family determinants. Based on a perspective that posits reciprocal or bi-directional influences in families (Anderson & Auslander, 1980; Minuchin, 1978), our analyses are guided by two broad questions: 1) What patterns of family interaction and family coping underlie variations (particularly *successful* adaptation) in the adolescent's diabetes management and psychosocial development; and 2) conversely, how does the level of parent and adolescent psychosocial development affect the child's diabetes management and family coping style?

The project is also in an excellent position to study resiliency because of the type of data we are collecting. Information in all three of the areas (personality, social, family) implicating resiliency in children at risk is gathered. Markers of outcome include physical measures such as metabolic control (hemoglobin Alc), medical providers' ratings of diabetic adjustment and compliance, and psychological measures such as the Diabetic Adjustment Scale (Sullivan, 1979a) and behavioral symptoms (Achenbach & Edelbrock, 1981). Those with superior outcomes on these measures can be considered our "resilient" adolescents.

Developmental and personality measures (e.g., self-esteem, locus of control, ego development) and intelligence test scores are obtained for all adolescents. Measures of the surrounding social milieu include a survey of recent life events (Coddington, 1972; Dohrenwend et al., 1982) and social support processes. For both major areas—personality and social milieu—similar measures are administered to parents. In gathering personality and social environment data on the parents as well as on the child, we have the opportunity to examine the *indirect* forces of the family in promoting resiliency. By following these individuals through a period of time crucial to the child's development—adolescence—we hope to isolate parental variables that influence their child's personality and social contacts, which, in turn, are likely to shape the child's resistance to the potentially negative consequences of the disease.

Direct family influences on resiliency are measured from three vantage points. In the tradition of previous research in this area, the parent and child's perception of the "family atmosphere" is measured (Moos, 1974). Family appraisal and coping processes are assessed through paper and pencil measures (McCubbin & Patterson, 1980), as well as through semi-structured family discussions, then coded for appraisal, problem-focused, and emotion focused coping strategies (Hauser et al., 1984b). Finally, on a "micro" level, family interactions are analyzed through coding family discussions with the Constraining and Enabling System (Hauser et al., 1984a).

By observing such an extensive array of psychological, social, and familial processes of these families as they adjust to a new chronic illness, we hope to move toward unraveling antecedents of resilient outcomes. We expect that these results should shed light on: 1) directions of causation in the development of resiliency; 2) *direct effects* from family factors; 3) *indirect effects* of the family on resiliency, by its mediating influence on personality and the social milieu; and 4) effects of the interaction of these factors with one another on stress resistance or invulnerability of the high-risk child. Through emphasizing healthy, optimal adaptation, our goal is to identify process or factors that may eventually be included in treatment plans for adolescent patients who are not effectively coping with their illness, so as to improve their adaptation.

Concluding Comments

In the course of development, many adolescents are exposed to situations or conditions that place them at risk for unsuccessful adaptation. In spite of these vulnerabilities, however, a great majority manifest no developmental arrests and appear to make an adequate and even superior adjustment. This positive or "healthy" side of psychosocial development has, in the last decade, become an increasingly prominent topic for investigation. Various personality factors, social milieu influences, and familial variables, as discussed in this review, have been found to be associated with resiliency. While it is probable that these sets of variables, in varying combinations, contribute to the development of stress resistance, our view is that the family plays a particularly significant role. Family processes impact upon the quality of development *directly* as well as *indirectly*, through their influences on the personality and social surroundings of the child.

Examining juvenile diabetes as a particular example of chronic illness, we have explored from conceptual and empirical standpoints how family variables might contribute to successful adaptation in adolescents at risk.

We reviewed research implicating "macro" level processes, such as household composition, parental attitudes, family patterns and roles, and the family atmosphere, as determinants of stress resistance. Also important, but less fully understood, are "micro" level processes in the family, such as various ways family members might interact or communicate to promote healthy outcome. The Health and Illness Project, a prospective study of the adaptation of adolescents and their families to juvenile onset diabetes, explores both levels of family functioning and provides a special opportunity to increase our understanding and knowledge of the process leading toward psychological health.

REFERENCES

ACHENBACH, T.M. (1979). The Child Behavior Profile: An empirically based system for assessing children's behavior problems and competencies. *International Journal of Mental Health, 7:* 24–44.

ACHENBACH, T.M., & EDELBROCK, C. (1981). Behavioral problems and competencies reported by parents of normal and disturbed children aged four through sixteen. *Monographs of the Society for Research in Child Development, 76* (1 serial No. 188.)

ANDERSON, B.J., & AUSLANDER, W.F. (1980). Research on diabetes management and the family: A critique. *Diabetes Care, 3:* 696–702.

ANDERSON, B.J., MILLER, J.P., AUSLANDER, W.F., & SANTIAGO, J.V. (1981). Family characteristics of diabetic adolescents: Relationship to metabolic control. *Diabetes Care, 4:* 586–594.

ANDERSON, B.J., & KORNBLUM, H. (1984). The family environment of children with a diabetic parent: Issues for research. *Family Systems Medicine, 2:* 17–27.

ANTHONY, E.J. (1974). The syndrome of the psychologically vulnerable child. In E.J. Anthony & C. Koupernik (Eds.), *The Child in His Family, Vol. 3, Children at Psychiatric Risk.* New York: John Wiley and Sons, pp. 529–544.

ANTONOVSKY, A. (1979). *Health, Stress and Coping.* San Francisco: Jossey-Bass Publishers.

BELL, R.Q. (1968). A reinterpretation of effects of studies of socialization. *Psychological Review, 75:* 81–95.

BENJAMIN, J.A. (1970). A study of the social psychological factors related to the academic success of Negro high school students. *Dissertation Abstracts International, 30* (8-A): 343.

BENOLIEL, J.Q., & QUINT, J. (1975). Childhood diabetes: The commonplace in living becomes uncommon. In A.L. Strauss & B.G. Glaser (Eds.), *Chronic Illness and the Quality of Life.* St. Louis: Mosby, pp. 89–98.

BLUELER, M. (1974). The offspring of schizophrenics. *Schizophrenia Bulletin, 8:* 93–107.

BLOCK, J.H., & BLOCK, J. (1980). The role of ego control and ego resiliency in the origins of behavior. In W.A. Collins (Ed.), *Development of Cognition/Minnesota Symposia on Child Psychology (Vol. 13).* Hillsdale, N.J.: Erlbaum Associates.

BOUCHARD, T.J., & McGUE, M. (1981). Familial studies of intelligence: A review. *Science, 212:* 1055–1059.

CEDERBLAND, M., HELGESSON, M., LARSSON, Y., & LUDVIGSSON, J. (1982). Family structure and diabetes in children. In Z. Laron & A. Galatzer (Eds.), *Psychological Aspects of Diabetes in Children and Adolescents.* Basel: S. Karger, (pp. 94–98).

CODDINGTON, R.D. (1972). The significance of life events as etiologic factors in the diseases of children. *Journal of Psychosomatic Medicine, 16:* 205–213.

COLE, R.E., AL-KHAYYAL, M., BALDWIN, A.L., BALDWIN, C.P., & FISHER, L. (1980). A cross-setting assessment of family interaction and the prediction of school competence in children at risk. Paper presented at the Schizophrenia High Risk Consortium Conference, San Juan, Puerto Rico.

COOPERSMITH, S. (1967). *The antecedents of self-esteem.* San Francisco: W.H. Freeman.

DOHRENWEND, B.S., KRASNOFF, L., ASKENASY, L., & DOHRENWEND, B.P. (1982). The Psychiatric Epidemiology Research Life Events Scale. In L. Goldberger & S. Breznitiz (Eds.), *Handbook of Stress.* New York: Free Press.

DRASH, A.L., & BECKER, D. (1978). Diabetes mellitus in the child: Course, special problems, and related disorders. In H. Katzen & R. Mahler (Eds.), *Diabetes, Obesity, and Vascular Disease. Advances in Modern Nutrition, Vol. 2.* New York: Wiley, (pp. 615–643).

DROTAR, D., CRAWFORD, P., & BUSH, M. (1984). The Family Context of Childhood Chronic Illness: Implications for Psychosocial Intervention. In M. Eisenberg, L. Sutkin, & M. Jansen (Eds.), *Chronic Illness and Disability Through the Life Cycle.* New York: Springer.

FIELD, T. (Ed.) (1980). *High-Risk Infants and Children.* New York: Academic Press.

GALATZER, A., & LARON, A. (1982). Psychological evaluation of newly diagnosed diabetics and their families. In Z. Laron & A. Galatzer (Eds.), *Psychological Aspects of Diabetes in Children and Adolescents.* Basel: S. Karger, pp. 51–57.

GALAZKA, S.S., & ECKERT, J.K. (1984). Diabetes mellitus from the inside out: Ecological perspectives on a chronic disease. *Family Systems Medicine, 2:* 28–36.

GARDNER, D.F., MEHL, T., EASTMAN, B., & MERIMEE, T.J. (1983). Psychosocial factors: Importance for success in a program of self-glucose monitoring. *Diabetes, 32:* 3A.

GARMEZY, N. (1979). Behavioral issues in chronic illness. In B.A. Hamburg, L.F. Lipsett, G.E. Inoff, & A.L. Drash (Eds.), *Behavioral and Psychological Issues in Diabetes: Proceedings of the National Conference.* Washington, D.C.: U.S. Department of Health & Human Services.

GARMEZY, N. (1981). Children under stress: Perspectives on antecedents and correlates of vulnerability and resistance to psychopathology. In A.I. Rabin, J. Aronoff, A.M. Barclay, & R.A. Zucker (Eds.), *Further Explorations in Personality.* New York: John Wiley & Sons, (pp. 196–270).

GARMEZY, N. (1983). Stressors of childhood. In N. Garmezy & M. Rutter (Eds.), *Stress, Coping and Development in Children.* New York: McGraw-Hill, (pp. 43–84).

GARMEZY, N. (1984). Stress-resistant children: The search for protective factors. In J.E. Stevenson (Ed.), *Recent Research in Developmental Psychopathology. Journal of Child Psychology and Psychiatry Book Supplement, No. 4.* Oxford: Pergamon Press, (pp. 213–233).

GARMEZY, N., MASTERS, A., & TELLEGEN, A. (1984). The study of stress and competence in children: A building block for developmental psychopathology. *Child Development. 55:* 97–111.

GARMEZY, N., & RUTTER, M. (1983). *Stress, Coping and Development in Children.* New York: McGraw-Hill.

HANSON, C.L., & HENGGELER, S.W. (1984). Metabolic control in adolescents with diabetes: An examination of systemic variables. *Family Systems Medicine, 2:* 5–16.

HARTER, S. (1982). The perceived competence scale for children. *Child Development, 53:* 87–97.

HAUSER, S.T., JACOBSON, A.M., WERTLIEB, D., BRINK, S., & WENTWORTH, S. (1985). The contribution of family environment to perceived competence and illness adjustment in diabetic and acutely ill adolescents. *Family Relations, 34:* 99–108.

HAUSER, S.T., & POLLETS, D. (1981). Psychological aspects of diabetes: A critical review. *Diabetes Care, 2:* 227–232.

HAUSER, S.T., POWERS, S., JACOBSON, A.M., WEISS, B., & NOAM, G. (1982). Family interactions and ego development in diabetic adolescents. In Z. Laron & A. Galatzer (Eds.) *Psychological Aspects of Diabetes in Children and Adolescents,* (pp. 69–76). Basel: S. Karger.

HAUSER, S.T., POWERS, S.I., NOAM, G.G., JACOBSON, A.M., WEISS, B., & FOLLANSBEE, D.J. (1984a). Family contexts of adolescent ego development. *Child Development, 55:* 195–213.

HAUSER, S.T., & SOLOMON, M.L. (1984). Coping with diabetes: Views from the family. In P. Ahmed & N. Ahmed (Eds.), *Coping with Diabetes.* Springfield, IL: Charles C. Thomas.

HAUSER, S.T., PAUL, E., DiPLACIDO, J., RUFO, P., SPETTER, L.D. (1984b). *Family Coping Processes Manual.* Boston: Unpublished coding manual.

HAUSER, S.T., PAUL, E., JACOBSON, A., WEISS-PERRY, B., VIEYRA, M., RUFO, P., SPETTER, L.D., DiPLACIDO, J., WERTLIEB, D., WOLFSDORF, J., HERSKOWITZ, R. (1988). How families cope with diabetes in adolescence: An approach and case analyses. *Pediatrician, 15,* 80–94.

JACOBSON, A., & HAUSER, S.T. (1983). Behavioral and psychological aspects of diabetes. In M. Ellenberg & H. Rifkin (Eds.), *Diabetes Mellitus: Theory and Practice* (3rd ed.) (pp. 1027–1052). New Hyde Park, NY: Medical Examination Publishing Co.

JACOBSON, A., HAUSER, S.T., POWERS, S., & NOAM, G. (1982). Ego development in diabetics: A longitudinal study. In Z. Laron & A. Galatzer (Eds.), *Psychosocial Aspects of Diabetes in Children and Adolescents.* Basel: S. Karger.

JACOBSON, A., HAUSER, S.T., WERTLIEB, D., WOLFSDORF, J.I., ORLEAN, S.J., & VIEYRA, M. (1985). Psychological adjustment of children with recently diagnosed diabetes mellitus. *Diabetes Care, 9:* 323–329.

JACOBSON, A., RAND, L., & HAUSER, S.T. (1984). Stressful life events and clycemic control among diabetics. *Psychosomatic Medicine, 46:* 83.

JOHNSON, S. (1980). Psychosocial factors in juvenile diabetes: A review. *Journal of Behavioral Medicine, 3:* 95–116.

KARP, S.A., WINTERS, S., & POLLACK, I. (1969). Field dependence among diabetics. *Archives of General Psychiatry, 21:* 72–76.

KAUFFMAN, C., GRUNEBAUM, H., COHLER, B., & GARNER, E. (1979). Superkids: Competent children of psychotic mothers. *American Journal of Psychiatry, 36:* 1398–1402.

KELLERMAN, J., ZELTZER, L., ELLENBERG, L., DASH, J., & RIGLER, D. (1980). Psychological effects of illness in adolescence. I. Anxiety, self-esteem, and perception of control. *Journal of Pediatrics, 97:* 126–131.

KOBASA, S.C. (1982). The hardy personality: Toward a social psychology of stress and health. In G.S. Sanders & J. Sols (Eds.), *Social Psychology of Health and Illness.* Hillsdale NJ: Erlbaum Associates, (pp. 3–32).

KOSKI, M. (1969). The coping process in childhood diabetes. *Acta Paediatrica Scandinavica Supplement, 198:* 199–214.

KOSKI, M. (1976). A psychosomatic follow-up. *Acta Paedopsychiatrica, 42:* 12–25.

LIEBER, D. (1977). Parental focus of attention in a videotape feedback task as a function of a hypothesized risk for offspring schizophrenia. *Family Process, 16:* 467–475.

LOEVINGER, J. (1976). *Ego Development.* San Francisco: Jossey-Bass.

MARRERO, D.G., LAU, N., GOLDEN, M.P., KERSHNAR, A., & MYERS, G.C. (1982). Family dynamics in adolescent diabetes mellitus: Parental behavior and metabolic control. In Z. Laron & A. Galatzer (Eds.), *Psychological Aspects of Diabetes in Children and Adolescents.* Basel: S. Karger.

McCUBBIN, H., & PATTERSON, J. (1980). *Systematic Assessment of Family Stress, Resources, and Coping: Tools for Research, Education and Evaluation.* St. Paul: University of Minnesota (offset).

MINUCHIN, S., ROSMAN, B. L., & BAKER, L. (1978). *Psychosomatic families: Anorexia nervosa in context.* Cambridge, MA: Harvard University Press.

MISHLER, E.G., & WAXLER, N.E. (1968). *Interaction in Families: An Experimental Study of Family Processes and Schizophrenia.* New York: Wiley.

MOOS, R. (1974). *Family Environment Scale.* Palo Alto: Consulting Psychologists Press.

MURPHY, L.B., & MORIARTY, A.E. (1976). *Vulnerability, coping, and growth from infancy to adolescence.* New Haven: Yale University Press.

NOWICKI, S., & STRICKLAND, B. (1973). A locus of control scale for children. *Journal of Consulting and Clinical Psychology, 40:* 148–154.

OLSON, D.H., PORTNER, J., & BELL, R. (1982). Family adaptability and cohesion evaluation scales. In D.H. Olson et al., *Family Inventories: Inventories Used in a National Survey of Families Across the Family Life Cycle* (pp. 5–24). St. Paul, MN: Family Social Science, University of Minnesota.

PIERS, E.V. (1969). *Manual for the Piers-Harris Children's Self Concept Scale.* Nashville: Counselor Records & Tests.

POND, H. (1979). Parental attitudes towards children with a chronic medical disorder: Special reference to diabetes mellitus. *Diabetes Care, 2:* 425–531.

QUINT, J.C. (1970). The developing diabetic identity: A study of family influence. In M.V. Batey (Ed.), *Communicating Nursing Research: Methodological Issues in Research, Vol. 3.* Boulder, CO: Western Interstate Commission on Higher Education.

RUTTER, M. (1972). *Maternal Deprivation Reassessed.* Harmondsworth, England: Penguin.

RUTTER, M. (1979). Protective factors in children's responses to stress and disadvantage. In M.W. Kent & J.E. Rolf (Eds.), *Primary Prevention of Psychopathology, Vol. 3. Social Competence in Children.* Hanover: University Press of New England, (pp. 49–74).

RUTTER, M. (1983). Stress, coping and development: Some issues and some questions. In N. Garmezy & M. Rutter (Eds.), *Stress, Coping and Development in Children.* New York: McGraw-Hill, (pp. 1–42).

RUTTER, M., COX, Z., TUPLING, C., BERGER, M,. & YULE, W. (1975). Attainment and adjustment in two geographic areas. I. The prevalence of psychiatric disorder. *British Journal of Psychiatry, 126:* 493–509.

SHOUVAL, R., BER, R., & GALATZER, A. (1982). Family social climate and the health status and social adaptation of diabetic youth. In Z. Laron & A. Galatzer (Eds.), *Psychological Aspects of Diabetes in Children and Adolescents.* Basel: S. Karger, (pp. 89–93).

SIMONDS, J. (1977). Psychiatric status of diabetic youth in good and poor control. *International Journal of Psychiatry Medicine, 7:* 133–151.

SIMONDS, J. (1977). Psychiatric status of diabetic youth matched with a control group. *Diabetes, 26:* 921–925.

STERKY, G. (1963). Family background and state of mental health in group of diabetic school children. *Acta Paediatrica Scandanavica, 52:* 377–390.

STIERLIN, H (1974). *Separating Parents and Adolescents.* New York: Quadrangle.

SULLIVAN, B.J. (1979a). Adjustment in diabetic adolescent girls: I: Development of the diabetic adjustment scale. *Psychosomatic Medicine, 41:* 119–126.

SULLIVAN, B.J. (1979b). Adjustment in diabetic adolescent girls: II: Adjustment, self-esteem and depression. *Psychosomatic Medicine, 41:* 127–138.

SWIFT, C.R., & SEIDMAN, H. (1969). Adjustment problems of juvenile diabetes. *Journal of the American Academy of Child Psychology, 3:* 500–515.

WERNER, E.E., & SMITH, R.S. (1977). *Kauai's Children Come of Age.* Honolulu: University of Hawaii Press.

WERNER, E.E., & SMITH, R.S. (1982). *Vulnerable but Invincible: A Study of Resilient Children.* New York: McGraw-Hill.

WERNER, E.E., BIERMAN, J.M., & FRENCH, F.E. (1971). *The Children of Kauai: A Longitudinal Study from the Prenatal Period to Age Ten.* Honolulu: University of Hawaii Press.

WHITT, J.K. (1984). Children's adaptation to chronic illness and handicapping conditions. In M. Eisenberg et al. (Eds.), *Chronic Illness and Disability Through the Life Span.* New York: Springer.

WILSON, H. (1974). Parenting in poverty. *British Journal of Social Work, 4:* 241–254.

WISHNER, W.J., & O'BRIEN, M. (1978). Diabetes and the family. *Medical Clinics of North America, 62:* 849–856.

WYNNE, L.C. (1967). Family transactions and schizophrenia: II: Conceptual considerations for a research strategy. In J. Romano (Ed.), *The Origins of Schizophrenia.* Amsterdam, Excerpta Medica (p. 165).

WYNNE, L.C., JONES, J.E., & AL-KHAYYAL, M. (1982). Healthy family communications patterns: Observations in families "at risk" for psychopathology. In F. Walsh (Ed.), *Normal Family Processes* (pp. 142–167). New York: Guilford.

WYNNE, L.C., SINGER, M.T., & BARTKO, J. (1977). Schizophrenics and their families: Recent research on parental communication. In J.M. Tanner (Ed.), *Developments in Psychiatric Research*. London, Hodder and Stoughton, Ltd. (pp. 254–286).

YU, P. (1979). Parental attributions as predictors of child competence in families with a parent with a hisotry of psychiatric disturbance. Unpublished doctoral dissertation. University of Rochester.

ZELTZER, L., KELLERMAN, J., ELLENBERG, L., DASH, J., & RIGLER, D. (1980). Psychological effects of illness in adolescents. II: Impact of illness in adolescents. *Journal of Pediatrics, 97:* 132–138.

7

Explorations of Vulnerability and Resilience: Case Studies of Diabetic Adolescents and Their Families

Joseph M. Schwartz, Alan M. Jacobson,
Stuart T. Hauser,
and Barbara Book Dornbush

In the first of our two chapters (chapter 6) we presented an overview of some of the key conceptual issues in the area of vulnerability and resilience in adolescence and reviewed the significant empirical findings from this burgeoning area of research interest. In addition to the more general review presented, one special focus of that chapter was on the research pertaining to a particular population at risk, *patients with insulin dependent diabetes mellitus* (IDDM) during a specific phase of the life cycle, *adolescence,* and to the contribution to vulnerable and resilient outcomes of one source of risk and protective factors, *the family.*

In this chapter we continue our focus on the adaptive strategies used by diabetic adolescents and on the factors in their family life that may facilitate or hinder the development of personal resources that aid the effective management of a chronic illness. We will pursue these issues through a detailed presentation of three case studies of diabetic adolescents. These cases are drawn from a large longitudinal study of family process and ego development in populations of psychiatrically ill, diabetic, and non-ill adolescents and their families. The cases will be considered in terms of a framework that is derived from three contexts: 1) the research findings reviewed in the previous chapter; 2) the developmental tasks of adolescence; and 3) the specific psychological constructs of central concern in the research project from which the cases were selected.

Research Overview

One aim of the present case study approach is to examine the extent to which the results of research on resilience in adolescence will be echoed in clinical interviews with diabetic teenagers. To facilitate consideration of the three cases from this perspective, we will briefly summarize the conclusions reached in the detailed review of the literature presented in the previous chapter.

Researchers have generally looked to three domains—the individual, the family, and the larger social environment—to identify those factors associated with the capacity to respond resiliently to stressful life experience. Personal attributes that have been linked with resilient outcomes in adolescence include: 1) well-developed verbal communication skills; 2) reflectiveness, impulse control, and the capacity to delay gratification; 3) self-esteem and a positive self-concept; 4) an internal locus of control and a sense of personal power; 5) interpersonal sensitivity and social responsiveness; and 6) intelligence. Resilient outcomes have been more frequently observed in those adolescents who have grown up in families characterized by: 1) a well-balanced approach to discipline and consistently enforced rules; 2) relationships that are warm, close, and understanding; 3) respect for individuality and autonomy; and 4) healthy communication patterns. High levels of possessiveness and anxiety within families have been correlated with less resilient outcomes in vulnerable teenagers. Those adolescents who were in communities with well-developed and accessible social support systems and were able to take advantage of such supports have generally fared better in managing stressful life events. The willingness to call upon agemates, older friends, clergy, and teachers for support and advice has been found to characterize teenagers who cope effectively with stress (cf. Werner & Smith, 1982).

In the discussion of the more limited research on resilience among adolescents with IDDM (generally defined in terms of good control of the illness), Hauser and colleagues (see preceding chapter) cite findings (cf., Simonds, 1977) which suggest that poor diabetic control is found in patients with high levels of psychiatric symptomatology. This conclusion also has been reached by Moran (1984) in his discussion of psychoanalytic treatment of diabetic children and adolescents seen at the Hampstead Clinic in London. His clinical experience as a psychoanalyst led him to formulate a reciprocal influence between diabetes and neurotic conflict. His impression was that diabetes influenced the nature of the psychiatric disorder that developed, while at the same time the management of the illness became a vehicle through which neurotic and family conflict was expressed. While others have challenged the notion that diabetes itself negatively influences personal adjustment (Dunn & Turtle, 1981; Jacobson, Hauser, Powers, & Noam, 1984; Jacobson, Hauser, Wertlieb, Wolfsdorf, Orleans, & Vieyra, 1985; Kellerman, Zeltzer, Ellenberg, Dash, & Rigler, 1981), there is far less doubt that psychopathology has a deleterious effect on adherence to prescribed treatment.

The quality of diabetic control may also be influenced by aspects of family life. Good illness management has tended to be found in families that value independence, autonomy, and self-sufficiency, encourage children to participate in social and recreational activities, permit open expression of feelings, and whose members are adaptable, supportive, and tolerant. Family attitudes of rigidity, overprotectiveness, overindulgence, perfectionism, and rejection have been linked with poor diabetic control. The mother-daughter interactions of female adolescents who are not adhering to treatment plans have been found to be characterized by intense emotional conflict, confrontation, and a relative inability to negotiate differences effectively (Bobrow, Avruskin, & Siller, 1985).

DIABETES AND THE DEVELOPMENTAL TASKS OF ADOLESCENCE

A second aim of this qualitative case study approach is to develop a deeper appreciation of the impact of insulin dependent diabetes mellitus on the developmental stresses of adolescence, and in turn how the developmental tasks of adolescence influence the management of this illness. For several reasons, IDDM is a particularly interesting stressor to study in relation to resilience in adolescence. When diagnosed in childhood or adolescence, it is an illness that requires a great deal of care by both child and family members. Discipline and deprivation are demanded of the child on a lifelong, daily basis. Inevitably, family routines are dramatically affected by the presence of a diabetic child in the household.

Further, the disease frequently has severe long-term sequelae, such as blindness, severe kidney illness, and heart disease. These dire consequences are common, but not inevitable. Such consequences are usually well known to children with diabetes and their families shortly after the illness is diagnosed. While good control of the illness through careful adherence to insulin usage, dietary restrictions, and exercise are emphasized, scientific evidence does not yet clearly support the value of tight diabetic control for averting these frightening long-range complications.

In recent years there have been compelling challenges to the previously widely held view that healthy adolescent development is characterized by intense turmoil (Masterson, 1967; Offer & Offer, 1975). Nonetheless, few would disagree that the developmental tasks of adolescence are formidable, even if many normal adolescents have sufficient ego strength and social supports to meet those tasks without the emotional upheaval that psychoanalytic writers have viewed as the essence of the adolescent process (Blos, 1962; Freud, 1946; Freud, 1958). It seems likely that a chronic illness like diabetes will complicate and amplify normal developmental stress.

One unique aspect of adolescence as a phase of the life cycle is that it is initiated by a discrete biological shift, the particular set of physiological and morphological changes involved in puberty. A variety of psychological consequences follow from the dramatic physical changes which produce the development of primary and secondary sex characteristics. The adolescent's psychic representation of his or her body must be reworked to take adequate account of this bodily revolution. This need to reconstruct the body image from that of child to that of adult is undoubtedly one source of the intense preoccupation of teenagers with the way their bodies look and work and of their often-observed exquisite sensitivity to any evidence of physical defect and deviation. It would not be surprising, then, if some diabetic teenagers reexperience in an especially painful way the narcissistic injury associated with having a body that is different and that chronically malfunctions and that they expect will deteriorate dramatically over the next 20 to 30 years. Furthermore, it is possible that the task of managing diabetes competently, depending as it does on the careful monitoring of internal physiological states, may be temporarily complicated by the flood of new sensations to which youngsters are exposed at puberty. In addition, if the newly reworked body image integrates a painful sense of defectiveness, self-consciousness about ac-

tively seeking sexual relationships may be especially acute, thus impeding one of the essential progressive thrusts of adolescence.

Another primary task of the teenage years has been described by Blos
(1967) as the "second individuation process of adolescence." This task
has many aspects. Chief among them are the development of a more
realistic image of parents, the reworking of childhood dependency on
parents toward ever-increasing degrees of autonomy, and the consolidation of a sense of oneself as an individual with one's own values,
strengths and weaknesses, and aspirations. When adolescence is stormy,
it is this process of identity acquisition that is frequently the root cause.
In addition, much family conflict is played out around the adolescent's
efforts to renegotiate the power balance with parents and other authority figures.

Diabetes may represent a significant added burden to this process of
separation and individuation. The youngster with diabetes may enter
adolescence with a history of unusually intense dependence on parents,
particularly if they have responded to their inevitable anxiety about the
illness by maintaining an excessively controlling attitude. Moran (1984)
has discussed cases of emotionally disturbed diabetic children who have
come to link the image of their anxious, overprotective parents with the
process of managing the illness. Hence, for them the care of their disease
becomes drawn into their efforts to separate from their parents, and
good diabetic control is sacrificed in the service of psychological and
interpersonal needs. Anna Freud (1952) noted in a discussion of the
psychic consequences of illness in adolescence, "At this last stage, before
independence is finally reached, recklessness in matters of health provides one of the familiar battle grounds for bitter struggles between the
adolescent and his mother (p. 79)." Within most families such struggles
are played out around minor illnesses and the temporary restrictions
such illnesses impose. Obviously, for the family with a diabetic teenager
the stakes involved in struggling over the management of the illness are
far higher. However, it is worth noting that such struggles may not be
typical. Indeed, one research group has reported data suggesting that
chronic illness may lead adolescents to develop ways of coping with the
anxiety aroused by physical illness (Zeltzer, Kellerman, Ellenberg, Dash,
& Rigler, 1980).

One additional task that must be mastered before adolescence can be
said to have been successfully completed is the development of a more
differentiated sense of one's future place in the human community (Erikson, 1956). Obviously, such matters as career choice and future social
role need not be settled in any final way by the end of adolescence.

However, the outlines of a life plan can usually begin to be discerned. Jacobson and Hauser (1983) have discussed the impact of the uncertain course of diabetes on patients' capacity to contemplate their future. Adolescents have often been viewed as managing their anxiety about the future by becoming excessively oriented to the present in ways that may self-destructively limit the options the future might hold for them. Jacobson and Hauser reported one case of a teenage diabetic who developed an irrational conviction that blindness was imminent. They noted that this 17-year-old boy's "response to his terror of disability was to try to forget he had diabetes by skipping nighttime injections—or to toy with dread by bouts of excessive drinking and fast driving. He especially loved the feel of driving too fast down winding roads, with the possibility that around any corner there would be another car and a fatal crash. Only at those moments did he feel released from his future disability (Jacobson & Hauser, 1983, p. 1042)." While such dramatic reactions are uncommon, the threat of future complications may be experienced as "waiting for the bombshell to explode" (Jacobson & Hauser, 1983, p. 1042). This experience of the future may have a subtle yet meaningful impact on career choice and on feelings about oneself (Hauser, Jacobson, Noam, & Powers, 1983).

The Adolescent and Family Development Study

A third aim of presenting these three cases is to allow us to take a more clinical approach to the specific foci of our own investigation of resilience and development in adolescence. The Adolescent and Family Development Study is a longitudinal study of adolescent ego development and family process. Subjects were drawn from populations of emotionally disturbed, diabetic, and normal early adolescents and were followed for three to four years. Each year, subjects responded to measures of ego development, self-esteem, and self-image formation. In addition, each year the adolescent participated in a clinical research interview. This semi-structured interview was usually conducted by the same member of the research staff each year and it attended to such topics as school life, family experience, relationships with friends, illness experience (where relevant), and ideas about the future. The underlying topic or theme in this interview was the identification of conflictual areas and the methods used to cope with conflict. These interviews were then coded and scored for levels of ego defenses and adaptive ego strengths. Each year, the adolescent and his or her parents also participated in tape-recorded discussions of their efforts to reach consensus about the solutions to moral dilemmas presented to them. These discussions were used to assess various family process dimensions.

Within this multifaceted project, two of the variables that have been studied intensively are *ego development,* an individual dimension, and *constraining and enabling interactions,* a family process dimension. In studying ego development we have closely followed the conceptualization formulated by Jane Loevinger (Loevinger, 1976) and have used the projective technique for measuring ego development that she developed. Within her approach, ego development is conceptualized as a unified underlying psychological dimension, perhaps best characterized as a framework of meaning through which experience is interpreted. According to Loevinger, this underlying dimension is reflected in the quality of impulse control, character, approach to relationships, thought contents, and cognitive style. Ego development is said to mature through discrete, successive stages which can be reliably discriminated using her measure, the Washington University Sentence Completion Test (Loevinger & Wessler, 1970). Evaluation of diabetic adolescents suggests that there are significant arrests in ego development, which persist over two-year follow-up in comparison to normal or non-ill adolescents (Jacobson et al., 1982). While these arrests or delays are not as serious as those found among our psychiatric patients (Hauser et al., 1983) and may not persist in adulthood, such developmental deviations appear to have important consequences for learning the tasks involved in managing diabetes (Barglow, Edidin, Budlong-Springer, Bendt, Phillips, & Dubow, 1983).

The particular family process dimension with which we have been most concerned measures what we have described as constraining and enabling interactions (Hauser, Powers, Noam, Jacobson, Weiss, & Follansbee, 1984). This framework is derived in part from Helm Stierlin's (1974) clinical analyses of the responses of disturbed parents to their teenager's efforts to separate. The major thrust of Stierlin's perspective is that the families of disturbed adolescents can often be distinguished by their prominent attempts to interfere with the autonomous and differentiated functioning of their children. Among these impediments to independent perceptions and actions are "binding" (constraining) interactions through which parents actively resist the differentiation of their children. We have substantially expanded this theory to account for forms of enabling interactions through which family members encourage or support the expression of more independent perceptions or thoughts. Among the types of constraining categories we have identified are those of distracting, devaluing, and indifference. The enabling interactions include such important interpersonal processes as explaining, accepting, and empathy.

At this point there is solid empirical evidence that ego development and constraining and enabling interactions are correlated. Several studies have consistently found that a variety of enabling interactions, particularly parental accepting behaviors, are associated with higher levels of ego development in psychiatrically impaired, diabetic, and normal early adolescents (Hauser, Powers, Jacobson, Schwartz, & Noam, 1982; Hauser et al., 1984). In particular, our initial findings suggest that families of diabetic adolescents functioning at high levels of ego development show a preponderance of explaining, accepting, and overall affective enabling behaviors, whereas families of adolescents with arrested ego development show numerous affective constraining behaviors (Hauser et al., 1984). Intuitively, it makes sense that both ego development and our family process dimension might very well be related to resilience among diabetic adolescents. For example, the capacity to take responsibility for control of impulses and to participate in more mature forms of interpersonal dependence are associated with higher levels of ego development and are likely to be positively related to stress resistance. It also seems reasonable that families that encourage and accept an adolescent's effort to think in a differentiated and well-articulated manner might be better able to support the kind of autonomous functioning that has been found to be associated with good diabetic control.

CASE STUDIES

The three teenagers we will be describing initially entered the project as early adolescents during brief inpatient stays at the Joslin Diabetes Center.* All three were admitted to have their treatment regimens assessed and adjusted and were given the opportunity to participate in a variety of educational groups and lectures about diabetes during their hospital stay. They were selected from our sample of 54 diabetic adolescents because they reflect the range of ego development represented in the study. Most of the material we will be using is drawn from the semistructured clinical interviews described previously. Two of the patients appear to be adapting well to their illness and represent "resilient" out-

---

*All names and certain other aspects of the case material have been altered to protect the confidentiality of subjects.

comes within this context. The third patient appears to be having considerably more difficulty with her illness and has been selected to help
highlight some of the differences between competent and problematic
adaptation to juvenile diabetes about which we have speculated.*

Mike

Mike was a 14-year-old eighth-grader when he entered the study. He
had been diagnosed as having diabetes two months before he became a
research subject. When first tested, Mike's ego development was already
at what Loevinger (1976) has labeled the Conscientious Stage, a stage
unusually high for a young adolescent. According to Loevinger, the qualities that are first present at this stage of ego development include a sense
of concern and responsibility for others, a recognition that rules can be
evaluated in terms of context, a sense of accomplishment rooted in personal goals and standards, and a rich, differentiated inner life. His family
discussions were characterized by high levels of accepting behavior on the
part of his mother and high levels of explaining behaviors toward Mike on
the part of both parents. Remarkably low levels of constraining behavior
were present in Mike's family throughout the discussions.

In his first-year clinical interview it was already evident that Mike was
showing a favorable adjustment to the recent news of his diabetes. He
described being surrounded by supportive and concerned people, family, friends, and treatment personnel. Furthermore, he was not reluctant
to use these people for support or for information. He communicated a
definite sense that other people were there to be utilized during his
personal crisis. This confidence in the availability of others seemed to
stem in part from his self-concept. He viewed himself as a person concerned about others and was already contemplating a career as a teacher:

> I like to hear people's problems and help them with them. . . . It
> seems that when you talk to people about their problems, so many
> times there's not necessarily the same exact problem but a common
> feeling or problem.

Regarding his friends he goes on to state:

> You always have the feeling that if there is anything I want to talk
> about I can talk to them or they can talk to me.

---

*For the purposes of the present study subjects' medical records were not consulted to
determine whether they were in good control of their illness. Rather, the clinical interview
material was used to determine subjects' self-assessed adaptation to their diabetes.

Because diabetes is an illness that may be inherited, often within the immediate and extended families of diabetics are other relatives with the illness. Such persons are potential repositories of much valuable experience with the disease. They are frequently in a position to provide emotional support and useful practical information about the management of the illness, although this will depend on the course their own illness has taken and on how effectively they have coped with it themselves. Mike did not have any diabetic relatives. However, in high school his two-year-older brother himself had to adapt to a chronic illness of his own, a painful hip problem caused by a serious automobile accident. Mike describes how his own illness deepened his understanding of his brother's struggle and how the two of them drew closer and provided one another with emotional sustenance:*

> I think it's since he, when he first got his brace, he had three years ago, I think about then. And at first he had to wear it 24 hours a day, and he wore it. He was really good, and people . . . you know . . . and people like his teachers think, think he really did great with it. But you know, being around home you could see the times when he used to kind of fight with mom and dad about it, and he didn't want to wear it and didn't really rebel, but he didn't want to do things, so he didn't want to and I never liked that. I always thought that he should wear it and do whatever he was supposed to do, 'cause I thought that he'd get out of it quicker and everything; but . . . and you know I used to give him a hard time and say you're supposed to wear it now and you're supposed to do this and do that. And he'd say, "But I don't want to." So we talked a little then, but when I got my diabetes it was kind of like we had something more in common, because it was the same thing like when people would say you're not supposed to eat that, you're not supposed to do that, and I'd say, "Well, it's my life. I can do with it what I want, you know." We got along better. It was kind of like we had something in common to talk about things. . . . I could . . . I could after I got my diabetes . . . I could understand why he acted like when he had his brace, and the reason he didn't want to do things that I never understood before, you know.

By the second-year interview Mike describes the support offered by his brother as particularly helpful in solidifying his tolerance of the

---

*All quotes are verbatim transcriptions from tape-recorded interviews. We have chosen not to smooth out awkward sentence construction in order to represent the dialogue as accurately as possible.

anxiety and uncertainty evoked by his diabetes. He tells the interviewer about his efforts to deal with his scary thoughts with an openness that is quite unusual:

> Well, when I first got out of the hospital, I was sure I was going to die, because everyone who had diabetes was going to die, right? So after a while you learn that that's not true, you are still going to be alive and live . . . and just thinking about . . . like you can have reactions when you have diabetes and it's becuase you don't have enough sugar in your system and just things like that. . . . At first, you get all these little pamphlets and you hear about all these people with their legs cut off or going blind. So these things are really scary in the beginning, but having someone to talk to and realizing that if you take care of it now, there is something that you can do about it right now that will help the future and things. Mostly, it's just knowing that there is someone that you can talk to right now and then just knowing with time everything . . . you will get used to everything a little more. . . .

Mike's special and empathic connection with his chronically disabled brother reflects a theme that appears in the protocols of several of the diabetic children in the study functioning at high levels of ego development. However, this relationship also seems congruent with Mike's other family ties. Recall that his family discussions were characterized by high levels of enabling interactions and low levels of constraining interactions. Mike's own view of his family is that members are very sensitive to one another's feelings. He articulates one difference between parents and children which was important to him in dealing with his illness. Parents invite you to lean on them, but are strong enough to not need to lean on you. In describing his parents' reactions to his diabetes he said:

> . . . and my parents just . . . I'd say they helped me the most . . . probably by not letting it upset them. But I think there is a big part to maybe parents' not letting you know how scared they are when something happens . . . and they kind of, I don't know, they kind of just stood there and stood back and gave me the support I needed. . . . They made sure that I had everything that I needed . . . to make it as easy as it could be when I was first getting used to having it.

Within the context of the research literature on resilience in adolescence, the program offered by the Joslin Diabetes Center can be viewed as a social support system available in the community. In that sense, all three of the patients have had the same opportunity to further develop their coping skills. We have a chance to observe how they view this opportunity and to note how other factors like ego development play a part in determining what advantage is taken of this experience. Mike's use of the program is entirely consistent with his high level of ego development and parallels his experience within his own family. He did not experience his stay in the hospital as a deprivation. Rather, he viewed it as an indicator of concern by his parents. Moreover, he reported actively using the program for support and education. He commented:

> I think it's really good just to . . . my doctor wanted me to come especially so soon after I got it . . . just to go to the lectures and learn everything. But I think I've gotten just as much out of meeting kids my age and talking to them about their diabetes and how, what from they had to go through and how they got it, as I have from the lectures.

In his third-year interview Mike describes one of his efforts to manage his illness more effectively. It clearly reflects all of the adaptive strengths that we have observed in him thus far—his confidence and autonomy, as well as his comfort in making use of the support and expertise of others. Mike described how he began to use daily blood tests rather than urine tests to regulate his glucose level more accurately. He initiated the change because of his dissatisfaction with the urine tests. He asked a family friend who worked at a diabetes clinic in another state about blood tests after having read about them in a magazine for diabetics. After talking to this family friend, he discussed the matter with a local pharmacist who went ahead and ordered a special kit for him. At that point he had some misgivings about the process he had initiated but realized that the special kit had already been obtained for him. He then talked to a neighbor active in an adult diabetic group who reassured him that he would be able use the kit himself, but offered to answer any questions that Mike might have. In fact, Mike found it easier to use this method of monitoring his illness and reported having fewer insulin reactions since making the change. While making this change he discussed the matter with his parents who were supportive of his wish to try this new monitoring system.

A number of other aspects of Mike's personality that emerge in his interviews bear mentioning. First is the wide range of activities in which he is involved and which he describes in a detailed, animated way. These include playing in a rock-and-roll band, participating in varsity athletics, and working as a volunteer in a local political campaign. He also appears well on the way toward narrowing down some career choices. Becoming a teacher or working with handicapped children seem like good possibilities to him. One possible area of modest anxiety appears to be involvement in dating girls. He was not involved with anyone in either of the first two years of the project. In the second year his younger sister already has a boyfriend, something which Mike says does not bother him. By the third year of the study Mike has begun to go out with a girl he dated several years earlier, in all likelihood before his diabetes was diagnosed. The interview data cannot help us confirm whether in some small way Mike's diabetes has contributed to some evident reluctance to get involved with dating, but the sequence of events is certainly consistent with such an interpretation. At worst, this may represent a small developmental delay that with time appears to be working out.

John

John first entered the study when he was 15 years old. Like Mike, he appears to have been in reasonable control of his diabetes, which was diagnosed at age 10. When first seen John's ego development was high, although not quite so high as Mike's. He was functioning at what Loevinger has labeled the "Self-Aware Level," one which is typical of adults in our culture. By comparison to lower levels of ego development, persons at the Self-Aware Level have more consciousness of themselves in relation to group norms and social expectations and a beginning sense of multiple options in relation to such expectations. In describing the Self-Aware person, Loevinger states that their "growing awareness of inner life is, however, still couched in banalities, often in terms of vague 'feelings' (1976, p. 19)." Thus, one would not expect to see the sensitivity to interpersonal nuances evident in Mike, who was functioning at the next level of ego development, in John's research protocols.

In the family discussions John's parents carried on a spirited and clear debate. This is reflected in high levels of enabling behaviors relative to constraining behaviors. Most prominent were explaining and accepting behaviors by mother and father. What was striking in these discussions was John's relatively low level of participation. At one point in frustration his father turned to John and said, "I want an opinion out of you." However, a few moments later during the discussion of the next dilemma, when John stepped outside the defined limits of the question to offer a novel solution, he was told in no uncertain terms that "you cannot make up your own alternative." This pattern of relatedness in the family, John's tendency to withdraw and test limits, and his parents' somewhat inhibiting response to his efforts to think for himself emerged as a major theme in John's clinical interviews.

John clearly was in the midst of a fairly intense struggle around separation and individuation with his parents. He expressed wishes for contact with his parents and apparently felt quite frustrated when he commented that his father hardly understood him at all and that he frequently found that he was unable to "speak what's on my mind." He is the youngest of four and echoed the often-heard youngest child's complaint that his parents have not changed with the times and still had the same expectations for him that they had for his older siblings. He also had some insight into family dynamics. When asked by the interviewer to describe his mother, John stated:

> She's very nervous. She's afraid if she agrees with my father, then I am going to hate her, and if she agrees with me, my father is going to hate her. So she is kind of stuck in the middle. If he says no, he means no, or if he says one thing, that's what he means. There's no changing his mind. He's very stubborn.

When the interviewer followed up on John's newly found interest in cycling, the following material emerged:

I: What do you like about cycling?

J: I don't know just . . . I don't like to be cooped up. I just like to get out. Whenever I get to feeling cooped up, I'll go out for a walk or start cycling.

I: What is it about the feeling of being cooped up that is unpleasant for you?

J: I don't like it. I feel like I'm just trapped and I don't like to feel or anything like . . . if I get into an argument with my mother or just anything.

I: Is that the sort of time that you might feel trapped and you go out and do your cycling?

J: Yeah.

I: What sorts of arguments do you have with your mom? I know most kids argue with their mom.

J: Oh, I don't know, all sorts of things.

I: Can anything come to mind?

J: Not really, no. It's just they start . . . ya know . . . when they start you can't remember what they started about. One thing leads to another.

I: How do you feel when one of these arguments just happened?

J: I'm just really upset and mad.

I: What about other situations that make you mad, anything come to mind?

J: Well, I don't know . . . when people just get on my back about . . . ya know . . . homework or quiz grades and school work or anything. Or . . . ya know . . . my friends, my parents, some of the friends I hang around with they don't like . . . and I mean I'm the one that's going to pick my friends and I'm the one that's going to live with them. They're not going to.

In other parts of the interview John revealed that his friends are "burnouts" and that one of them has an older brother with a police record. He also stated that he had been caught cutting classes and that recently his grades had fallen. A major focus of contention between John and his parents was his wish to attend vocational high school and become a plumber. Despite the anger generated by these disagreements and John's need to separate from his mother, he has been able to use variety of parent surrogates to assist him. He reported a very positive connection with a woman guidance counselor at school who had begun to help his parents see John's point of view. His brother-in-law also emerged as someone John had been able to talk to about "anything." He became noticeably upset when talking about his brother-in-law's recent move away from the area in which John lived.

Even in the presence of his more conflicted feelings about his parents, John described ways that his family members continued to serve as important resources for him. From the start there had been much support for him adapting to his diabetes. He reported managing his insulin by himself from the time of diagnosis. He also attended a summer camp for diabetics for three summers, experiences he viewed as extremely positive ones. His older sister is diabetic and he found her consistently available during his initial adjustment to the illness:

> Well, my older sister was a diabetic, so all I could think was taking a shot every day. You know, I didn't know why she had to take one and what was wrong with her. But you know, she was always there

if I ever needed help with something, you know, cause she had been through it herself. So it was pretty easy.

This positive attitude toward the management of his illness was also reflected in his attitude toward his stay in the hospital. He recognized that his blood sugars had been running high and saw the hospitalization as an opportunity to replace his old diet with one over which he could be in better control and lose weight as well. At the time of the interview he proudly reported having already lost several pounds and having made some new friends among the other diabetic adolescents he had met. Thus, while it appeared that John was involved in a fairly typical, if somewhat intense, adolescent conflict with his family, this struggle did not impede his capacity to function competently in the area of his diabetes.

Becky

Becky was 13 years old when she first participated in the research project. Her diabetes was diagnosed when she was four years old. Of the three teenagers we present, she was in poorest control of her diabetes and was having the most difficulty complying with treatment. An additional chronic illness, epilepsy, was discovered approximately one year prior to her entering the study. When first assessed, Becky was functioning at a relatively low level of ego development, one that Loevinger (1976) has labeled the "Self-Protective Stage." This stage represents an advance over previous stages in that impulse control is no longer completely externally imposed. The person functioning at the Self-Protective level "understands that there are rules. . . . His main rule is, however, 'don't get caught' " (Loevinger, 1976, p. 17). Such persons have difficulty accepting responsibility for their actions, tending instead to look to place blame elsewhere. Over the three years of her participation in the project, Becky did show modest, but measurable, gains in ego development.

Becky's family discussions of moral dilemmas were strikingly different from those of the two prior cases. Most noteworthy about the first year's family discussion was Becky's extremely limited participation. During the discussion of several questions posed to the family, Becky barely said a word. Her father had much difficulty tolerating any difference of opinion. He came across as very aggressive in trying to get all family members to agree with him. In one instance he concluded that the family had reached consensus without Becky ever expressing an opinion. In another discussion, after lecturing Becky on the merit of his own point of view, he said to Becky, "I think you'd better change your answer, don't you?" Striking imbalances occurred in the family profile of constraining and enabling behaviors. Becky's father expressed more constraining and enabling behaviors than any other family member. His constraining behaviors were rated primarily as distracting and devaluing. His enabling behaviors were rated primarily as explaining, although a more qualitative analysis suggests that 'lecturing' might be a more apt label. Accepting behaviors were much more limited in Becky's family than in Mike's or John's.

The picture of Becky and her family that emerges from her clinical interviews is largely congruent with her level of ego development and her family's mode of interacting in the moral dilemma discussions. In her first clinical interview Becky came across as nice but not very reflective. She seemed constricted and to be using much denial around her illnesses. She did acknowledge that her diabetes was not in good control, but professed little concern about it. Her experience of her parents around the care of her illnesses was that they were controlling, overprotective, and too "strict." Although it was apparent Becky was having difficulty living within the dietary constraints imposed by her diabetes, her mother refused to buy sugar-free soda and ice cream because of her fear of cancer. In essence, she was attempting to protect her daughter from a remote danger, while undermining Becky's efforts to cope with a real and present illness.

Becky viewed her mother, in particular, as interfering with her autonomous strivings in other arenas as well. For example, Becky reported an interest in interior decorating and a variety of related hobbies like drawing and collecting doll houses. Her mother was critical and prohibiting of these interests, even though these were activities Becky said helped her deal with the temptation to cheat on her diet. Her mother's interference with her autonomy even included mandating that a drawing Becky had made in art class be given to her older brother to decorate his bedroom. Becky indicated feeling hopeless about getting her mother to change her mind. This general sense of ineffectiveness was further evident in her response to the interviewer's query about her upcoming transition to high school: "I don't really know, it's a bigger school so I'll probably get lost."

Within Becky's family, there are two members who might be in a position to help her cope with her chronic illnesses. Like Becky, one of her uncles is diabetic. When the interviewer inquired about whether they talk about diabetes Becky tersely stated that her uncle "doesn't say nothing." One of Becky's two older sisters has epilepsy and the following exchange took place when the discussion turned to how Becky learned she had epilepsy:

B: Well, my sister has it and . . . you know . . . so . . . and I noticed that the . . . like I stared and when I'd come back . . . and I didn't really know what the heck was going on. So I told the . . . my doctor and he said to have . . . have an EEG. And they found out I had epilepsy.

I: What is epilepsy?

B: Umm, it's about the . . . your brain. Does something to the brain. So I don't really know.

I: Did he explain it very much?

B: The doctor?

I: Yeah.

B: No.

I: But your sister, she has the same thing?

B: Yeah.

I: And she's had it for a long time, I guess, hasn't she?

B: Yeah, she's had it since she was only 13, too.

I: How old is she now?

B: Nineteen.

I: So . . . ah . . . six years. Did . . . did . . . what did she tell you about it?

B: Nothing.

I: Nothing?

B: Nothing. Probably doesn't know too much about it anyway.

In any event it is not clear how good a model Becky's sister would be around tolerating the restrictions of epilepsy. Becky reported that her sister had had difficulty managing her frustration about not being able to get a driver's license and had driven on a number of occasions without a license. Perhaps Becky was merely being prudent in not turning to her sister for advice. However, her own difficulty seeking support from the environment is suggested by her perception of the program at the Joslin Diabetes Center as an opportunity to have fun, and by her parents having to force her to ask her math teacher for help with material she could not grasp, something she did only with considerable embarrassment.

By Becky's third year in the study some progressive trends began to be evident. She had confronted her mother around the issue of her career path. Her mother had been in favor of her pursuing training in nursing, although Becky was not interested in it. She had told her mother she wanted to go into interior decorating and felt that her mother had accepted this aspiration. On the recommendation of her physician she was now using blood tests to monitor her glucose level and as a consequence was in better control of her diabetes. She required help from her mother in taking the blood tests. However, she seemed to view her mother's involvement less as an intrusion than as a support. She was still using some denial around her illness. She told the interviewer that she was better able to deal with the restrictions of her diabetes because she expected a cure to be found in five or 10 years. However, this kind of denial was far more adaptive than her previous self-indulgent involvement in fantasies that she could always get away with eating just a little bit more.

Discussion

Our intention in presenting the cases of Mike, John, and Becky was to explore the degree to which material drawn from clinical interviews with diabetic adolescents would enrich our understanding of factors involved in promoting stress resistance in adolescence. The cases can now be viewed in terms of the initial framework which involved consideration of: 1) the research literature on resilience in adolescence; 2) the developmental tasks of adolescence and how these might be affected by the presence of a chronic illness like diabetes; and 3) the dimensions of ego development and constraining and enabling family interactions which were of prime interest in the Adolescent and Family Development Study from which the cases were drawn.

As we examine the case material, Mike emerges as a textbook exemplar of a resilient adolescent. He is coping with a significant stressor by bringing to bear all of his considerable resources. Indeed, these resources appear to be just those that the research findings have found to be involved in distinguishing those adolescents who are resilient from those who are vulnerable. For example, he is quite clearly skilled in communicating his feelings through words, is insightful and empathic, and has a sense of being able to exercise control over his environment through his own efforts. Like Werner and Smith's (1982) resilient adolescents, Mike is quite willing to make use of the available supports in the environment. Recall his deepening connection to his chronically disabled brother, his positive response to the program at the Joslin Diabetes Center, and his use of diabetic adults to help him make the transition to blood test monitoring of sugar levels. At least as Mike saw them, his family, too, possessed the qualities that researchers have concluded relate to good diabetic control. He felt that his family valued his autonomy and independence, were interested in hearing about his feelings, encouraged his involvement in a variety of recreational activities, and were supportive and available to him.

Becky's clinical interviews also seem to illustrate issues that have been linked with resilience and vulnerability by researchers. Certainly by comparison to Mike and to a somewhat lesser degree, John, Becky seemed quite limited in her capacity to verbalize her feelings and was far less reflective. What emerged most centrally during the first two years of her participation in the study was a sense of helplessness and a perception of herself as unable to influence others, especially her mother. Becky's view of her family certainly illustrated findings from the research literature associated with vulnerability. Her uncle and older sister, potential supports around her diabetes and epilepsy, were emotionally unavailable. It also was apparent that Becky felt her mother to be too controlling and overprotective. In addition, one area of maternal rigidity—her concern about the carcinogenic potential of sugar substitutes—removed a potential adaptive outlet from a girl who was having difficulty complying with her diet.

Blos (1967) has described the process of individuation as an aspect of "psychic restructuring that winds, like a scarlet thread, through the entire fabric of adolescence" (p. 162). This developmental theme is the one which is most evident in the clinical material. What seems to vary is the degree of turmoil that accompanies this process. With Mike the process seemed to be unfolding in a pattern which Offer and Offer (1975) have labeled "Continuous Growth." That is, Mike appeared to be moving with little emotional upheaval toward a clearer and more differentiated sense of himself and the goals he wished to pursue. Not surprisingly, his diabetes management had not been contaminated by the need to separate from his parents.

On the other hand, John seems involved in a stormy process of separation and individuation. He and his parents were involved in disagreements about his friends, his career interests, and his school performance. Nonetheless, he was able to keep the care of his illness outside the arena in which the separation struggle was being enacted. Perhaps his history of having been supported in taking care of his diabetes himself and of having been provided with much familial support around his illness (e.g., being sent to summer camp for diabetics) helped keep his diabetes psychologically neutral with respect to his evident adolescent conflicts.

In her early interviews, Becky was chafing under the restrictions of her parents, who were seen as too strict. Her wish to individuate was evident enough, but she seemed unable to envision any way of becoming her own person. Although not manifestly symptomatic, she, like the emotionally disturbed children with IDDM described by Moran (1984), seemed to overidentify the care of her diabetes with the person of her mother. One might speculate that some degree of her poor diabetic control served her need to find some way of achieving independence from her. By the third year of the study she had established some degree of individuation by fighting successfully for her own career choice. Perhaps this degree of autonomy allowed her to enter a more collaborative relationship with her mother around her illness, as manifested by their cooperation in making the change from urine screens to blood test monitoring.

Within this small sample of diabetic teenagers, ego development emerged as a reliable correlate of psychosocial maturity, in general, and of resilience, in particular. Becky, the patient with the lowest level of ego development, was clearly having the most difficulty separating from her parents and keeping her diabetes under good control. Ego development as conceptualized by Loevinger may indeed be an underlying general trait which can serve as a predictor of resilience. Certainly, many of the particular factors found by researchers to predict resilience and illustrated so clearly in Mike's protocols are ones which are at the heart of Loevinger's description of persons operating at relatively high levels of ego development. An important theoretical question here is whether high levels of ego development are to be conceptualized as a *marker* of resilient outcome or as a *protective factor* promoting resilient outcome. There is no simple answer to this question. It is reasonable to view ego development as an achievement in and of itself and hence as a positive developmental outcome. However, once attained, ego development can in turn serve a protective function as it permits far more sophisticated modes of adaptation to stressful life experience.

There are many obvious limitations to the case study approach pursued in this chapter. Small numbers of cases, no matter how carefully selected, are likely to differ from one another in ways that are bound to qualify the conclusions that are drawn from comparing and contrasting them. Obvious uncontrolled factors in our cases include the length of time these adolescents had been diabetic, the presence within the family of other members with diabetes, and socioeconomic status. Certainly, Becky's attitude toward her illness is bound to reflect some enduring effects of having had to first grasp its meaning with the mind of a four-year-old child. On the other hand, John was first diagnosed as diabetic at age 10 and Mike first faced his illness with all of the sophisticated cognitive apparatus of a bright 14-year-old. The clinical approach to the case material presented in this chapter is, of course, no substitute for more systematic data analysis. Conclusions reached via this research methodology must be offered cautiously. However, linked to more traditional quantitative research methods, this case study approach can enrich the meaning and allow for a deeper appreciation of our empirical findings.

REFERENCES

BARGLOW, P., EDIDIN, D. V., BUDLONG-SPRINGER, A. S., BENDT, D., PHILLIPS, R., & DUBOW, E. (1983). Diabetic control in children and adolescents: Psychosocial factors and therapeutic efficacy. *Journal of Youth and Adolescence, 12:* 77–94.

BLOS, P. (1962). *On Adolescence: A Psychoanalytic Interpretation.* New York: Free Press.

BLOS, P. (1967). The second individuation process of adolescence. *The Psychoanalytic Study of the Child, Vol. 22.* New York: International Universities Press.

BOBROW, E. S., AVRUSKIN, T. W., & SILLER, J. (1985). Mother-daughter interactions and adherence to diabetes regimens. *Diabetes Care, 8:* 146–151.

DUNN, S., & TURTLE, J. (1981). The myth of the diabetic personality. *Diabetes Care, 4:* 640–646.

ERIKSON, E. H. (1956). The problem of ego identity. *Journal of the American Psychoanalytic Association, 4:* 56–121.

FREUD, A. (1946). *The Ego and the Mechanisms of Defense.* New York: International Universities Press.

FREUD, A. (1952). The role of bodily illness in the mental life of children. *The Psychoanalytic Study of the Child, Vol. 7.* New York: International Universities Press.

FREUD, A. (1958). Adolescence. *The Psychoanalytic Study of the Child, Vol. 13.* New York: International Universities Press.

HAUSER, S. T., JACOBSON, A., NOAM, G., & POWERS, S. (1983). Ego development and self-image complexity in early adolescence: Longitudinal studies of psychiatric and diabetic patients. *Archives of General Psychiatry, 40:* 325–332.

HAUSER, S. T., POWERS, S., JACOBSON, A. M., SCHWARTZ, J., & NOAM, G. (1982). Family interactions and ego development in diabetic adolescents. In Z. Laron & A. Galatzer (Eds.), *Psychological Aspects of Diabetes in Children and Adolescents.* Basel: S. Karger.

HAUSER, S. T., POWERS, S. I., NOAM, G. G., JACOBSON, A. M., WEISS, B., & FOLLANSBEE, D. J. (1984). Family contexts of adolescent ego development. *Child Development, 55:* 195–213.

JACOBSON, A., & HAUSER, S. T. (1983). Behavioral and psychological aspects of diabetes. In M. Ellenberg & H. Rifkin (Eds.), *Diabetes Mellitus: Theory and Practice.* New Hyde Park, NY: Medical Examination Publishing.

JACOBSON, A., HAUSER, S. T., WERTLIEB, D., WOLFSDORF, J. I., ORLEANS, J., & VIEYRA, M. (1985). Psychological adjustment of children with recently diagnosed diabetes mellitus. *Diabetes Care, 9:* 323–329.

JACOBSON, A., HAUSER, S. T., POWERS, S., & NOAM, G. (1982). Ego development in diabetic adolescents. *Pediatric and Adolescent Endocrinology, 10:* 1–8.

JACOBSON, A. M., HAUSER, S. T., POWERS, S., & NOAM, G. (1984). The influence of chronic illness and ego development on self-esteem in diabetic and psychiatric adolescent patients. *Journal of Youth and Adolescence, 13:* 489–507.

KELLERMAN, J., ZELTZER, L., ELLENBERG, L., DASH, J., & RIGLER, D. (1981). Psychological effects of illness in adolescence I. Anxiety, self-esteem, and perception of control. *Journal of Pediatrics, 97:* 126–131.

LOEVINGER, J. (1976). *Ego development.* San Francisco: Jossey-Bass.

LOEVINGER, J., & WESSLER, R. (1970). *Measuring Ego Development, Vol. 1.* San Francisco: Jossey-Bass.

MASTERSON, J. F. (1967). *The Psychiatric Dilemma of Adolescence.* Boston: Little, Brown. (Reprinted by Brunner/Mazel, NY, 1984.)

MORAN, G. S. (1984). Psychoanalytic treatment of diabetic children. *The Psychoanalytic Study of the Child, Vol. 39.* New Haven: Yale University Press.

OFFER, D. & OFFER, J. (1975). Three developmental routes through normal male adolescence. In S. C. Feinstein & P. L. Giovacchini (Eds.), *Adolescent Psychiatry, Vol. 4.* New York: Jason Aronson.

SIMONDS, J. (1977). Psychiatric status of diabetic youth matched with a control group. *Diabetes, 26:* 921–925.

STIERLIN, H. (1974). *Separating Parents and Adolescents.* New York: Quadrangle.

WERNER, E. E. & SMITH, R. S. (1982). *Vulnerable but Invincible: A Study of Resilient Children.* New York: McGraw-Hill.

ZELTZER, L., KELLERMAN, J., ELLENBERG, L., DASH, J., & RIGLER, D. (1980). Psychological effects of illness in adolescents II: Impact of illness in adolescents. *Journal of Pediatrics, 97:* 132–138.

8

Action and Acting Out: Variables in the Development of Resiliency in Adolescence

Timothy F. Dugan

Certain patterns of action and acting out, in contrast to certain types of inaction, cooperativeness, and restraint, are factors predicting resiliency and favorable development during adolescence. While the concept of acting out is often used in a pejorative manner and seen as psychopathological, acting-out behavior may also be an indicator of hope and potential for success in the face of adversity.

Winnicott (1956), in order to illustrate his theory of the "antisocial tendency," describes a case consultation to a mother of an adolescent who had been stealing. He tells the mother, "Why not tell him that you know that when he steals he is not wanting the things that he steals but he is looking for something that he has a right to; that he is making a claim on his mother and father because he feels deprived of their love"

The author would like to acknowledge the assistance of Steven Ablon, M.D., Anton Kris, M.D., and David Van Buskirk, M.D., who reviewed earlier drafts of this chapter.

(p. 307). Winnicott goes on to say that the "antisocial tendency implies hope . . . that it represents a tendency toward self-cure . . . and that the nuisance value of the antisocial child is an essential feature . . . a favorable feature" (p. 311) in that it compels the environment to respond to the child and, ultimately, to the deprivation sustained by the child.

The communicational aspects of acting out, that is, the "cry for help" formulation, and the restitutive aspects of acting-out behavior (Ornstein, Gropper, & Bogner, 1983) have been well delineated within the psychoanalytic literature. Concepts of developmental resiliency can point the way to understanding acting out as one of the ingredients of a healthy outcome. From a psychopathological point of view, Winnicott's notion of the antisocial tendency can be explained by using the concepts of "repetition compulsion" or of "passive/active reversals" as they have to do with the mastery of early traumatic events. From the viewpoint of resiliency, however, it would be important to note, in Winnicott's example, the boy's capacity to maintain an outgoing and ongoing object-relatedness, a sense of desire and need (even if unconscious), and a purposefulness of action. The concept of resiliency in children and adolescents is used to describe those individuals demonstrating factors "typically associated with a heightened probability of present or future maladaptive outcomes but which are not actualized in some children whose behavior instead is marked by patterns of behavioral adaptation and manifest competence" (Garmezy & Rutter, 1983, p. 73). In this chapter, I focus on the adaptive capacity of being able to act in relationship to others, even when such behavior results in provocation or annoyance.

In this context, acting-out behaviors and the capacity to be active or to "act up" provide evidence of preserved ego functioning, rather than solely ego weakness. Certain patterns of inhibition, inaction, and compliance are shown to foreshadow the development of a sense of helplessness and despair. I will explore these issues after presenting a case vignette around which I will organize my later discussion.

CASE VIGNETTE

Henry, a white male, was 18 years old when he began a twice weekly psychotherapy. He came for psychiatric care because he had recently quit college (during the spring of his freshman year) and returned home, depressed and suicidal. He told me of his fantasy of committing suicide: "I would leave the state and head west to Colorado. There I would walk in the woods, leave no trail behind me, and walk until I dropped dead of starvation and exposure." He said that he had done average work during the first semester of his freshman year in college until he began to feel sick in December. It had taken the University Health Service two months to diagnose mononucleosis. In the four months prior to seeing me he had been feeling increasingly depressed, angry with himself, ashamed of his body, and overcome with the sense of being weak and damaged. He was unable to concentrate because of racing thoughts and had left school without telling his friends or room-mates. He could not envision a return to school or involvement in the outside world "for the rest of my life." He had temper tantrums focused on criticisms of his father and felt identified with his mother as a "victim of my dad."

His parents told me that he had been a difficult infant who "spit out all of his food" from ages eight months to 17 months. This had coincided with a maternal, postpartum depression which had resolved itself with-out treatment. When Henry was 17 months old, the paternal grand-mother had come to live with the family, and she had assisted in the child-care duties over the past 18 years. While this grandmother was silent and intimidating and critical of the mother, his parents noted that Henry was and continued to be quite close to his grandmother. The grandmother had had a serious myocardial infarction shortly before the patient's matriculation in college and was currently quite weak and dis-abled. The parents wondered whether the grandmother's presently de-bilitated state might be contributing to their son's depression. Otherwise, the parents noted that he had had a "happy childhood" and a successful adolescence. In high school, he had many male friends whom he did not keep up with after matriculating in college, and he had been a very good athlete. In particular, they mentioned very warm and close relationships with two athletic coaches. The father raised a concern about his son's insecurity around females and mentioned that while Henry had dated several girls, he had never "gone steady." Also, the father noted that he did not consider his son "smart." In fact, he did not believe his son had any intellectual interests, but rather was quite concrete in his thinking and pragmatic in his choice of courses at school.

Within one month of beginning psychotherapy, Henry began to feel some relief. However, upon contracting a mild upper respiratory illness, he again felt depressed and experienced an overwhelming feeling of being weak and damaged. We were able to weather this storm and he began to plan to return to college the following September. He had no sense of what he would like to major in, nor was he confident that he could be successful in his academic endeavors. He was feeling relieved and we were faced with a common dilemma for therapists who see adolescents: Is it better for him to go back to school with the hope of linking up with peers and mentors and of making a connection with another therapist, or is it better for us to continue the psychotherapy, deal with the regression implicit in living with his family, and gradually help him make plans in his hometown? He was too anxious and fearful of his sense of weakness and dependency longings to tolerate a plan to stay at home, and his parents had a wish for him to "get back on the horse that bucked him." So he returned to school.

His arrival at school was overwhelming and traumatic. He lasted two days, became extremely agitated, suicidal, and despairing, and left school precipitously. He told his parents by phone, "I am going to Colorado to die," and then promptly hung up. Two days later, having created a considerable "nuisance" (in Winnicott's terms) to his family and me, and leaving me with the sense of having erred in agreeing to his return to college, he called his father and requested, "Will you come get me?" The father, an amateur airplane pilot, immediately jumped into his plane and rescued his son. They returned to the family home where the patient erupted, hit his father, broke furniture, and had to be taken to a local psychiatric hospital by the police where I met the patient and his family.

The patient appeared disheveled and hypervigilant as he sat with his back to a wall. He was dissociated and offered no spontaneous words, except for repetitively saying, "I'm dead. I'm already dead. I'm dead." At no time was he frankly psychotic by mental status exam or projective testing. He became more animated and was discharged from the hospital in six weeks with plans to live at home, work in his father's business, and resume twice-per-week psychotherapy with me.

In the following months he missed a number of appointments with me. All the misses were preceded by some sense of weakness on the patient's part and his belief that I would find him undesirable. I would call him, offer the rescue that he had requested of his father, and he would quickly return. Following an acute knee sprain, the patient left town without notifying his parents or me and made a solo 10-hour ascent of a snow-covered mountain. He did this without gloves, wearing a flannel shirt and sweater, and without a map or previous familiarity with the mountain.

Within four months after the outset of treatment, the patient and I agreed that there was a repetitive pattern following his perception of a physical insult to his bodily integrity. Also, with some embarrassment, he was able to admit to a persistent fantasy in his journey to the mountain:

that I would have been there waiting for him at the summit of the mountain or that he would call his dad for an airplane rescue. Following the exploration of this issue, the patient was able to consistently attend all appointed hours. Of importance here is the presence of the centrifugal flight away from a very real, present sense of injury to his self-esteem. Ornstein, Gropper, and Bogner (1983) comment on this lack of self-cohesion as a precipitant for an episode of shoplifting in their adult patients.

The transferences were mixed at this point. On one hand, I was the active, rescuing father who would protect Henry from danger, respond to his needs and plights, and give him the feeling of being valued as a man by a man. Also, I was like his grandmother who could nurture him and care for him. However, there was also a strong, negative maternal transference. I was like a depressed, incapable mother who could not respond to him particularly after he had sustained an insult to his body and self-esteem and felt depleted. He had to escape from this depressed mother and search out a connection to someone else who could sustain him.

At the end of the first year of psychotherapy, Henry submitted an application to a local college. He refused an offer of money from his father, quit the job at his father's factory, and got a job at a local fast-food restaurant saying, "I don't make much money, but enough to get by on. I'm there to meet people and test out whether you've been telling me the truth. I'll see whether I can actually talk to people about how I'm feeling. Fifteen other kids work there and plenty of kids come in there for fish and chips. We'll see." At work, he met a male friend and they moved into an apartment together. The appeal of an extrafamilial social role was noticeable. There was a prominent counterdependent theme as well, as he searched for a sense of himself amongst peers, and a look to the outside for affiliation, involvement, and affective connection. He had consolidated a strong, positive paternal transference with me and had begun to internalize these new identifications.

After two-and-a-half years of twice-per-week psychotherapy, Henry had arrived at some peace with his father and said, "I still mistrust him. However, if I had to live with a mother like he grew up with, I wouldn't say much to people either. I'd stay by myself. . . . You know, there is a sense of being 'above all the mess' when we're up there in that plane." We had survived two or three upper respiratory infections, one fractured thumb while playing basketball, and joked about his being able to be satisfied with a local emergency room rather than having to "freeze my rear end off, climbing that entire mountain, looking for a doctor at the summit." He ran uncontested for a seat on the Student Council of a community college and unsuccessfully ran for president of the Student Council. He continued to feel quite depressed at these moments of failure, but used me and his roommate for solace. He remained anxious around girls, exhibiting a labile self-esteem in their presence. He told me, "This has something to do with my mother and I'm terrified to look at it. She's a really cold person. I always thought I wanted too much. No wonder I felt dead. I couldn't feel anything because there was no point to it. She can't feel anything, she's cold, why should I risk feeling anything? It was easier to feel dead."

As he ended his third year of psychotherapy, Henry was able to continue his exploration of these observations of his mother and his feelings toward her of rage, longing, and disappointment. He was able to see the stabilizing influence of his actions and the need he had for the rescue efforts of fathers and grandmothers. Additionally, he could remember the importance of his high-school athletic coaches. We again had an opportunity to recall his need for me to hospitalize him, his missed appointments and wishes that I call him to reschedule, and his worries that I would lose interest in him or become too depressed to sustain my efforts on his behalf. At one point he said, "Without athletics and Coach Jones I would have sat around all day hating myself and waiting for my mother to feed me."

We have been able to explore his issues around his sense of early maternal deprivation and understand better how his actions in relationship to others have been in the service—as formulated by Winnicott—of recouping that which he had lost. Henry's actions of the past have become his vehicles for communication in the present and the road to early memories of wish, desire, and deprivation. At the time of the writing of this chapter, Henry had applied to transfer to several competitive universities with the intention of majoring in history and going on to complete a doctorate in this area of study. With much affection he told me, "Well, it's no surprise that I am interested in the relevance of history. That's been my major since I met you."

RESILIENCY IN ADOLESCENCE

Generally, those adolescents brought to us have been "acting out" and are in conflict with people and institutions in their environment. As clinicians, we therefore see a highly selected group of adolescents. When we retrospectively review their histories we are not surprised to find much evidence of prior difficulty, long-standing problems, many failed attempts at solutions, and a failing self-esteem at the time of presentation. These adolescents and their families provide fertile soil for psychopathological formulations and predictions of doom. The question asked within the resiliency literature, however, is "What are the protective factors that tend to support mental health, competence, and successful adaptation in the face of adversity?" These ideas, concerning the maintenance of successful adaptation, are quite different from the ideas generally presented in the clinical, psychoanalytic literature which are focused upon explanations of pathological behavior.

I offer a brief review of this literature to present examples of these "protective factors." Rutter (1975a) identified successful school attainment as predicting a positive childhood outcome. Whereas IQ and cognitive capacity predict good outcome according to Long and Vaillant (1984) and Garmezy, Masters, and Tellegen (1984), childhood school attainment does not predict better adulthood outcome according to Vaillant and Milofsky (1980). A good relationship with one parent who is described as warm and noncritical is considered protective (Rutter, 1979). Both Garmezy (1981) and Werner and Smith (1982) cite internal locus of control (a sense of inner responsibility, absence of projection), reflectiveness, and positive sense of self as predictors of good adolescent outcome. Kauffman et al. (1979), in their study of psychotic mothers, state that highly competent kids, whom they refer to as "Superkids," may develop when the mother is warm, even if bizarre, and when she has been able to maintain her nonfamilial social relationships, rather than regress to states of social isolation. Hauser et al. (1985) cites "enabling interactions through which family members encourage or support the expression of more independent perceptions or thoughts" (p. 88) as predicting enhanced ego functioning and presumably resiliency during adolescence. Of interest, Vaillant and Milofsky (1980) report that the level of childhood psychological trauma, childhood social class, and childhood educational level do not predict male adult health at the age of 47. And Long and Vaillant (1984) and Vaillant and Vaillant (1981) report that adolescent work history predicts good psychological adjustment in adulthood and predicts attainment of a higher social class during adulthood. In this regard, there are large possible discontinuities between childhood adaptation and adolescent or adulthood adaptation and large possible discontinuities even between later adolescent adaptation and adulthood adaptation.

I cite these factors because they raise questions about how similar developmental insults, such as maternal postpartum depression in

Henry's case, can have such widely different outcomes in adolescence and adulthood. The prior studies tend to focus on specific individual or family variables and I want to now focus on more extrafamilial, social factors. Specifically, I will refer to two longitudinal studies: the New York Longitudinal Study (Chess & Thomas, 1984) and the work presented by Vaillant (1977), Vaillant and Milofsky (1980), Vaillant and Vaillant (1981), and Long and Vaillant (1984), in which adaptation from adolescence to adulthood is described.

Chess, in her chapter "Defying the Voice of Doom" (this volume), describes four older adolescents whose early developmental history and temperamental difficulties would have predicted "doom" in adolescence. Three of these children were quite successful, and Chess attempts to isolate the qualitative factors that seemed to account for their ability to turn the tide. She mentions several factors: one boy's musical abilities, which allowed his involvement in a college music program and which necessitated his working to support his college expenses; another boy's ability to develop relationships with peers and parents of peers and his ability to use their counsel, as opposed to the counsel of his quite chaotic family; and one girl who had a very disturbed suicidal mother who was able to maintain a close, warm, and noncritical relationship with an older sister, mother surrogate, and her father in lieu of any contact with her mother. Chess highlights the theme of a capacity to develop a distance "from noxious familial onslaughts and underminings, of leaving behind irreconcilable conflicts and substituting alternative constructive social involvements which have the power to protect and to provide a second, or even a third, chance" (p. 198, this volume).

Vaillant and Vaillant (1981) and Long and Vaillant (1984) similarly cite the capacity to work as an adolescent and to engage in alternative social roles as a predictor of adulthood positive mental health and adulthood socioeconomic success. In supporting such observations, Vaillant and Vaillant (1981) cite Brown and Harris (1978): "Like Erikson, Brown and Harris successfully united Freud and Marx when they wrote, 'For it is in the perception of oneself successfully performing a role that inner and outer worlds meet and internal and external resources come together' " (p. 1440).

Another similar finding, reported in a study of "invulnerable" children of psychotic mothers (Musick et al., 1984), is that children whose mothers facilitate their involvement with outside social agencies and whose mothers feel positively about such outside social contact are much more competent than children with less social contact and with similarly ill mothers. Having access to outside others by virtue of having a special skill, economic need, or inner determination allows for a mutative experience in which failings of the past can be contended with, possibly mastered, probably repressed, and success achieved beyond that which would have been predicted.

Henry had suffered from an eating disorder in infancy, which coincided with a maternal, postpartum depression. However, his adolescent outcome was not that of an inactive, dysphoric, depressed youth, but rather that of an active, friendly teenager of above-average intelligence. Factors that can readily be identified as promoting this "resilience" include: the presence of a substitute caretaker, Henry's paternal grandmother, from infancy through his adolescence; his considerable athletic abilities; his object-relatedness and ability to involve himself with two male athletic coaches; and his persistent involvement in his afterschool athletic program which provided distance from his family. His outcome, over and above what might be predicted, provides evidence of his resiliency.

However, once these growth-supporting factors were lost in college, certain elements of his underlying psychopathology became evident. Upon matriculating college, he lost daily contact with his paternal grandmother; her permanent loss to him was threatened by her myocardial infarction; he lost the containment of his high school athletic program and two special male coaches; and his already damaged body image was assailed by mononucleosis. His decompensation included a massive regression and suicidal, near-psychotic depression.

I present this case because it raises many questions. To what extent are factors promoting resiliency merely temporizing and to what extent do they allow for permanent character change and stabilization? One could argue that these behaviors are merely temporizing and serve to avoid confrontation with the underlying pathology. On one level, this view is accurate as we see the depths of Henry's acute oral regression. However, it does seem that his ability to engage caretakers, grandmother, and athletic coaches, even in the face of depressive affect and sense of deprivation, and to create a considerable nuisance to engage an additional caretaker, a psychiatrist, are obvious strengths that appear to be part of his character. Rather than being someone "who has been neglected," he is "someone who has been found." He has a belief about himself and his life that "all is not lost. Even if you get forgotten, you can be found."

I link this concept of resiliency with the psychoanalytic notions of action and acting out because of the similar questions each of these concepts present. Are the behavioral patterns seen in resilient adolescents or acting-out adolescents persistent or transitory? Are these behavioral patterns merely "cover-ups" which obfuscate the still lingering unresolved pathology? In Henry's case, the ongoing issue of his perception of his mother's coolness and aloofness and his feeling deadened in relationship to her took nearly four years of twice-weekly psychotherapy to uncover. Was this issue masked under a veneer of resiliency and avoided by his actions or was this issue contended with by his ability to engage caretakers and then allowed permanent resolution in the context of having caretakers, one of whom was a psychiatrist?

ACTION AND ACTING OUT

In the case of Dora, the first reported analysis of an adolescent, Freud (1905) first uses the phrase "acting out" in the postscript where he says, "Thus she acted out an essential part of her recollections and fantasies instead of reproducing it in the treatment" (p. 119). She displaced her feelings of revenge for being deceived and deserted by another man onto Freud—"acting out"—and prematurely terminated treatment. Freud (1914) undertakes the first discussion of acting out in his paper, "Remembering, Repeating, and Working Through." He states that the "patient yields to the compulsion to repeat, which now replaces the compulsion to remember" (p. 151). And in his paper, "The Technique of Psychoanalysis," Freud (1940) states, "We think it most undesirable if the patient acts outside the transference instead of remembering. The ideal conduct for our purposes would be that he (the patient) should behave as normally as possible outside the treatment and express his abnormal reactions only in the transference" (p. 177), meaning only in the office. Freud is clear in his desire that motoric activity be inhibited and the impulses be contained within "the psychical field" (Freud, 1914, p. 153).

Freud used the term "acting out" to describe a variety of behaviors: first, in reference to the transference, as the patient "acts it before us, as it were, instead of reporting it to us" (Freud, 1940, p. 176); second, when describing the patient's repetition compulsion within the transference and outside the transference with other people in his or her life, actions that constitute a resistance to the treatment. Anna Freud (1968) reminds us of the context of psychoanalytic theory within which such a definition existed, a theory based on drive derivatives and repression. If id drives are not gratified, then repressed memories and oedipal conflicts return to consciousness for analysis. However, she reminds us that the clinical and theoretical focus has shifted, so that there is now increased interest in preoedipal pathology, which is nonverbal, cannot be remembered, and must be relived in action (see also Atkins, 1970; Greenacre, 1950,

1962). Today's patients who enter treatment are already in action in the external environment and secondarily are drawn into treatment. Anna Freud points to our interest in the transference analysis of impulse-ridden subjects and infantile elements which necessitate tolerance for extreme forms of "acting out." Anna Freud says that "acting out" is age-adequate in adolescence; and even Offer and Offer's work (1976), often cited for documenting the norm of a less-than-tumultuous adolescence, states that at least one-third of their subjects have tumultuous ("acting-out") adolescences.

Anna Freud (1968) further states that the term "acting out" is no longer applied to repetitions within the transference at all, but is reserved for reenactments of the past outside of the analysis. While going along with some of this redefinition to include transference enactments, she would like the term confined to description of behavior within an analytic context to include a description of behaviors representing past memories and preverbal experiences which must be lived through and interpreted. She would prefer actions outside of the analysis being called "reality actions." I agree with this. As an example, in describing the behavior of adolescents, she replaces the phrase "acting out" with the word "acting" and says that the fact that an adolescent "carries his actions beyond the confines of the analytic situation reflects his developmental need to seek experience outside his family" (p. 169). This is the sine qua non of an evolving sense of identity. This quality of being active in relationship to others (objects) should not be referred to by a psychopathological label. In fact, the ability to act can be a protective variable and lead to the development of resiliency.

Henry offers us a case in point. Because of his own self-criticism and the intensity of his dependent feelings, he had to leave home, return to college, and interrupt his psychotherapy prematurely. However, his actions of "going to Colorado," of climbing a cold mountain, and of missing appointments when experiencing bodily pains became a clear communication that he was hurting and needed to be rescued, and yet he desired to be an independent man on his own two feet. He oscillated between coming to me and wanting me to come to him. These actions pointed to separation-individuation conflicts within the transference and assisted in developing a formulation about the etiology of the conflict. Rather than delaying the process, Henry's actions facilitated our understanding of his predicament vis-à-vis his family. The acting-out aspect of this behavior was manifest in the office when he would gloss over the details of his journeys, focus on extraneous detail, and avoid any reference to his internal feeling states or fantasies. Not until he was certain that I would value him in a way similar to his high-school basketball coach would he then grant me entrance to his internal world. As Boesky states (1982, p. 52), acting out is inseparable from the transference and, therefore, psychoanalytic treatment cannot occur without acting out. Henry's actions often preceded our understanding and his insight.

Fenichel (1945) mentioned three factors involved in the predisposition to acting out. One factor is "an alloplastic readiness," by which he means a unique involvement of the acting-out person with the outside world, usually involving an excessive dependency upon the reactions of the outside world to his actions. The second factor refers to the primacy of oral conflicts, represented by impetuousness and urgency and low frustration tolerance. The third factor refers to early trauma as a prerequisite for acting out. Fenichel points to the excessive dependence upon the reactions of the outside world of the action-prone individual. However, a theorist such as Erikson (1956, p. 122), who is particularly interested in the complexity of interplay between an individual and the outside world, emphasizes in his comments about identity formation that the reactions of the outside world are essential for an adolescent's development of a personal sense of identity. The question of "how much is enough and how much is too much?" is raised. One could venture the hypothesis that the amount of involvement with outside others is directly proportional to the gravity—meant both as a physical principle describing "pull" and as an adjective connoting severity—of early developmental failures.

Greenacre (1950) highlights the existence of preoedipal trauma as a genetic antecedent to acting out and elaborates three more predisposing factors to acting out: 1) the patient presents a special emphasis on visual sensitization and a bent for the dramatic; 2) there is an unconscious belief about the "magic of action"; and 3) there is a distorted relationship between action and its relationship to speech and verbal thought. Blos (1963) paraphrases Greenacre and says, "Under such conditions (of preoedipal trauma), the function of language has miscarried and the action language of earlier stages continues to operate side by side with it as a form of communication and problem solving" (p. 170).

As to the specificity of the trauma, Schwartz (1968), citing observations on a cohort of acting-out children at the Hampstead Clinic, reports the frequency of "a break in the mother/child relationship at the very height of the ambivalent phase of development (age 18–30 months)" (p. 181). Continuing this theme of trauma, separation, and loss, Grinberg (1968) states that experiences that determined earlier mournings that were not worked through were the "essential roots" (p. 171) of acting out.

Grinberg elaborates on Greenson's point that acting out is "like a dream that could not be dreamt" (p. 177) including the wish fulfillment aspects of regaining the lost object. These papers refer to preoedipal trauma sustained within early object relationships that cannot be described or remembered within a verbal or cognitive mode. Malone (1963) describes acting-out children within multiproblem families as having a delayed progression toward secondary process thinking and delayed symbol formation. Words are not available to these individuals at the time of the traumas and are not available to them in memory at the time of their presentations to our clinics for treatment. It is here that actions speak louder than words and actions must suffice as a communicational mode in lieu of other modes.

Henry's history is populated with involvement with people in his external world. He does present an interesting question as to whether these involvements are better categorized by Fenichel (1945) as "too dependent" or by Erikson (1956) as "necessary." As I was able to become a participant in these interactions, it was clear that Henry was always asking me in one way or the other, "Do I matter to you? Do you feel the urge to pursue me when I run away?" These action statements communicated a history of feeling neglected or discarded, and they seemed clear in their content and genuine in their affect. These actions, owned by him, became the fulcrum around which we could challenge his experience of being "done to" in the world with the notion of his active agency in these current matters. Schafer (1979) states that "character refers to the actions that people typically perform in the problematic situations that they typically define for themselves" (p. 875). Over time, Henry and I could agree that he was the type of person who would act even more independently when he was in fact feeling more needy.

Given Fenichel's (1945) and Greenacre's (1950) formulations of preoedipal trauma as a predisposing factor to acting out in adulthood, one could conceptualize the prominence of acting out in adolescence as a means of coming to terms with unresolved issues within a family that must be communicated within and without the family, as an individual begins to feel conflicts around identity formation and senses the urge to leave his family behind and set out on his own path. Again, Grinberg's (1968) thoughts about failed mourning are helpful, and Blos's (1968) observations about the second separation individuation phase in late adolescent development are instructive and consistent with Anna Freud's notion (1968) of the age-adequacy of acting out in adolescence. Erikson (1956) conceives of adolescence as a time of repudiating the past, of embracing the new, of determining the "me" and the "not-me," and of struggling with these issues via experimenting with roles in relationship to parents, peers, teachers, bosses, mentors, and institutions. These trial experiences and practicing modes are essential to the process of adolescent development.

Although describing the process of psychoanalysis with adult patients, Vanggaard (1968) introduces the notion of "trial-and-error" behavior. By this he means behavior evidenced "at an advanced stage of a successful analysis, when defenses have been modified and bound energy released, new aggressive and sexual impulses make their demanding appearance in the patient . . . he (the patient) has to learn from experience (of action) before acquiring a new level of integration" (p. 207). Blos (1968) states, "We can see that the fixed ego attitude of dealing with danger (via 'avoidances' and avoiding people) has broader, more inclusive scope than a character trait derived from drive transformations, e.g., 'obstinacy' " (p. 248), which poses an issue between people. In comparing two character traits, avoidance and obstinacy, Blos favors the trait that involves a less fixed attitude within the ego, such as obstinacy which would be interpersonally problematic, over a trait involving avoidance which could behaviorally manifest itself as restraint, deliberateness, or even cooperativeness. From the point of view of adolescent development, trial-and-error actions are a necessity. Whether such actions will allow conflicts to be delineated in order to be worked through or to be avoided cannot be known until the action is experienced, described, and understood. In this case, differentiating between trial-and-error actions and the treatment resistance of acting out cannot be accomplished until a period of time well after the event has occurred.

Rangell (1968) articulates a position of respectfulness and tolerance toward actions, saying, "We do not forbid 'thinking out' and 'feeling out' " (p. 200) and alerts us to the "moralistic attitude on the part of some analysts toward 'action' . . . (which may result in) a generalized and more permanent inhibition of action which outlives the analysis and may go on to long-lasting deleterious effect" (p. 200). He also mentions the comments of Deutsch (1966) on the "fate neurosis" where an inhibition of action is the major problem.

Greenacre (1968) refers to acting out within analysis as "playful practice" and compares it to periods in earlier childhood development when "growth proceeds in stages with fluctuations of activity" (p. 213). She admonishes us to not prohibit such behaviors in our patients because of the flow of material and memories that will be squelched. While the line has to be drawn at behaviors injurious to self and others, adolescent patients in their ways of "play acting," temporary role experimentation, trial and error behaviors, and playful practicing must be tolerated so that the attendant memories can become manifest and allowed to be worked through in treatment. Otherwise, we run the risk of prematurely halting the presenting identity crises of our patients and their exploration of options and encouraging premature foreclosure, as Erikson (1956) warns against.

In the case of Henry, as we continued to understand the communicational aspects of his behavior, he did again "join the world." In his usual counterdependent fashion, he took a stand against his father, refused all monetary assistance, and began working at a local fast-food restaurant. Quite deliberately, he articulated a "trial-and-error" plan as he told me of the number of peers, males and females, that he would encounter and the number of bosses with whom he would have to contend. He met a male friend, a college graduate, through his job, with whom he took an apartment, thereby moving out of his home. However, he quickly got into some difficulties with a male boss and returned to his father's business for employment until the following summer when he took a job coaching children in athletics. He also began to ask girls out for dates, always telling me, "This is like an experiment in life. I'm always scared. I don't know why. But maybe we'll be able to figure it out."

As he approached girls with greater intention and sometimes urgency, a change was noted on how he felt on subsequent visits to see his parents. He was feeling increasingly satisfied with his father and began to report an increasing awareness of his mother's emotional unavailability. He was now able to restate his early presentation to me as "dead" within the context of an enhanced sense of personal agency, "I keep myself dead so I can't feel anything. No wonder. If I knew how I felt around my mom and how I wanted her to respond to me, like I was a real living person, I would just get so angry and feel so frustrated." This is an example of character change as described by Schafer (1979), as it refers to a very different construction of Henry's reality.

At this time, the transference to me was largely positive and paternal. As he felt more identified with me, he also felt closer to his own father. Additionally, he identified with my tolerance for his actions by initiating more actions of his own. He developed "trial-and-error" strategies and was more direct and purposeful in his actions. His actions in relationship to girls led to an increased awareness of his conflicts with his mother and permitted him the opportunity to find words to describe earlier and ongoing feeling states in relationship to her.

CONVERGENCE OF "ACTING OUT" AND RESILIENCY CONCEPTS

Henry summed up the dilemma quite well. He said, "I just got through high school. Whenever I was upset, I would stay at (athletic) practice later or shoot baskets for four hours at a time. I never knew that I was disappointed in my mother." Which side of the coin to look at—the psychopathology avoidance or the growth-producing features—depends upon our frame of reference. I agree with Boesky (1982) when he says it is not possible to define acting out adequately. Actions cannot be classified solely as resistances, nor solely as evidence of growth.

Resiliency might be considered synonymous with the positive aspects of acting out as described in the preceding section. Trial-and-error actions, playful practicing, action as communication, and action as restitution would be psychoanalytic terms describing growth-producing actions in relationship to objects.

Throughout this chapter, I have attempted to describe one patient's method of dealing with an early disturbance in the mother-child interaction and his successful attainment of distance from his mother and his feelings about her. This capacity to achieve distance may be one area where the concepts of resiliency and the positive side of "acting out" converge.

As I have mentioned previously, Stella Chess describes her resilient adolescents' abilities to "develop distance from noxious familial onslaughts" (p. 198, this volume). Long and Vaillant (1984) cite the capacity to work and engage in alternative social roles during adolescence as a predictor of adulthood positive mental health. Musick et al. (1984) tell us that "invulnerable children" of psychotic mothers have had the benefit of extrafamilial, social agency contact.

Returning to the psychoanalytic literature on adolescent development, Blos (1968) states, "We cannot fail to notice how (adolescent) character takes shape silently, how it consolidates proportionate to the severance from and dissolution of infantile ties: like Phoenix rising from its ashes" (p. 250). And Blos continues, in the same paper, "Again, we observe a tendency toward internalization or conversely, toward a disengagement (on the ego level) from the adult caretaking environment (usually the family) which has acted as the trustee and guardian of the immature ego of the child" (p. 257). And Erikson (1956) describes the similar time of life for an adolescent conflicted between his ties to the past and wishes for the future and states, "It must be remembered that the counterpart of intimacy is distantiation, i.e., the readiness to repudiate, to ignore, or to destroy those forces and people whose essence seems dangerous to one's own. Intimacy with one set of people and ideas would not be really intimate without an efficient repudiation of another set (of people)" (p. 81).

So, in this concept of the attainment of distance, there is a convergence between the psychoanalytic theoretical writings of Erikson, Blos, and Winnicott, the resiliency literature as seen in the writings of Chess and Vaillant, and the sociological work of Brown and Harris. This idea of distance is on a continuum between the notion of internal psychological distance from old introjects and internalizations, access to peers in contemporary culture, and social distance in the world in terms of work involvement and social role functioning.

In high school, anchored by his athletic talents and involvement with his high-school coaches in a school environment that rewarded such athletic success, Henry felt capable and happy. His school performance was average, although his thinking processes tended to be somewhat concrete and his peer relationships included little sustained involvement with girls. His actions and activities outside of his family were protective and stabilizing and lent to him a quality of resiliency. Under the pressures of his separation from this extrafamilial containing environment, he was unable to sustain himself and returned to his own family and the regressive experiences of times past. With the help of psychotherapy and his own willingness to construct behavioral experiments, Henry was able to construct an upward cycle of social interaction, role experimentation, and enhanced self-esteem. In particular, he was able to throw himself back into college, again move away from home, and begin making contact with girls. Buttressed by his enhanced self-esteem and successful role performance, he has been able to let himself feel his feelings around women, recover early memories of deprivation at the hands of "my cold mother," and begin to link up his running away and his centrifugal tendency with his experience of childhood frustration and deprivation. He has begun to cry about and grieve the unfairness of growing up with a mother whom he perceives to be emotionally cold.

These memories could not be recalled in the absence of extrafamilial object relationships and actions to allow for displacement of affect and enhanced self-esteem. Also, they could not have been attained solely within the transference because of the unacceptability of the dependency and regression-proneness in adolescence. Actions were as necessary in this process as were words.

SUMMARY

The realm of actions and their meanings in adolescent development were discussed. Excerpts from the four-year psychotherapy of an 18-year-old male were offered as a means of focusing the discussion. While data were offered showing how actions provided a resistance to encountering certain negative affects and thereby constituted a resistance to treatment, the positive benefits of actions were stressed. The main thesis of the chapter is that certain actions and acting out are desirable qualities to the extent that the behaviors increase a patient's involvement with others; allow for experimentation with new ideas, people, and propositions; and allow for the progressive resolution of earlier developmental traumas. The resiliency literature provided descriptions of certain adolescent activities, i.e., exercise of special skills and adolescent employment, which were considered growth-producing.

Furthermore, it was suggested that successful psychotherapy and psychoanalysis including the development of transference necessitated a certain level of action and acting out. In fact, the concept of transference is based on the necessity of acting out.

REFERENCES

ATKINS, N. (1970). Action, acting out, and the symptomatic act. Report of Panel. *Journal of the American Psychoanalytic Association 18:* 631–643.
BLOS, P. (1963). The concept of acting out in relation to the adolescent process. In E. Rexford (Ed.) *A Developmental Approach to Problems of Acting Out.* New York: International Universities Press, 1978, pp. 153–174.
BLOS, P. (1968). Character formation in adolescence. *Psychoanalytic Study of the Child, 23:* 245–263.
BOESKY, D. (1982). Acting out: A reconsideration of the concept. *International Journal of Psycho-Analysis, 63:* 39–55.
BROWN, G., & HARRIS, T. (1978). *Social Origins of Depression: A Study of Psychiatric Disorder in Women.* London: Tavistock.
CHESS, S., & THOMAS, A. (1984). *Origins and Evolution of Behavior Disorders: From Infancy to Early Adult Life.* New York: Brunner/Mazel.
DEUTSCH, H. (1966). Discussion of paper by P. Greenacre. In E. Rexford (Ed.) *A Developmental Approach to Problems of Acting Out.* New York: International Universities Press, 1978, pp. 234–245.
ERIKSON, E. (1956). The problem of ego identity. *Identity and the Life Cycle.* New York: W. W. Norton.
FENICHEL, O. (1945). Neurotic acting out. *Collected Papers, Vol. II.* New York: Norton, 1954, pp. 296–304.
FREUD, A. (1968). Acting out. *International Journal of Psycho-Analysis, 49:* 165–170.
FREUD, S. (1905). Fragment of an analysis of a case of hysteria. *Standard Edition VII:* 3–124.
FREUD, S. (1914). Remembering, repeating, and working through. *Standard Edition XII:* 145–155.

FREUD, S. (1940). An Outline of Psychoanalysis. *Standard Edition XXIII:* 140–207.

GARMEZY, N. (1981). Children under stress: Perspectives on antecedents and correlates of vulnerability and resistance to psychopathology. In A. Rabin, J. Arenoff, A. Barclay, & R. Zuckar (Eds.), *Further Explanations in Personality.* New York: John Wiley, pp. 196–270.

GARMEZY, N., & RUTTER, M. (1983). *Stress, Coping, and Development in Children.* New York: McGraw-Hill.

GARMEZY, N., MASTERS, A., & TELLEGEN, A. (1984). The study of stress and competence in children: A building block for developmental psychopathology. *Child Development, 55:*97–111.

GREENACRE, P. (1950). General problems of acting out. In *Trauma, Growth, and Personality.* New York: International Universities Press. 1969, pp. 224–236.

GREENACRE, P. (1962). Problems of acting out in the transference relationship. In E. Rexford (Ed.) *A Developmental Approach to Problems of Acting Out.* New York: International Universities Press, 1978, pp. 215–234.

GREENACRE, P. (1968). The psychoanalytic process, transference, and acting out. *International Journal of Psycho-Analysis 49:* 211–218.

GRINBERG, L. (1968). On acting out and its role in the psychoanalytic process. *International Journal of Psycho-Analysis,* 49: 171–178.

HAUSER, S., VIEYRA, M., JACOBSON, A. & WERTLIEB, D. (1985). Vulnerability and resilience in adolescence: Views from the family. *Journal of Early Adolescence: 5:* 81–100.

KAUFFMAN, C., GRUNEBAUM, H., COHLER, B., GAMER, E. (1979). Superkids: Competent children of psychotic mothers. *American Journal of Psychiatry, 136:* 1398–1402.

LONG, J., & VAILLANT, G. (1984). Natural history of male psychological health, XI: Escape from the underclass. *American Journal of Psychiatry. 141:* 341–346.

MALONE, C. (1963). Some observations on children of disorganized families and problems of acting out. In E. Rexford (Ed.) *A Developmental Approach to Problems of Acting Out.* New York: International Universities Press, 1978, pp. 21–43.

MUSICK, J., STOTT, F., SPENCER, K., GOLDMAN, J., & COHLER, B. (1984). The capacity for enabling in mentally ill mothers. *Zero to Three, 4(4):* 1–6.

OFFER, D. & OFFER, J. (1976). Three developmental routes through normal male adolescence. *Adolescent Psychiatry, 4:* 121–141.

ORNSTEIN, A., GROPPER, C. & BOGNER, J. (1983). Shoplifting: An expression of revenge and restitution. *The Annual of Psychoanalysis, Volume XI.* New York: International Universities Press, pp. 311–331.

RANGELL, L. (1968). A point of view on acting out. *International Journal of Psycho-Analysis, 49:* 195–201.

RUTTER, M., COX, A., TUPLING, C., BERGER, M., & YULE, W. (1975). Attainment and adjustment in two geographic areas. I: The prevalence of psychiatric disorder. *British Journal of Psychiatry, 126:* 493–509.

RUTTER, M. (1979). Protective factors in children's responses to stress and disadvantage. In M. Kent & J. Ralf (Eds.) *Primary Prevention of Psychopathology, Vol. 3. Social Competence in Children.* Hanover, N.H.: University Press of New England.

SCHAFER, ROY (1979). Character, ego-syntonicity, and character change. *Journal of the American Psychoanalytic Association, 27:* 867–891.

SCHWARTZ, H. (1968). Contribution to symposium on acting out. *International Journal of Psycho-Analysis, 49:* 179–181.

VAILLANT, G. (1977). *Adaptation to Life: How the Best and Brightest Came of Age.* Boston: Little, Brown & Co.

VAILLANT, G., & MILOFSKY, E. (1980). Natural history of male psychological health, IX: Empirical evidence for Erikson's model of the life cycle. *American Journal of Psychiatry, 137:* 1348–1359.

VAILLANT, G., & VAILLANT, C. (1981). Natural history of male psychological health, X:

Work as a predictor of positive mental health. *American Journal of Psychiatry, 138:* 1433–1440.

VANGGAARD, T. (1968). Contribution to symposium on acting out. *International Journal of Psycho-Analysis, 49:* 206–210.

WERNER, E., & SMITH, R. (1982). *Vulnerable but Invincible: A Study of Resilient Children.* New York: McGraw-Hill.

WINNICOTT, D.W. (1956). The antisocial tendency. In *Through Paediatrics to Psycho-Analysis.* New York: Basic Books, 1975, pp. 306–315.

WINNICOTT, D.W. (1971). Case XIII. "Ada" at 8 years. In *Therapeutic Consultations in Child Psychiatry.* New York: Basic Books, pp. 220–238.

Part IV

DEFYING THE VOICE OF DOOM: FROM ADOLESCENCE TO ADULTHOOD

9

Defying the Voice of Doom

STELLA CHESS

Child psychiatry, embedded in the medical model, has as its objective the treatment and prevention of behavioral disturbance. Pathological behavior, when it is extreme, is not difficult to identify. Disagreements as to the correctness of pronouncing a child behaviorally disturbed arise when the actions of such children differ from the expected to only a slight degree. It is then that it becomes crucial to know the range of normative behavior in developmental contexts, so that the behavioral pattern of the child undergoing diagnostic study can be compared with normal peers. In the course of this comparison, there may be disagreement as to how far from the average or modal behavior the concept of the norm is to be extended. Studies of both range of abilities and styles of functioning can help determine when differences from the average simply constitute nuisances or normal variability, or are in actuality evidences of pathology. Such investigations of normative behaviors and continuous versus discontinuous patterns of growth and maturation are, in fact, a major discipline of crucial importance.

The study presented in this chapter was supported in part by a grant from the National Institute of Mental Health (MH-31333).

As the range of normative patterns of development continues to be explored, and as modes of intervention to eliminate or ameliorate pathology continue to be refined and modified, the possibilities of prevention become increasingly clear. Thus, there are now important studies of risk, of those features within the child that appear to foreshadow actual behavioral disturbance, as well as those features of the environment that seem to influence the overt appearance of behavioral pathology. The identification of risk factors is a powerful method in pointing to priorities of action before waiting for risk to become actuality, even though in substantial percentages of children at risk, even without intervention, risk may not turn into actual disorder.

Studies of risk have progressed especially with the technique of longitudinal research starting in childhood. Such studies permit the identification of group trends, as well as the examination of the life course of the individuals making up the groups at different developmental points. With such simultaneous study of individuals, of environments and of the interactions between individual and environment, we have become increasingly aware that not only is it the identification of risk that is important, but also it is necessary to analyze the course of those subjects who are at risk and yet develop normally. Such individuals defy the voice of doom, even though they are as vulnerable as far as the presence of risk factors is concerned as those whose unfavorable outcomes are responsible for the finding of the statistical correlations. However, they defy this statistical predictive finding and have healthy rather than morbid outcome.

Prevention then assumes another responsibility. While continuing to avoid, where possible, risk factors from occurring, and while taking measures to minimize the pathological consequences of known risks, there is now added the very important study of the resilient ones, those whose risks have not led to disaster. What are the features of children who, in the presence of known potentials for disaster, have managed nevertheless to sustain healthy development? What are the features of the environment that have potentiated these healthy outcomes? What interactions and mutual influences of child and environment have provided protective and buffering effects? The Clarkes (1984) have provided a tight summation of the task: "So there are at least four interacting and transecting headlines in human development: the biological trajectory, the social trajectory, the effect of the individual on his environment which, by a feedback cycle, acts upon him, and finally the chance event" (p. 194).

The individual whose name stands out as a pioneer investigator who began to focus subject risk and outcome studies on resiliency against misfortune has been Norman Garmezy (Garmezy 1981, 1983; Garmezy & Neuchterlein, 1972). He was among the first to emphasize that, no matter how high the risks, morbid outcome does not reach 100%. It is those whose existence was acknowledged only by the leftover variance after predictive correlations were established who are now receiving the spotlight of attention from an increasing group of investigators. The identification of resiliency and the capacity for effective coping is part of the essence of prevention. Its usefulness lies not in a message for inaction, with the argument that the strong can preserve themselves. Rather, it calls for action to strengthen those features of effective coping in all children so as to lower the power of risk factors to achieve a reality of morbid outcome.

Such longitudinal studies as those by Long and Vaillant (1984), Werner and Smith (1982), and Chess and Thomas (1984) have made possible the identification of both vulnerability and resiliency in individual children. Factors that constitute a risk for one kind of individual may not be so for another with differing personal characteristics or differing environmental milieu. Similarly, the factors that lead to healthy mastery of particular stresses not only differ from group to group, but also from individual to individual. Thus, the very same events that had been identified as significant traumas when a population's outcomes as a group are being studied may have heightened power for one person in the group and given no power at all for another.

These are important facts, and as is so often the case, each new solution brings its new issues. Just as the studies of risk must be subdivided into separate functional factors, so the study of resiliencies must also be examined in terms of the individuals who possess them. It is also possible to conduct a study in which the multiplicity of traumata is correlated with adverse and pathogenic behavioral response. It still remains necessary to examine separately the effects of specific traumata such as parental separation in producing anxiety, social withdrawal, aggressiveness, or academic failure. One would also not expect that the proportions of different symptoms would be the same were the traumatic event to be the catastrophes that accompany war, the consequences of nutritional deprivation, or the effects of ethnic discrimination.

It also remains necessary to separate children into different age and developmental periods, inasmuch as for each traumatic situation cognitive, emotional, and perceptual abilities, as well as past events, will influence the type of behavioral reactions and the potential for healthy mastery. The acuteness or chronicity of adverse circumstances is also an issue. And so are the numerous features of personal individuality: temperament, cognition, prior experience, support systems, and cultural expectations. And, in some situations, certain of these individual factors will be pertinent to the question under examination, while others will be unessential if placed into the equation. We gain new insights from such studies as responses to divorce by Hetherington (1980), and by Wallerstein and Kelly (1980); to the stress of parental conflict by Wallerstein (1983), Chess and colleagues (1983), to psychological health as well as pathology in children with psychotic parents by Graham, Rutter, and George (1973) and Anthony (1974); to firstborn children's reactions to the birth of a sibling (Dunn, Kendrick, & MacNamee, 1981); to familial identification as members of the "underclass" (Long & Vaillant, 1984); to ego control and resiliency by Block and Block (1980); and to the examination of physiological correlates of certain behavioral reactions to stress by Kagan (1983).

In what might at times appear to be a contradiction of neat correlations yet confounding outcomes, we are well advised to keep in mind the Clarkes' commentary noted above.

In a longitudinal study that starts in early infancy and moves into early adult life, it is possible to examine scientific interest in risk issues from a number of vantage points. The New York Longitudinal Study, having followed 133 subjects through this developmental interval, with frequent waves of data collection, has been able to identify quantitative factors in childhood that have led to optimum adult adaptive outcome within the sample as a whole and also those that have potentiated poor adult functioning. It has been of special interest to note those individuals whose adult functioning has defied the group trends, whose early risk features predicted poor adult outcome, but who, nevertheless, had above-average adult adaptation.

THE NEW YORK LONGITUDINAL STUDY

The New York Longitudinal Study (NYLS) was initiated in 1956 for the purpose of studying both normal and problem development in the members of its cohort. The focus was on individual styles of behavior, the *how*, rather than the *what* (capacities) or the *why* (motivations). It had appeared to the founders of the study, Drs. Stella Chess and Alexander Thomas, that individual differences in behavioral styles or temperament had been insufficiently studied with respect to their influence upon developmental outcomes. It was postulated that temperamental individuality resulted in variability in the impact of different events and attitudes upon children; that children's temperamental qualities influenced their caretakers, provoking differing attitudes and experiences for children of different temperaments as a consequence. It was these mutually interacting features of both child and environment, either goodness or poorness of fit, that were postulated to influence the quality of adaptation of children as they went through sequential developmental stages and also fostered the creation of behavior disorder.

As the cohort of 133 individuals moved from infancy through the stages of childhood, adolescence, and now early adulthood, the specific interactions occurring in each individual were recorded. During infancy and the first three years, the basic tool for the gathering of information was parental interviews. These were constructed around functional features of the lives of babies and young children, such as eating, sleeping, being bathed, and, as they grew older, play with children and adults, and speech. The scope of areas covered was extended as the children grew older to conform with their expanded activities and capacities. Interviews were held with both parents every three months at first, starting at two to three months of age. By age three, interviews were carried out at six-month intervals, then at yearly intervals until age eight. During adolescence the subjects were interviewed directly by a time-related interview with the parents covering similar material. At ages 18 to 22, the most recent interview was held with all of the 133 subjects and, with their permission, with their parents—again covering similar areas.

The validity of the early parental interviews was confirmed by comparison with time-related observations in the home in 22 subjects, each designed so as to permit rating of seven of the nine temperamental qualities that had emerged from the original interview data by inductive content analysis. Confirmatory qualitative direct observations also occurred during the interviewing, which was done at the subjects' homes for the most part. At ages three and six, all subjects were administered a standard intelligence test plus several additional tasks specifically designed to bring out styles of problem solving. A subgroup was also given intelligence tests at age 11, when academic functioning was also assessed. Each child whose parents had behavioral concerns that merited clinical study was given a full diagnostic workup by myself and, where indicated, a clinical diagnosis was made. Whenever parents wished advice on their handling of a child, whether the youngster was a clinical problem or not, such advice was given and followed up both short-term and a year after the last clinical contact. All children with behavior disorder at any time were followed up as frequently as was required, and during the adolescent and early adulthood interviews as well.

Data on parental attitudes and practices were obtained both from the routine interviews and from a specially designed parent discussion when the child was age three. The three-year-old special parent interview was carried out by two investigators who had not otherwise been involved in the study, who talked simultaneously with each parent in separate rooms so as to ensure that the opinion of each would be independent.

The nine temperamental characteristics derived from the early interviews and rated in all later inquiries are:

1. Activity Level

This category describes the level, tempo, and frequency with which a motor component is present in the child's functioning, providing individual scores ranging from low, through moderate, to high activity level.

2. Rhythmicity

Scoring for this category was based upon the degree of rhythmicity or regularity of repetitive biological functions. Information regarding sleep-wake cycles, restful and active periods, hunger and extent of appetite, and bowel and bladder function were all used in the scoring. Ratings extend from highly regular, through variable, to highly irregular and unpredictable.

3. Approach or Withdrawal

This rates the child's initial reaction to any new stimulus, be it food, people, places, toys, or procedures. Behaviors in this category range from high approach to the new, through moderate or variable movement toward, to high withdrawal from stimuli.

4. Adaptability

When considering adaptability, one is concerned with the sequential course of responses a child makes to new or altered situations. In contrast to the previous category, it is not the initial response that is scored but rather the ease or difficulty with which the initial pattern of response can be altered in the direction desired by the parents or others.

5. Intensity of Response

In this category interest is directed to the energy content of the response, irrespective of its direction. Thus, whether the mood be positive or negative, the intensity level may range from highly intense, through moderate intensity, to mild energy level of expressiveness.

6. Threshold of Responsiveness

Interest here is in the level of extrinsic stimulation that is necessary to evoke a discernible response. It is irrelevant to scoring whether the response be approaching or withdrawing, mild or intense. The rating of high, medium, or low reflects the intensity of stimulus required to evoke a response.

7. Quality of Mood

Rated here is the amount of pleasant, joyful, friendly behavior as contrasted with unpleasant, crying, and unfriendly actions. In scoring mood quality, the intensity is not taken into consideration. Scoring ranges from highly positive to highly negative.

8. Distractibility

This category refers to the effectiveness of extraneous environmental stimuli in interfering with, or in altering the direction of, ongoing activity. Ratings range from highly distractible, through moderately or inconsistently so, to highly undistractible.

9. Attention Span and Persistence

This double area includes two subcategories that are related. Attention span refers to the length of time a particular activity is pursued, and must be judged in terms of the child's age and the average attention span typical of such age. Ratings range from long attention span, through average, to short attention span. Persistence indicates the child's maintaining an activity in the face of obstacles to its continuation. Thus, a child may be highly persistent in task accomplishment along with long attention span, but might also be distracted from the task yet return to it periodically and highly persistently until it has been accomplished. For each of these subcategories, ratings range from high degree of expression, through moderate, to low degree of expression.

In the quantitative analyses our subjects' temperamental qualities were placed on a continuum from easy temperament to difficult temperament. The easy temperament cluster includes high regularity; high degree of approach; quick adaptability; low or moderate intensity of mood expressiveness; and predominance of positive mood. By contrast, difficult temperament is defined as the clustering that includes high irregularity; high degree of withdrawal from new situations, people, and objects; slow adaptability; high intensity of mood expressiveness; and predominance of negative mood. While this continuum fails to take into account other clusters, for the purposes of quantitative analyses this organization of data has been highly useful. Consideration of the richness of other aspects of temperamental individuality required qualitative examination.

Data on these temperamental qualities were obtained not only from parent interviews, but also from teacher interviews and school observations each year of nursery school and kindergarten and the first three years of grade school.

Quantitative Analysis of Data

In order to examine features of earlier functioning that made for high, moderate, or low risk for later disordered behavior, a number of ratings were made. Those relevant for this discussion included:

a) adaptation at age three;
b) difficult to easy temperament on a continuum at age three;
c) presence of a behavior disorder at various ages of childhood and adolescence;
d) degree of parental conflict found present at age three;
e) degree of parental permissiveness reported at age three;
f) divorce or death of parents before age 12.

For outcome measures in early adulthood, ratings included:

a) adult adaptation;
b) difficult to easy temperament on a continuum;
c) presence of a clinical diagnosis.

Both multiple regression and set correlation analyses identified difficult-easy temperament at age three and parental conflict at age three to be significantly correlated with early adult adjustment. Parental divorce, after partialing out the effect of parental conflict, was not a significant risk factor nor was parental permissiveness versus nonpermissiveness. Thus, the three-year-olds with both difficult temperament and marked parental conflict should be at high risk for unfavorable outcome in early adult life.

Since risk means a potentiality and not a fixed irrevocable fate, it is of interest to identify those subjects at high risk who, nevertheless, achieved good adult functioning. By examining features of the lives of these subjects and finding what types of interactions, relationships, and/or fortuitous happenings proved either to be long-term buffering features or unanticipated events creating beneficial turning points, one can gain an understanding of those seemingly invulnerable individuals who have appeared in study after study flouting the voice of doom. Thus, in the NYLS we identified the subjects who were in the extreme quartiles for both difficult temperament and high severity of parental conflict but yet in adult life scored above 6.01, the median adjustment score for our sample in the adult period.

First, some comments are in order on the group trends that appeared in our high risk group. For the NYLS in toto, 43% had developed a behavior disorder at some period in childhood or adolescence, with an overall average age of onset of seven years. (Most of these cases were mild and would probably not have been identified if the children had not been subjects in our longitudinal study.) The five high-risk subjects, in contrast, had an 80% rate of behavior disorder, with four years as their average age of onset. Further, while there were no significant sex differences in the overall NYLS sample, for this high risk group, four out of five subjects were male. There was also a predominance of males in the intermediate risk group with easy temperament but high parental conflict—but no sex differences in the intermediate group with difficult temperament but low parental conflict. These data, although the numbers are small, tend to be in agreement with those of Hetherington (1980), and of Wallerstein and Kelly (1980) that boys are more vulnerable to parental conflict than girls.

Qualitative Examples of High-Risk Subjects with Good Outcome

Michael was interviewed at age 22. From this interview, an adult adjustment rating score of 6.21 was given him. While this score is not dramatically above the median adjustment score of 6.01, this relatively good outcome is of importance in view of his status as a high-risk subject. With temperament ratings in the difficult cluster each year throughout child-hood, Michael was diagnosed to have an Adjustment Disorder at age four. The major symptom area was nursery school where he was a non-participant, withdrawn, slowly adaptive, with a mixture of low- and high-key intensity of responses. The high parental conflict was identified from the three-year-old independent parental interviews and confirmed by Michael himself during the early adult interview at age 22. At that time he recalled his parents' relationship to have been volatile with much overt conflict.

The nursery school problem had appeared to be independent of the parental friction and related to the poorness of fit between Michael's temperamental qualities and the demands of school adjustment. Falling into the difficult child group, albeit with variability of intensity of mood expressiveness from high to low, Michael had always withdrawn from new experiences, adapted only after a long-drawn-out period, and shown pre-dominance of negative mood. Rhythmicity had been variable. At the be-ginning of the previous nursery school year at age three, he had remained at the periphery of the group for many weeks and then gradually had become a participator. His parents were not surprised when Michael, at age four, once again showed a reluctant school beginning, but had ex-pected that, as before, he would gradually adapt. However, at age three he had had very few illnesses, and adaptation had been aided by the regular-ity of the school experience. In contrast, at age four Michael suffered from upper respiratory infections with great frequency and each had a long duration. Thus, he attended school for one week and then was out for two. On each return to school his behavior reverted to that which had characterized his initial sideline watching and nonparticipation. By mid-winter the nursery school teacher had become quite concerned over this failure of adaptation and participation, and concluded that Michael was an anxious child who needed psychiatric treatment.

It was at this time that Michael's parents initiated the clinical consulta-tion. They were surprised particularly at the contrast between the child's behavior at nursery school and at the neighborhood playground, which could be seen from his bedroom window. With an older sister and brother, Michael's mother had used this playground frequently, and Michael, from his carriage days, had been taken to this playground many times each week. When he had begun to walk and to use the equipment himself, he had appeared at ease, and at age four, despite the nursery school timidity, his behavior when at the playground continued to be free, sociable, and zestful. In fact, this contrast of behavioral style in these two contexts contributed to an understanding of the sources of his problem.

In the clinical interview, Michael was initially very shy, refusing to come into the playroom. When his mother was invited to enter and inspect the toys, Michael trailed her and remained in close proximity, wordless. I had asked the mother to bring from home a favorite toy, and when I asked whether I might see it, a small hand emerged from behind her protective barrier and handed me a paper bag. I examined the snap-together large beads and began manipulating them, making obvious and clumsy mistakes. Michael darted out and said, "You do it like this," and began demonstrating. After a few moments of cooperative interaction, he suddenly became aware of his stance and quickly retired again behind his mother. However, through similar opportunities for modest approaches and easily available withdrawals, gradually the two of us became engaged in several activities with verbal interactions mounting in quality and friendliness. Although not totally at ease after an hour, when I stated that we must now replace the toys since it was time for him to leave, Michael flung himself against his mother's chest and whispered in her ear, gesturing at the interviewer, and then waited for her to transmit his message. This was an urgent request to stay longer so that he could continue to play.

Thus, in the microcosm of the office evaluation, Michael had demonstrated both his initial high withdrawal with negative mood and his ability to adapt, albeit slowly. He had also demonstrated that, with adaptation, there was a rising positive involvement and zest to his play and sociability. Further, given this opportunity for gradual familiarization, there had been no indication of anxiety, although there had been watchful wariness initially. While the colds had interfered with visiting the neighborhood playground as much as with nursery attendance, since Michael could monitor the activity of the playground from his bedroom window, his return to the playground had not included the loss of familiarity, as had been the case with interrupted nursery school attendance.

Full clinical history failed to reveal any indices of anxiety in home behavior. There were no regressions of skills, no language regression or other speech difficulties; neither fears nor nightmares had put in appearance. The clinical judgment was, therefore, that this was an Adjustment Disorder, in which, due to temperamental qualities, the episodic nursery school attendance and the pressure there to participate quickly in planned activities constituted a psychosocial stressor. Soon there was to be a winter recess, and then in several weeks spring would be coming. It

was suggested that with the warm weather Michael's respiratory infections would disappear and his school attendance would then become
regular. Familiarity would grow and nonparticipation would end, since
the excessive stress would have terminated. And, indeed, this proved to
be the case.

In middle childhood, Michael's functioning was good. He attended the
same neighborhood school throughout, and although the initial phase of
each school year was characterized by subdued or complaining attitude,
this lasted a shorter and shorter time with each passing year. Since there
was no family move, the school building and his schoolmates remained
unchanged, so that no major new adaptations had been required of him.
The move from grade school to the junior high school building had been
in the company of the same group of children. Although other schools
also fed into this junior high school with the addition of new schoolmates, the pattern of learning expectations had not altered in their essence and the presence of his old friends were buffering aspects of the
new areas of demand for adaptation.

In adolescence, matters changed. He had been, in his own words, "at
the tail end of the counterculture" but had managed nevertheless to be
caught up in it. By age 16, Michael was experimenting with marijuana,
cocaine, LSD, and other drugs. While one might think that, due to his
withdrawal from the new, he might have some protection from the lure
of drug experimentation, one must also take into account that adolescents are highly conforming—that is, to the behaviors regarded as praise-
worthy by other adolescents. Thus, with ample opportunity to watch
peers experiment and to gain familiarization with first the idea and then
the experience of being spaced out, Michael became involved to an ominous degree. School grades suffered, relationships with his parents deteriorated as a consequence, and confrontations becoming an increasingly
characteristic part of home life. At the urgent request of his parents, a
full clinical study was done. Not only did Michael's functioning indicate a
behavior problem, it was also in marked contrast to that of his highly
respected father and his well-functioning older brother and sister. A
diagnosis of Avoidant Disorder of Adolescence was made. Psychotherapy was recommended but refused by Michael. It was not forced on him
inasmuch as, without his motivation for treatment, or at least acquies-
cence, psychotherapy could not be useful. Treatment sessions would
have become in essence a further battleground of confrontation.

At the time of the young adult interview, at 22, we found a remarkable
change. One is reminded here of the Clarkes' fourth point, "the chance
event." An interest in music, which had begun at age nine but, at that

age, without any remarkable qualities, had now turned into talent, which Michael was pursuing seriously. Whether talent is to be classified as a chance event may be debatable, but it is a feature of competence that is unpredictable and, unlike mere routine performance, not to be acquired by practice alone. In Michael's case, awareness of his high level of ability and its recognition by others and their admiration of it and him led to high motivation and enjoyment. This led to a desire to study in a conservatory of music, which was backed by his parents. When we interviewed him at age 22, he was working toward a degree in music with evidence of successful functioning in his studies. He had now made friends amongst those with interests similar to his own. Since his musical direction was not that which any of his family had followed, he now had a place of respect that was entirely his own. His social life and sexual experiences were both fulfilling. Although supported in tuition and major living expenses by his parents, Michael had held several part-time jobs. He reported that he still experienced stress and uneasiness in new situations, especially when performing. With his high motivation, however, he had learned to persevere until at ease. This sequence had become an acquired pattern through which he achieved adaptation to circumstances he judged worthy of special effort. It was evident during the interview that Michael had acquired social charm and grace. Indeed, Michael indicated a substantial measure of self-esteem, declaring that he now liked himself, respected himself, and was respected by others.

The correlation of holding a job during adolescence with positive adult functioning has been indicated in the work of Long and Vaillant (1984) for youths from families identified as belonging to the "underclass" who, from a predictive point of view, would have been expected to function marginally at best in adult life. In Michael's case no such dramatic issue of class membership existed. Nevertheless, if the decision to earn money and become self-supporting by one's own efforts is an indicator of self-respect, this goal was a fact of Michael's late adolescent and young adult functioning. The development of special talent provided the opportunity for him to regain the self-respect that had been eroding during the period of "counterculture" dedication and the turning of his back upon family standards of academic and behavioral functioning. Of course, talent by itself does not guarantee a dedication to the hard and persistent work needed to make an actuality of the promise. The phenomenon of the promising young man or woman who, with the passage of the years, has turned into the embodiment of lost opportunity is not an unfamiliar one. On the other hand, the almost criminal adolescent or young adult or would-be family parasite whose newly discovered unusual abilities point to a way out of a vicious cycle of downward spiraling functioning is also a well-known, if less common, phenomenon.

That such a benign outcome may be impossible without some special feature to lift the individual out of a deteriorating developmental course has also been exemplified in the NYLS sample. This was the case of Norman, with easy temperament and high parental conflict. With a mild Adjustment Disorder in childhood, beginning at age four, the temperamental qualities that contributed to a poorness of fit between himself and his parents were those of short attention span and high distractibility. Although actual academic functioning in middle childhood was adequate, from the very beginning of school the parental demand for dedicated studying with lengthy attention span and low distractibility acted as a severe psychosocial stressor for this child. Self-respect grew less and less, as attested by such statements as "My father doesn't respect me, and let's face it, why should he?" Depressed in adolescence, by young adulthood Norman had thrown off the depression by means of massive denial. Although a repeated college dropout, and with jobs requiring minimum skill held just long enough to merit unemployment insurance after achieving the necessary status of being fired, Norman reported great expectations just around the corner. He described an assortment of itemized pipe dreams, revolving primarily around musical talent which he intended to work at when he got around to it. His plans for exploitation of this talent were clearly grandiose and unrealistic and never came to fruition. Norman's life in fact was parasitic, which he maintained by a charm that was disarming and highly useful in freeloading on relatives and friends.

Whether or not Norman did in fact have musical talent is unknown. He may have been as talented as Michael. What was clear was that he was unable to work at developing his potential. As a child he was capable of good functioning. Had there not been the continuous psychosocial stressor of rigid demands and expectations that were unattainable in view of his temperamental cluster, he most probably would have pursued a positive developmental course. Instead, his inability to meet his parents' standards led to increasing self-devaluation and pessimism within himself with regard to any substantial work achievement. A self-fulfilling prophecy was achieved, with retreat into parasitism and massive defensive denial.

The contrast with Michael is striking. Both young men had intellectual levels well above average, so this was not a confounding factor. Indeed, Norman had been accepted by, and then dropped out of, a prestigious college. But actually his family had pressured him into applying, against his attempts to delay past the deadline. By contrast, Michael's application to the conservatory had been his own decision, and he had worked hard to attain it. Basic to the difference in their functioning in adult life was the continuous erosion of self-respect Norman suffered through his parents' destructively critical attitudes. Michael, on the other hand, had a positive developmental course through middle childhood. Even though his adolescence was stormy, unhealthy, and filled with conflict with his parents, once he set his goal on a musical career and began to work seriously to accomplish this, he gained his parents' support and respect, as well as his own self-respect. One can say that Michael and Norman's contrasting attitudes toward work were the result of their own levels of self-respect and their family attitudes, and at the same time helped to shape their self-evaluations and family judgments.

Is it still possible that some new chance factor may create a dramatic turnabout in Norman? It seems unlikely, but we still have much to learn about human potential and the factors that unlock it. The interaction of temperament, talent, and motivation with environment is not the only dynamic that shapes life competence.

A second example of a subject with childhood high-risk features but good adult outcome is Stanley. In early adulthood he received an adjustment score of 7.31, well above the median of the total NYLS sample. Despite the high-risk combination of difficult temperament and severe parental conflict at age three, Stanley had never shown symptoms of a behavior disorder either during childhood or in adolescence. From the separate parental attitude interviews done when the children were age three, we had characterized his mother as compulsively intrusive and controlling, while his father had retired from the constant mother–child altercations and in the family context had appeared to be passive and aloof. In the course of the direct adolescent interview, Stanley had confirmed this, commenting upon his parents' many arguments, mostly initiated by his mother. He had indicated also that his mother had a bothersome habit of asking him personal questions about his father and brother. At age 20, he characterized his mother as sarcastic and cynical, but also as talented and bright, while his older brother (also in our study) called their mother controlling, nagging, and intrusive. This older brother, a highly distractible boy, had been throughout childhood and adolescence the target of their mother's ire and energetic venom. She, a clinically compulsive individual, had a distinct poorness of fit with the brother, whose "forgetfulness," really his easy distractibility, had been interpreted by her as deliberate sabotage with intent to make her life miserable. All of our discussions with her did not change this conviction, even though we pointed out the many occasions when he forgot dates he had made with his friends. Stanley, although possessing a difficult temperament, was not distractible and, in his mother's idiosyncratic hierarchy of values, was a model obedient son.

Both brothers had, as soon as their ages permitted, turned their interests and close relationships toward peers and their family groups where they were welcomed. Each had a different circle of friends, and consequently their daily paths diverged. Stanley, throughout middle childhood and adolescence, spent as much time as he could outside of the family, although, when at home, interactions were reasonably peaceful, but not important to him.

At the time of the young adult interview, at age 20, although meriting a high adjustment score on the basis of work, friendship patterns, capacity for sexual fulfillment, and goal-directed activity, Stanley remained at a distance from his family. He was friendly with his brother, but not close. He was distinctly emotionally detached from both parents, maintaining the focus of affective relatedness toward peers as in his earlier years. His selection of college and of vocational interests had been arrived at by himself in consultation with those of his friends and their parents whose opinions he valued. Competent, but not possessing any unusual talents, Stanley had achieved a harmony of functioning. Important in this favorable situation had been his ability to distance himself from the distasteful home relationships. Partly, also, he had been buffered by the fact that his brother had absorbed the bulk of their mother's obsessive and intense emotional pressures. Simply keeping his room neat, remembering his homework and dental appointments, and hanging up his jacket had been sufficient to satisfy his mother in her campaign for behavioral conformity. That he was absent from home much of the time had been, for her, no issue. And the father stayed on the sidelines and thus evaded his wife's pressure to enter battle against his sons in support of demands that he himself did not feel to be important. A battle with his mother had been fought by the older brother when he had refused to allow her to know his college plans. When Stanley followed the same strategy, little fuss resulted.

Left alone by this focus on his brother, Stanley had been allowed to make adjustments at his own speed. With consistency of friendships and school settings, new situations had been mastered in the company of friends who were marching to the same tune. Familiarization had permitted initial negative mood reactions to become positive. And high intensity of mood expressiveness had been forgiven him in view of the widespread knowledge of his mother's intrusive behavior, which appeared explanation enough to friends and teachers. With regard to the presence in his life of parents in high conflict, Stanley is one of a number of our subjects who were able to distance themselves from an extremely stressful home environment. Such distancing provided a buffer that was protective of developmental course, of self-esteem, and of ability to acquire constructive goals.

Qualitative Examples of Intermediate High-Risk Subjects

While less dramatic, it is instructive to examine qualitatively the life courses of members of the intermediate-risk subjects with positive adult outcome: those in the extreme quartile for difficult temperament but without parental conflict, or those with extreme parental conflict but with easy temperament. Two such examples will be given.

Kathy, in early adulthood, was second highest in adult adjustment score of the entire NYLS sample, with a rating of 9.49. Her early home adjustment at ages three and five had not been remarkable but at age five her school adjustment score had been notably high. Indeed, teachers from nursery through second grade had all commented upon Kathy's remarkable intellectual ability, her maturity, and her sociability, as well as her helpfulness toward classmates and her popularity with them. Both Kathy and her sister (also a NYLS subject) had characterized their mother as the disciplinarian and their father as trying to be the "good guy." This opinion confirmed the data from the parent attitudes interviews held when each child had become three years old. Kathy had, according to our accumulated data and also in terms of her adult recollection, managed to maintain a positive relationship with both parents. At the same time, she was clear that she had, from very early on, learned to keep an emotional distance from each. Not only did she prefer to spend her time with her friends, but she also turned to them for intimate confidences. This had not caused problems with her parents, each of whom saw her as a private individual who had a right to maintain such privacy, especially as she did so pleasantly. Despite parental differences, by this maneuver of personal distancing from her parents, Kathy had protected herself from the potentially disturbing task of trying to adapt to contradictory parental attitudes. She had not, fortunately, generalized this ability to maintain emotional distance to the outside world. Not only did she have a selection of close friends, but she also had the ability to form satisfying heterosexual relationships. She developed a clear vocational goal requiring dedicated study, and in this also she was succeeding at a high level. In the adult interview, her poise and self-awareness were of note. Her assessments of situations and people have been, so far, quite accurate, and her resources for both self-protection and openness were selective and uninhibited.

Another of our young women subjects, Laura, was in the intermediate-risk group in view of difficult temperament but low conflict between her parents. At the time of her early adult interview her adaptation merited a rating of 7.91. At age seven, Laura had been diagnosed as having a mild Adjustment Disorder. Characteristic of her difficult temperament, she flared up quickly over minor as well as major disappointments, and each new event or set of demands led to high and noisy withdrawal. This in itself did not constitute the Adjustment Disorder, but when there was negative feedback from classmates and fears developed, these were of sufficient dimension to be classified as a clinical problem.

Matters were not helped by the fact of her mother's severe psychiatric disorder, which included multiple suicide attempts, usually with an accusatory element as to the individual and actions that "made her" want to end her life. Both parents did make great efforts to keep Laura from feeling that she contributed in any way toward the mother's self-destructive actions. However, the home atmosphere was always a tense one, as these maternal suicide attempts kept occurring and the father tried unsuccessfully to monitor the presence of sedatives in life-threatening quantities. He was also conciliatory and overprotective toward his wife, and Laura resented his admonitions to keep from upsetting her mother. At the same time, she wondered whether she bore any responsibility for her mother's suicidal attempts, which sometimes followed closely upon altercations between her mother and herself. Although Laura did have some reasonably good friendships, these were not sufficiently close or trusting to become her sources of positive psychological support. On the other hand, one of Laura's older sisters, who was very aware of the stresses at home, acted as a surrogate mother, and buffered Laura as best she could against these tensions, and did become to some extent her confidante.

At the time of the adolescent interview, Laura's clinical status had worsened and she was given the diagnosis of Adjustment Disorder of Adolescence. Her mother's suicidal episodes had not only continued, but also became more frequent, and when she finally drowned in her bath when Laura was still a teenager, it was not certain whether she had been confused by an overdose of sedation or had had an independent cardiac episode but was unable to get help. She was found dead by another family member just as Laura was returning home from school. Subsequently, after several years, her father remarried. Laura and her sisters had a stormy relationship with their stepmother and this marriage, for independent reasons, as well as the rift in what had been close daughter-father relationships, ended in divorce.

During these stressful events, Laura's functioning deteriorated. She moved into significant experimentation in drug use, her academic interests waned, and her achievement level fell. Relationships with peers was indifferent to bad. Her older sister, however, remained a supportive influence, and her father, through all his troubles, remained dedicated to Laura's interests and there was mutual warmth between them. Many somatic symptoms such as chronic back pain were persistent and no organic bases had been found.

By early adulthood, Laura had recovered from her clinical psychiatric disorder. She was now pursuing a vocational goal of her own choosing and one that had the respect of father and older sisters. To gain the training needed, Laura had improved her scholarship and had been admitted to the specialized training where she was functioning satisfactorily. Although there had been several earlier unsatisfactory heterosexual relationships, she was now positively involved with a young man whom she later married. The pains and aches had receded. Indeed, had they remained, she would not have been able to move into her self-selected field. Laura had received psychotherapy for a period during middle childhood, with good response. With the reappearance of symptoms, psychotherapy had been resumed during adolescence, but with minimal response and much resentment. It was, therefore, terminated at that time.

In older adolescence, following her own formulation of a vocational goal and desire for a different lifestyle, Laura herself requested psychotherapy. This was instituted, but with a different therapist, so as to avoid a recurrence of her earlier negativistic reaction to therapy. Psychotherapy this time met with Laura's active cooperative participation in gaining insight and changing her maladaptive behavior. A progressive rise in adaptive functioning followed, until, at age 22, her level of adaptation was judged to be well above average. There had been, in fact, several fortuitous meetings with me between the formal data-gathering procedure of adolescence and that of early adulthood. In these meetings, Laura had been friendly and affectionate, and had reported her growing interests with pleasure. It was evident that she was ready to learn what was necessary in order to fulfill her own standards of functioning. Thus, we were aware that her positive change in early adulthood had not been a sudden conversion, but rather the result of a gradual process of change and a growing sense of inner strength and direction. All of this had received enthusiastic support from Laura's family. Further, in the course of her training and her awareness of the type of functioning her profession would require, she had simultaneously been making a determined effort to curb the outward expression of intense negative initial reactions. She had succeeded in establishing a benign cycle, in which positive functioning stimulated new positive efforts, and success of effort led to further positive functioning accompanied by a growing self-esteem and awareness that she had truly earned the respect of others. With all of the psychosocial stressors evident in the case of Laura, the basic love and support of family members had been a powerful force in retarding the negative influence of difficult temperament.

Such dramas have been better told by novelists like George Eliot, whose insights have preceded by many decades the New York Longitudinal Study. In the final chapter of *Middlemarch*, aptly called "Finale," George Eliot (1872) says, "Every limit is a beginning as well as an ending. Who can quit young lives after being long in company with them, and not desire to know what befell them in their after-years? For the fragment of a life, however typical, is not the sample of an even web. Promises may not be kept, and an ardent outset may be followed by declension; latent powers may find their long-awaited opportunity; a past error may urge a grand retrieval" (p. 573).

Although, like George Eliot, we have difficulty in quitting young lives with which we have been long in contact, there is nevertheless a limit, in view of our own mortality, in knowing what their full after-years will bring. Nevertheless, Michael, Stanley, Kathy, Laura, and others of our sample have a message of use to our professions. When asked to help a youngster in trouble, our efforts now have a greater assurance. The choice of a therapeutic strategy, of course, is still determined by the specific factors of each individual case. But we now have a stronger belief in the power of reinforcement of work dedication, whether it be a direction of interest or a spectacular talent. There is also a time to lean heavily on familial support, but there is also in certain circumstances a high virtue in distancing from noxious familial onslaughts and underminings, in leaving behind irreconcilable conflicts, and in substituting alternative constructive social involvements which have the power to protect and to provide a second—or even a third—chance.

REFERENCES

ANTHONY, E.J. (1974). The syndrome of the psychologically invulnerable child. In E.J. Anthony & C. Koupernik (Eds.), *The Child in His Family: Children at Psychiatric Risk*. New York: John Wiley.

BLOCK, J.H., & BLOCK, J.G. (1980). The role of ego-control and ego-resiliency in the organization of behavior. In W.A. Collins (Ed.), *Development of Cognition, Affect and Social Relations. The Minnesota Symposium on Child Psychology (Vol. 13).* Hillsdale, N.J.: Lawrence Erlbaum Associates.

CHESS, S., & THOMAS, A. (1984). *Origins and Evolution of Behavior Disorders: From Infancy to Early Adult Life.* New York: Brunner/Mazel.

CHESS, S., THOMAS A., MITTELMAN, M., KORN, S., & COHEN, J. (1983). Early parental attitudes, divorce and separation, and young adult outcome: Findings of a longitudinal study. *Journal of the American Academy of Child Psychiatry, 22*(1): 47–51.

CLARKE, A.D.B., & CLARKE, A.M. (1984). Constancy and change in the growth of human characteristics. *Journal of Child Psychology, Psychiatry, 25*(2): 191–210.

DUNN, J., KENDRICK, C., & MacNAMEE, R. (1981). The reaction of first-born children to the birth of a sibling: Mother's reports. *Journal of Child Psychology, Psychiatry, 22:* 1–18.

ELIOT, G. (1872). *Middlemarch.* New York: W.W. Norton, 1977.

GARMEZY, N. (1981). Children under stress: Perspectives on antecedents and correlates of vulnerability and resistance to psychopathology. In A.I. Rabin, J. Aronoff, A.M. Barclay, & R.A. Zucker (Eds.), *Further Explorations in Personality.* New York: John Wiley.

GARMEZY, N. (1983). Stressors of childhood. In N. Garmezy & M. Rutter (Eds.), *Stress, Coping, and Development in Children.* New York: McGraw-Hill.

GARMEZY, N., & NEUCHTERLEIN, K. (1972). Invulnerable children: The fact and fiction of competence and disadvantage. *American Journal of Orthopsychiatry, 42:* 328–329.

GRAHAM, P., RUTTER, M., & GEORGE, S. (1973). Temperament characteristics as predictors of behavior disorders in children. *American Journal of Orthopsychiatry, 43:* 328–339.

HETHERINGTON, E.M. (1980). Children and divorce. In R. Henderson (Ed.), *Parent-Child Interaction: Theory, Research, and Prospect.* New York: Academic Press.

KAGAN, J. (1983). Stress and coping in early development. In N. Garmezy & M. Rutter (Eds.), *Stress, Coping and Development in Children.* New York: McGraw-Hill.

LONG, J.V.F., & VAILLANT, G. (1984). Natural history of male psychological health. XI: Escape from the underclass. *American Journal of Psychiatry, 141:* 341–346.

RUTTER, M. (1983). Stress, coping and development: Some issues and some questions. In N. Garmezy & M. Rutter (Eds.), *Stress, Coping and Development in Children.* New York: McGraw-Hill.

WALLERSTEIN, J.S. (1983). Children of divorce: The psychological tasks of the child. *American Journal of Orthopsychiatry, 53*(2): 230–243.

WALLERSTEIN, J.S., & KELLY, J.B. (1980). *Surviving the Break-up: How Children and Parents Cope with Divorce.* New York: Basic Books.

WERNER, E.E., & SMITH, R.S. (1982). *Vulnerable but Invincible: A Study of Resilient Children.* New York: McGraw-Hill.

10

Escape from the Underclass

JANCIS V.F. LONG and GEORGE E. VAILLANT

Among the most at-risk children in our society are those born to conditions of entrenched urban poverty. The ominous word "underclass" is being increasingly used to describe this significant population, characterized by chronic underemployment and often affected by chaotic family life, alcoholism, drug use, criminality, or mental illness. It is the latest name for an old concern: the problem of a permanent, irreversibly impoverished social stratum whose sins of omission and commission toward its children guarantee psychological unpreparedness for self-improvement. Simultaneously, society's attitudes toward this population guarantee fewer improvement opportunities than society provides the rest of its members. For while it is agreed that individuals born at the bottom of the social hierarchy face almost insuperable barriers to upward mobility, the idea that their own moral failings keep them in poverty appears as strongly today as it has for two centuries.

Early in the nineteenth century, distinctions were already being made between "paupers"—those apathetically adapted to poverty—and the

---

The material in this chapter is revised with permission from *The American Journal of Psychiatry, 141*(3), 341–346, March 1984. Copyright 1984, The American Psychiatric Association.

"poor," who strove through hard work to minimize it. Later, Marx's "lumpenproletariat" and the "undeserving poor" of Victorian England foreshadowed the more recent conceptions of the "hard to reach," and "lower lower classes," and the "unstable poor." Although each label had a slightly different connotation, they had in common the idea of a problematic, disreputable class who differed in attitude and opportunity from the "honest," "hardworking," "socially conscious," "stable" working class (Matza, 1966). In the early 20th century, there was said to be a class of people "without self respect and ambition, who rarely if ever worked, who are aimless and drifting, who like drink, who have no thought for their children" (Hunter, 1912, p. 18). In 1970 a similar characterization described an underclass "lacking the education and the skills and other personality traits they need in order to become effectively in demand in the modern economy" (Myrdal, 1970, p. 32).

Auletta (1982) has described a small group of hard-core welfare recipients in New York City whose extreme alienation and hopelessness an educational program was trying to remedy. Despite the vivid humanity of the participants, a generally despairing view emerged of recalcitrant poverty, criminality, and personal chaos. The impression inexorably builds of an entrenched underclass who have at best sporadic employment, long stretches of dependence on public welfare, unstable family life, unreliable working habits, and a disproportionate incidence of criminality, alcoholism, and drug abuse.

While it is well-known that some children emerge intact from the worst backgrounds, research and experience demonstrate the strong tendency for underclass families to reproduce their hopelessness, alienation, and antisocial behavior. Such traits obviously tend to produce poor school performance and poor work attitudes, thus supporting the notion of a self-perpetuating "culture of poverty" (Lewis, 1964). But what is happening here? How can we disentangle the psychological disadvantages conveyed by the underclass child's family from the acquired disadvantages of poor neighborhoods, inadequate schools, and a job market that discriminates against the impoverished urban teenager? The fact is that despite increasing work (Grinker & Sviridoff, 1980; Rutter & Madge, 1975) to assemble and quantify our knowledge of the effects on adult lives of various kinds of childhood, some reported elsewhere in this volume that the parameters are still unclear.

This chapter presents information we feel to be relevant to understanding family versus social influences on the life course. It derives from a study of an underclass sample chosen prospectively who appeared by midlife to have overcome the comparative disadvantage of their childhood. Although when chosen for a longitudinal study at 14 they lived in families characterized by chronic unemployment and a variety of other deeply unfavorable conditions, by the age of 47 the majority had attained the same levels of occupational success and psychological well-being of other members of the study whose parents had been members of the more stable and steadily employed urban working class. While the results of this study we feel are optimistic in demonstrating that not only the exceptions, but the majority of an underclass childhood population *can* achieve upward mobility, the major interest of the chapter may lie in what can be learned from considering the factors that may have allowed this particular cohort to escape.

METHOD

A longitudinal prospective study established by Glueck and Glueck (1950) in 1940 made it possible to compare midlife outcomes for children from more and less disadvantaged working-class homes. Glueck and Glueck had selected a sample of 456 Boston inner-city junior high school youths (ages 12–16 years) as a nondelinquent control group for their study of an equal number of boys remanded to reform school. Half the sample came from homes lacking hot water, central heat, a bathroom, or an inside toilet. Few parents had white-collar work, and fewer could be called middle-class. Their selection for nondelinquency (the delinquent counterparts were not followed beyond young adulthood) meant that this sample does not represent boys who had been arrested prior to 14 or those considered by teachers to be in the most delinquent fifth of their classes. But because they lived in poor neighborhoods and were selected for average or lower IQ (mean = 94) they did not include those members of their class most likely to achieve upward mobility through attendance at the elite Boston public high schools. Eventually, 19% of these nondelinquent subjects spent at least one night in jail and 7% met Robins' (1966) criteria for sociopathy. The major way in which this sample was not representative of the entire urban poor of Boston at that time is that it was male and white. Most members of this sample were reinterviewed when they were in their early twenties and early thirties (Glueck & Glueck, 1968). When they were approximately 47 years old, extensive data were gathered on 87% of the original sample, and the majority were reinterviewed (Vaillant, 1983; Vaillant & Milofsky, 1980; Vaillant & Vaillant, 1981).

To compare the experiences of the "underclass" in this sample with the "working class," four family categories were identified based solely on the ratings of childhood family conditions: 1) chronically dependent (N=71), meaning that family income had been provided mainly through social agencies for several years; 2) multiproblem (N=75), men from families that manifested 10 or more problems on a 25-item scale (Glueck & Glueck, 1950)—representative problems included dependence on nine or more social agencies, early loss of a parent, parental cruelty, criminality, mental deficiency, neglect, and frequent moves (34 men met the criteria for inclusion in both groups); 3) nondependent, nonproblem (N=344), all the men who did not come from dependent or multi-problem families; and 4) a subcategory of the preceding group, class V nondependent, nonproblem (N=86), the men whose families were from social class V (Hollingshead & Redlich, 1958) but who did not meet the criteria for the problem groups.

Raters blind to the childhood data rated these four groups as adults in terms of socioeconomic measures and measures of criminality and global mental health. They used Hollingshead and Redlich's (1958) method of assigning weights to different levels of education, income, and quality of residence to divide the men into five social classes. In general, members of class V were defined by having completed less than 10 grades of education, being unemployed or unskilled laborers, and living in slum housing. Robins' (1966) 19-point scale, which measures delinquent, cruel, antisocial, rebellious, and grossly impulsive behavior from life history data, was used to assess sociopathic symptoms. A global mental health rating was made according to Luborsky's Health-Sickness Rating Scale (HSRS) (Luborsky, 1962). This instrument uses 34 case illustrations to assist raters in placing subjects on a 100-point continuum ranging from total institutional dependency to absence of psychological dysfunction. Life history data, psychiatric records, evidence of social integration, and statements of inner well-being or discomfort were used to make the assessment. Multiple replications have shown this technique to be very reliable (Luborsky & Bachrack, 1974). Months spent in jail and percentage of life spent unemployed at ages 25, 32, and 47 were estimated from interviews with the men or with family members and from the men's criminal records. Further descriptions of the measures and assessment methods are available elsewhere (Vaillant, 1983; Vaillant & Milofksy, 1980; Vaillant & Vaillant, 1981).

RESULTS

When the subjects were children, the intergroup differences were very clear; the two most socially disadvantaged groups manifested more problems of every kind (see Table 1). Descriptions of these homes in the research notes included many such entries as: "Home is in a huge tenement block, rubbish and garbage block the hallways"; "Home is little more than a place to hang one's hat. Parents are highly incompatible, much quarrelling, screaming, and physical force"; "Father has had 31 arrests for alcoholism, mother is dirty and lacking self-respect"; "Police believe parents not competent to care for children"; "Family lives by bootlegging."

Table 2 shows that by age 47 the children of chronically dependent and multiproblem families were, by the measures used, almost indistinguishable from those without such initial disadvantages. This was true for income, employment, and global mental health. Criminality showed a slight association with multiproblem-family membership. Thus, by these measures, a majority of the children of the underclass fared as well as the children of stable working-class parents. Unemployment and being on welfare at midlife were infrequent exceptions, not the rule. For the 64 men whose family data are shown in Table 1 but who, due to attrition, are excluded from Table 2, we had complete mortality data, fairly comparable arrest records, and data on 50% for sociopathy and social class. Unfavorable factors among these men were statistically high, but in absolute terms they would not amount to more than about four excess deaths and four excess cases of sociopathy or membership as an adult in social class V.

Although there was no significant difference in average adult social class attainment among the populations studied, the distribution of adult social class was not without some parental influence (see Table 3). First, fewer dependent and multiproblem family offspring left class V than did those from class V families who were not so disadvantaged (see Table 3). All three groups (dependent, multiproblem, and class V origin) sent fewer children into the white-collar ranks of class III and above than did the remainder of the sample.

Although the focus of this paper is the experience of a class rather than on individually different experiences within the group, it is interesting to note some of the factors that seemed to promote upward and downward mobility. Both childhood IQ ($r=.34$) and childhood coping skills—a measure of social, family, and school integration (Vaillant & Milofsky, 1980)—($r=.25$) correlated with upward social mobility signifi-

TABLE 1*

Characteristics of Chronically Dependent, Multiproblem, Nonproblem, and Class V Nonproblem Families

	Type of Family									
Characteristic	Chronically Dependent (N=71)		Multiproblem (N=75)		Nondependent Nonproblem (N=344)		Class V Nondependent Nonproblem (N=86)		All Families (N=456)	
	N	%	N	%	N	%	N	%	N	%
Alcoholism in immediate family	28	39	44	58	58	17	16	19	109	24
Delinquency in immediate family	4	6	14	18	17	5	2	2	27	6
Mental illness in immediate family	4	6	7	10	7	2	3	3	14	3
Chronic economic dependency	71	100	34	45	0		0		71	16
Multiproblem family	34	48	75	100	0		0		75	16
Poor budget planning	49	69	60	80	124	36	37	43	205	45
Dropout, death, or too few data[a]	13	18	22	29	34	10	8	9	64	14

[a] These data refer to the men, not their families.
*Reprinted with permission from Long & Vaillant (1984), The American Journal of Psychiatry, 141 (3), 341–346. Copyright 1984, The American Psychiatric Association.

TABLE 2*
Midlife Outcomes for Men from Chronically Dependent, Multiproblem, Nonproblem, and Class V Nonproblem Families

Type of Family[b]	Midlife Outcome[a]											
	Social Class (I–V)		Income (1978 dollars)		Percent of Adult Life Employed		Months in Jail		Number of Sociopathic Symptoms		Health-Sickness Rating Scale Score	
	Mean	SD	Mean	SD	Mean	SD	Mean	SD	Mean	SD	Mean	SD
Chronically dependent (N=58)	3.6	.9	15,500	8,700	92.6	17	6	13	2.8	2	73	12
Multiproblem (N=53)	3.8	.7	15,000	8,000	90.1	16	8	10	3.1	2	72	14
Nondependent, nonproblem (N=310)	3.4	.8	15,100	9,000	94.6	12	5	3	2.3	2	75	12
Class V nondependent, nonproblem (N=78)	3.6	.7	14,700	7,400	93.4	15	5	3	2.3	2	73	14
All families (N=392)	3.5	.8	15,600	8,700	93.6	14	5	12	2.4	2	75	13

[a] Differences in midlife outcomes for all the populations and variables in the table were nonsignificant except for months spent in jail, which for men from multiproblem families was significantly higher, $t=3.22$, $p < .001$.

[b] Sample numbers represent those men at age 47 for whom all the variables in the table could be calculated. The differences between these totals and those in Table 1 are a rough measure of attrition from the original sample through death, loss, and refusal to participate, although for some of these subjects partial information was available. The meaning of intergroup differences in attrition rates is discussed in the text.

*Reprinted with permission from Long & Vaillant (1984). *The American Journal of Psychiatry*, 141 (3), 341–346. Copyright 1984, The American Psychiatric Association.

TABLE 3*

Adult Social Class of Men from Chronically Dependent,
Multiproblem, Nonproblem, and Class V Nonproblem Families

Men in Each Type of Family	Classes I and II		Class III		Class IV		Class V	
	N	%	N	%	N	%	N	%
Chronically dependent (N=58)[a]	5	9	19	33	23	39	11	19
Multiproblem (N=53)[a]	4	8	16	30	25	47	8	15
Nondependent, nonproblem (N=310)[a]	31	10	146	47	121	39	12	4
Class V nondependent, nonproblem (N=78)[a]	3	4	31	39	39	50	5	7
All families (N=425)[b]	38	9	179	42	166	39	42	10

[a] For the chronically dependent sample the distribution was significantly different from that of men from nondependent families, x^2=10, df=3, p < .05. For men from multiproblem families the difference was not significant.
[b] The total N is larger here than in Table 2 because information from which social class could be calculated was available for some subjects who could not be interviewed.
*Reprinted with permission from Long & Vaillant (1984), *The American Journal of Psychiatry, 141* (3), 341–346. Copyright 1984, The American Psychiatric Association.

cantly and independently. For the men from dependent and multi-problem families, IQ bore an even stronger relationship to upward social mobility (r=.48 and r=.46, respectively). For men from multiproblem backgrounds, childhood coping skills appeared to be relatively less strongly associated with upward mobility (r=.14). When IQ and child-hood coping skills were held constant, the social class of the subjects' parents did not explain any further variance in the subjects' adult social class. This finding suggested a search for variables that might affect IQ, or mutually affect IQ and upward mobility. However, none of five possi-ble variables checked—Anglo-American ethnicity, English-speaking par-ents, and the absence of familial alcoholism, delinquency, or mental illness—predicted upward mobility or affected IQ scores in this sample.

The *absence* of upward mobility from the lowest socioeconomic level, however, as well as downward drift in this period of overall generational improvement, was unequivocally associated with alcoholism or mental illness, despite the fact that there were also alcoholics among the most upwardly mobile.

Only 19% (N=16) of the men who were in social class V as adults had as children belonged to multiproblem families. In contrast, 41 of the 42 men in class V as adults were alcoholics or mentally ill. Over half of the class V adults suffered two or more of the following: alcoholism, antiso-cial personality, IQ less than 80, disabling physical illness, schizophrenia, or HSRS score of less than 65. Thus, in this cohort—*where racism and high unemployment rates were not factors*—the mechanism for transmitting disad-vantage would seem to be alcoholism, whose heritability among these men has been presented elsewhere (Vaillant, 1983), depression and men-tal retardation. Far from being a self-perpetuating cycle of disadvantage, the underclass of the men's childhood was largely escaped in adulthood, while the most disadvantaged of the adult men had inherited or acquired specific disabilities rather than economic deprivation per se.

Before discussing the relevance of these optimistic results for the vul-nerable children of today's underclass, it is worth noting some of the subjective experiences of the men involved. For them there was nothing automatic about their gradually improving conditions of life. Most recalled years of hardship and hard work. Some had felt keenly the diffi-culties of accepting responsibility as they moved further from the slum environment and accepted work promotions. Others felt, as keenly, the frustration of years of repetitive work and low earnings. Many felt "cheated of a good education." Others pointed, with mixed pride and resentment, to years of night school squeezed between full-time work and family responsibilities. Although the relative advantages enjoyed by their own children were for the most part a profound pleasure to which they could see their own contribution, in some this also stirred up resentment.

In accounting for the capacity of these men not to reproduce their unfavorable childhoods, the men themselves acknowledge a combination of ego strengths and helpful external factors. The capacity to work hard, the desire to excel, a lifetime interest in "finding out how things work," and "shrewd money sense" were different ways men had seen carrying them forward. But a mother who maintains standards, an uncle who substitutes for an absent father and, above all, the character of spouses for those for whom marriage had worked well were subjectively often thought to be key to a man's ability to keep going.

In the subjective as well as the statistical results, the same factor stands out. When opportunity presented itself, either in the form of steady or of upwardly mobile work, the majority of the children of this particular underclass proved to have the ego strengths necessary to avail themselves of it, and to establish homes and lifestyles very different from the chaotic conditions of their youth.

DISCUSSION

At first, the certainty of a self-perpetuating underclass appears so obvious as to require no proof. It seems that deprivations in childhood—which may include malnutrition, abuse, overcrowding, unstable living situations, gross neglect, and inferior education and socialization—can only produce young adults with low levels of education and work skills and with high levels of social distrust, hostility, and alienation. The larger society seems to compound this problem. Schools in the poorest areas are notoriously bad. Discriminatory wages and hiring practices serve to perpetuate disadvantages of upbringing. Social workers, probation officers, and drug counselors know well that their most difficult and disturbing clients frequently come from chaotic homes and provide similarly unfavorable conditions for their own children.

Thus, in the mid-1960s Oscar Lewis introduced the idea of a "culture of poverty" and proposed that a key factor in the transmission of extreme disadvantage was a "design for living which is passed down from generation to generation" (Lewis, 1964, p. 83). Among the traits that Lewis believed were transmitted from one generation to another were inability to save money or defer gratification and "strong feelings of powerlessness, marginality and helplessness" (p. 84).

However, the extent to which the children of the underclass do in fact inherit their parents' ways of life, which aspects are most likely to be inherited, and which adult experiences mitigate the inheritance factor have not been adequately studied. The proportion of an original population represented by any given adult outcome cannot be determined retrospectively. For example, a social worker's underclass caseload may all have come from deprived backgrounds; but unless we also know the proportion of similarly deprived children who were upwardly mobile, the impact of deprivation on adult outcome cannot be calculated. Too brief a follow-up may also conceal information. Studies that demonstrate the vicious cycle of extreme poverty by comparing the socioeconomic status of fathers with that of their sons in early adulthood (Blau & Duncan, 1967; Schiller, 1970) leave open the question of how far these differences will continue in later life.

Clearly, prospective studies of the sort presented in this paper become a necessity. For the men in this study, the transmission of their parents' chaotic or dependent lifestyles was not inevitable or even very likely. If their backgrounds are accepted as having the characteristics of an underclass, then the study refutes the hypothesis that the chances of escape from such a class are always minimal. The transmission of disorganization and alienation that seems inevitable when a disadvantaged cohort is studied retrospectively appears to be the exception rather than the norm in a prospective study that locates the successes as well as the failures. The chaos, unemployment, and extreme poverty of the most disadvantaged subjects in our study had not affected the capacity of the majority of them to obtain jobs, maintain them, and be promoted. Indeed, equal ratings for social class and psychological well-being among the four groups suggest unexpected resilience. Estimation of a subject's HSRS score was based on a wide variety of life history data. It included the results of a two-hour interview that ranged over intimate details of a man's health, feelings about his wife, family, and friends, and his sources of pleasure and pain. If the sense of marginality, hopelessness, powerlessness, or lack of self-respect that the literature claims is transmitted from one generation to the next had been directly or obliquely expressed by the majority of the disadvantaged groups, such a sense would have been reflected negatively in the 100-point HSRS scale. This was not the case. These optimistic results, however, require a closer look before estimating their relevance to understanding and making policy for today's children of poverty.

First, the problem of inherited disadvantage for the minority of socially deprived children is not eliminated by the escape of the majority. Men from multiproblem families died sooner, were more delinquent, and experienced worse health. It took 30 years of effort for them to achieve the success reported here. That the majority of the world's population reach midlife without pediatricians or obstetricians does not diminish the value of these professions to the early years.

Second, while it is satisfactory that these men did no worse than their inner-city peers, it should not be overlooked that only 10% of the entire sample had by midlife reached the secure middle-class status of classes I and II. Even in a time of a quantitatively and qualitatively expanding job market, the barriers to upward mobility for the working class remain strong.

Third, and most important for generalizing from these results, is consideration of how this may have been a particularly favored underclass. Four factors stand out. The people studied were white, male, and selected for relative nondelinquency and had moved from childhood to midlife in the United States between 1940 and 1975. Being white and male unquestionably favored the upward mobility of all four populations. The immense importance of race in the opportunity structure of the United States has been painfully documented (Hauser & Featherman, 1974) and far more painfully experienced. Current statistics also indicate a preponderance of women among the poorest segment of our society. But, unless one is prepared to say that white men from severely disadvantaged backgrounds do not count as an underclass, the results merit at least some optimism, even for those for whom the escape routes are more difficult. The importance of IQ, especially for disadvantaged youth, is consistent with Jencks' (1979) findings.

The bias resulting from selection for nondelinquency at age 14 is more difficult to evaluate. Certainly, the men were different from the Boston youth remanded to reform school (Glueck & Glueck, 1968), but compared with national averages the men in this study did not represent a particularly law-abiding group. Moreover, because this group was selected for low IQ, escape through access to higher education was in general denied.

The most serious problem in generalizing from these data may be that the men belonged to a favored historical cohort. It can be claimed that families who were chronically dependent in 1940, after a decade of universal economic depression, were less alienated and socially deviant than families whose dependency occurs during boom times. Furthermore, the fact that half of the men's parents were foreign-born made them what Matza (1966) has described as the most temporary members of the "disreputable poor." But even if true, these arguments do not explain the resilience of children from multiproblem families.

A second feature of the favored historical cohort is the fact that these men entered the work force in the late 1940s, when employment levels were high, national wealth was increasing, and the occupational structure was expanding in the middle ranges (Duncan, 1979). Furthermore, some of the men had experienced a break with their family background in the form of service in the armed forces and were able to benefit from the GI Bill of Rights for occupational and educational training. These factors may have given this birth cohort some special escape routes that were less available to later cohorts. On the other hand, current sociological analyses of mobility tables (Hauser et al., 1975; Hope, 1982) favor a view of vertical social mobility as constant between classes over time. By this view the absolutely better position of the sons in our cohort than that of their fathers is explainable by changes in the occupational structure, but the relatively equal positions of the more and less disadvantaged (particularly in regard to income) is not explained by economic good times. It is unlikely that the post-World-War-II economic prosperity unequally favored the most disadvantaged.

From the practical point of view, we see a danger that these hopeful findings could be taken to suggest that extreme poverty ultimately presents no problems to the next generation or that benign neglect is an appropriate solution to desperate social problems. Our conclusions from the data are entirely to the contrary. The overwhelming impression from this study of lives is that early, continuous, and improving work opportunities enable most people to overcome even the worst starts to life. If deprived family backgrounds do not necessarily permanently disable the majority of urban children, the intervention and concerted provision of economic opportunity become a less hopeless and more urgent task.

REFERENCES

AULETTA, K. (1982). *The Underclass.* New York: Random House.

BLAU, P.M., & DUNCAN, O.D. (1967). *The American Occupational Structure.* New York: John Wiley & Sons.

DUNCAN, O.D. (1979). How destination depends on origin in the occupational mobility table. *American Journal of Sociology, 84:* 793–803.

GLUECK, S., & GLUECK, E. (1950). *Unravelling Juvenile Delinquency.* New York: The Commonwealth Fund.

GLUECK, S., & GLUECK, E. (1968). *Delinquents and Nondelinquents in Perspective.* Cambridge, MA: Harvard University Press.

GRINKER, W., & SVIRIDOFF, M. (1980). *Report of Manpower Demonstration Research Corporation.* New York: MDRC.

HAUSER, R.M., DICKINSON, P., TRAVIS, H., et al. (1975). Structural changes in occupational mobility among men in the US. *American Sociology Review, 40:* 585–598.

HAUSER, R.M., & FEATHERMAN, D. (1974). White and nonwhite differentials in occupational mobility among men in the US, 1962–72. *Demography, 11:* 247–265.

HOLLINGSHEAD, A.B., & REDLICH, F. (1958). *Social Class and Mental Illness.* New York: John Wiley & Sons.

HOPE, K. (1982). Vertical and nonvertical class mobility in three countries. *American Sociology Review, 47:* 99–113.

HUNTER, R. (1912). *Poverty.* New York: Macmillan.

JENCKS, C. (1979). *Who Gets Ahead?* New York: Basic Books.

LEWIS, O. (1964). The culture of poverty. In J. De Paske & S.N. Fisher (Eds.), *Explosive Forces in Latin America.* Columbus: Ohio State University Press.

LUBORSKY, L. (1962). Clinicians' judgments of mental health. *Archives of General Psychiatry, 7:* 407–417.

LUBORSKY, L., & BACHRACK, H. (1974). Factors influencing clinicians' judgments of mental health. *Archives of General Psychiatry, 31:* 292–299.

MATZA, D. (1966). The disreputable poor. In R. Bendix & S. Lipset (Eds.), *Class Status and Power.* New York: Free Press.

MYRDAL, G. (1970). *The Challenge of World Poverty.* New York: Pantheon Books.

ROBINS, L. N. (1966). *Deviant Children Grown Up: A Sociological and Psychiatric Study of Sociopathic Personality.* Baltimore: Williams & Wilkins.

RUTTER, M., & MADGE, M. (1975). *Cycles of Disadvantage: A Review of Research.* London: Heinemann.

SCHILLER, B.R. (1970). Stratified opportunities: The essence of the "vicious circle." *American Journal of Sociology, 76:* 426–442.

VAILLANT, G.E. (1983). *The Natural History of Alcoholism.* Cambridge, MA: Harvard University Press.

VAILLANT, G.E., & MILOFSKY, E. (1980). Natural history of male psychological health, IX: Empirical evidence for Erikson's model of the life cycle. *American Journal of Psychiatry, 137:* 1348–1359.

VAILLANT, G.E., & VAILLANT, C.O. (1981). Natural history of male psychological health, X: Work as a predicator of positive mental health. *American Journal of Psychiatry, 138:* 1433–1440.

Name Index

215

Subject Index

Abandonment fears, 82, 88
Abuse, *see* Drug abuse; Physical abuse;
    Sexual abuse
Achievement, 125
Acting out, 86, 166–174
    communicational aspects of, 158
    predisposition to, 168
    resiliency and, 157–158, 165, 167, 172
    within analysis, 170–171
Activity level, 184
Adaptability, 184, 189, 191
Adaptive distancing, 95–102, 194–195,
    198
Adjustment Disorder, 188–189, 192, 196
Adolescent and Family Development
    Study, 139
Adolescent Health and Illness Project, 126,
    129
Adolescents, *see also* Children
    acting out and, 167, 169–171
    of alcoholic families, 86–88
    capacity to work, 163–164, 172–173
    diabetic:
        autonomy and, 135, 138, 141, 145,
            150, 152, 154
        developmental tasks and, 136–139
        ego development, 140–154
        family effect on resiliency, 121–126
        neurotic conflict and, 136
        psychological risks, 121–122
        puberty and, 137–138
        self-esteem and, 124–125, 127, 135,
            139
        separation issues and, 138, 147,
            153–154

distancing from the family, 164–165,
    172–173
parental impact on maturation of,
    118–119
personality and, 113–114, 127–128
street children as, 77
Affect:
    alcoholic families and, 94–95
    motivational role of, 16–21
Aggression, 64, 85
Alcoholic families:
    affect in, 94–95
    individuation in, 91–92
    interventions for, 101–104
    nonalcoholic spouse and, 100–101
    physical abuse in, 94, 99–100
    power structure, 89–90
    reality in, 93–94
    risk for children, 82–88
    role of oldest child in, 100
    separation and loss in, 92–93
    socioeconomic status, 98–99
    variability in, 89
Alcoholism, 81, 88
    causes of, 103
    the underclass and, 200–201, 204, 208
Alienation, 201, 211
Ambivalence, 14, 21
Anger, 94
Antisocial personality, 208
Antisocial tendencies, 157–158
Anxiety, 49, 84, 144, 189
    mastery of, 96
    physical illness and, 138
Attention deficit disorder, 84, 98

219

Psychopathology:
  family, 75
  in street children, 71
Psychosocial development, 72, 127
Puberty, 137

Rationalization, 39, 50
Reality, 93–94
Reality testing, 76
Reciprocity, 39
Regression, 165, 173, 189
Reparation, 30, 32–33, 35
Repetition compulsion, 158, 166
Resiliency, 181
  acting out behavior and, 157–158, 165, 167, 172
  competence and, 112–113
  definition, 3–4, 112
  diabetic adolescents and, 123–129, 134–136, 141, 152–154
  ego development and, 154
  in the family system, 11–16
  family's role in, 116–120
  moral climate of families and, 40
  social milieu and, 115–116
  street children and, 59, 71–78
  variables related to, 113
Responsiveness, 185
Rhythmicity, 184
Rigidity, 122, 125
Rituals, 92–93
Role performance, 173
Role reversal, 25
Runaways, 87

Salutogenesis, 111
Schizophrenia, 208
School environment, 115
School performance, 81, 84–85, 163, 201
Secondary process thinking, 169
Secrets, 102–103
Self-Aware Level, 146
Self-cohesion, 161
Self-concept, 142
Self-destructive behavior, 86
Self-esteem, 75, 114, 161, 173, 191
  children of alcoholic families and, 84–85
  diabetic adolescents and, 124–125, 127, 135, 139
  family effects and, 120
  street children and, 73–74
Self-fulfilling prophecy, 192
Self-image, 139
Self-Protective Stage, 149

Self-respect, 193
  the underclass and, 210
Separation-individuation, 82, 86, 167
  alcoholic families and, 92, 102
  diabetic adolescents and, 138, 147, 153–154
  second phase of, 169
Sex roles, 62
Sexual abuse, 65, 81–82
Sexual identity, 83, 99
Shame responses, 94–95, 98
Single-parent families, 90, 99
Social class, 163, 204, 207, 210
Social milieu, 115–116, 120
  diabetic adolescents and, 127–128
Social mobility, 204, 208, 212
Social skills, 114
Social support systems, 135, 137, 145, 152, 182
Socioeconomic status, 98–99, 123, 154
Sociopathy, 202–204
Somatic symptoms, 197
Stepfathers, 64
Stereotypy, 10
Streetwise International, 58
Stress, 26, 40, 182
  manageable, 73
  personal attributes and, 120
Stress resistance, 110–113, 120, 126, 128–129, 141, *see also* Resiliency
Substance abuse, *see* Alcoholic families; Drug abuse
Suicidal behavior, 85–88, 99–100, 158–160, 165, 196
Superego, 24
Survival strategies, 67–69, 72
Symbol formation, 169

Talent, 191, 193
Temperament, 7, 10, 181–188, 192–193, 195–196
  diabetic adolescents and, 120
  street children and, 65, 71
Trial and error actions, 170–172
Transference, 127
  acting out and, 161, 166–168, 171, 173–174
Trauma, 181
  level of childhood psychological, 163
  preoedipal, 168–169

Underclass, 200–201, 210
  compared to the working class, 203
Unemployment, 204